The Vampire Doodle Diaries

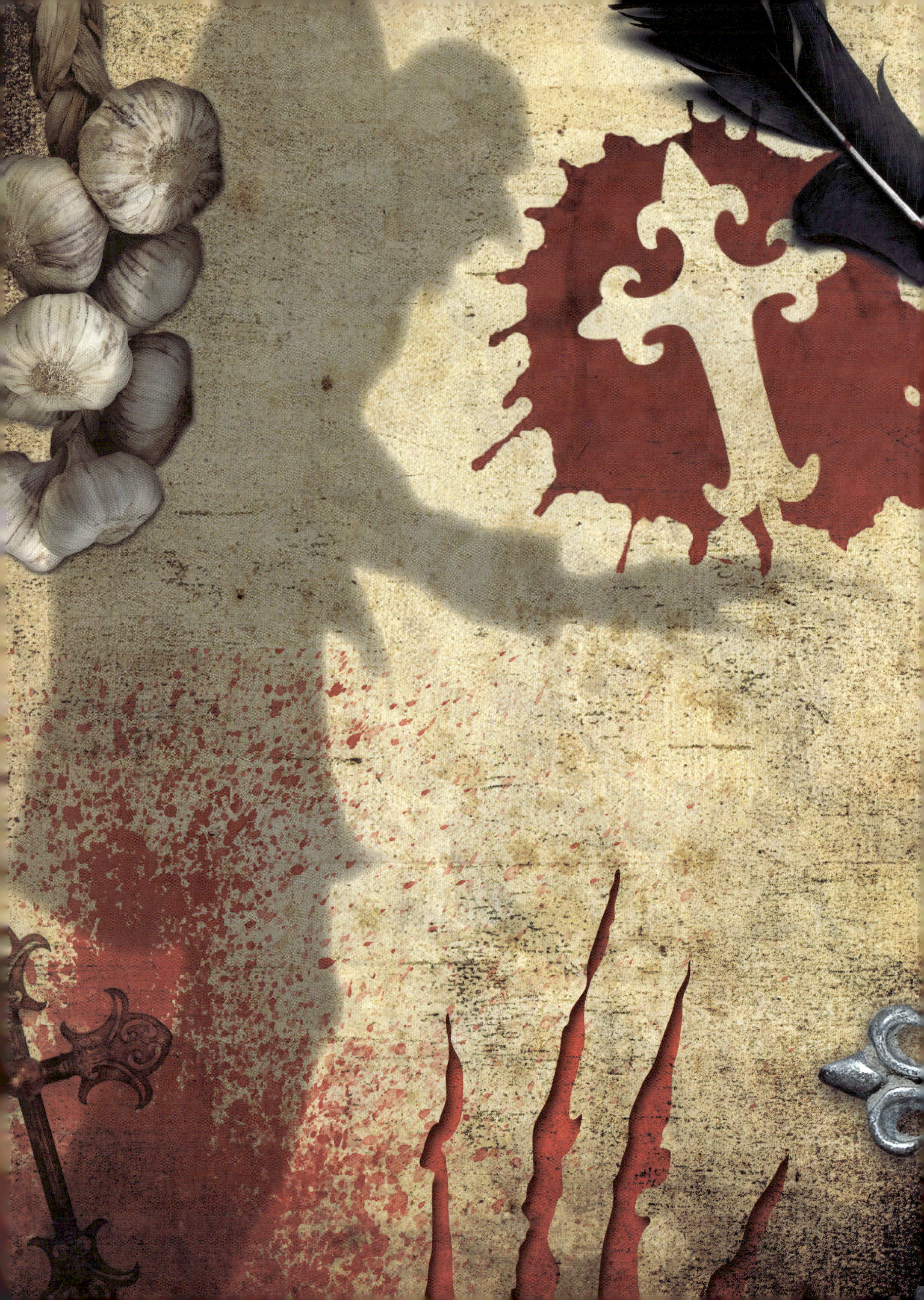

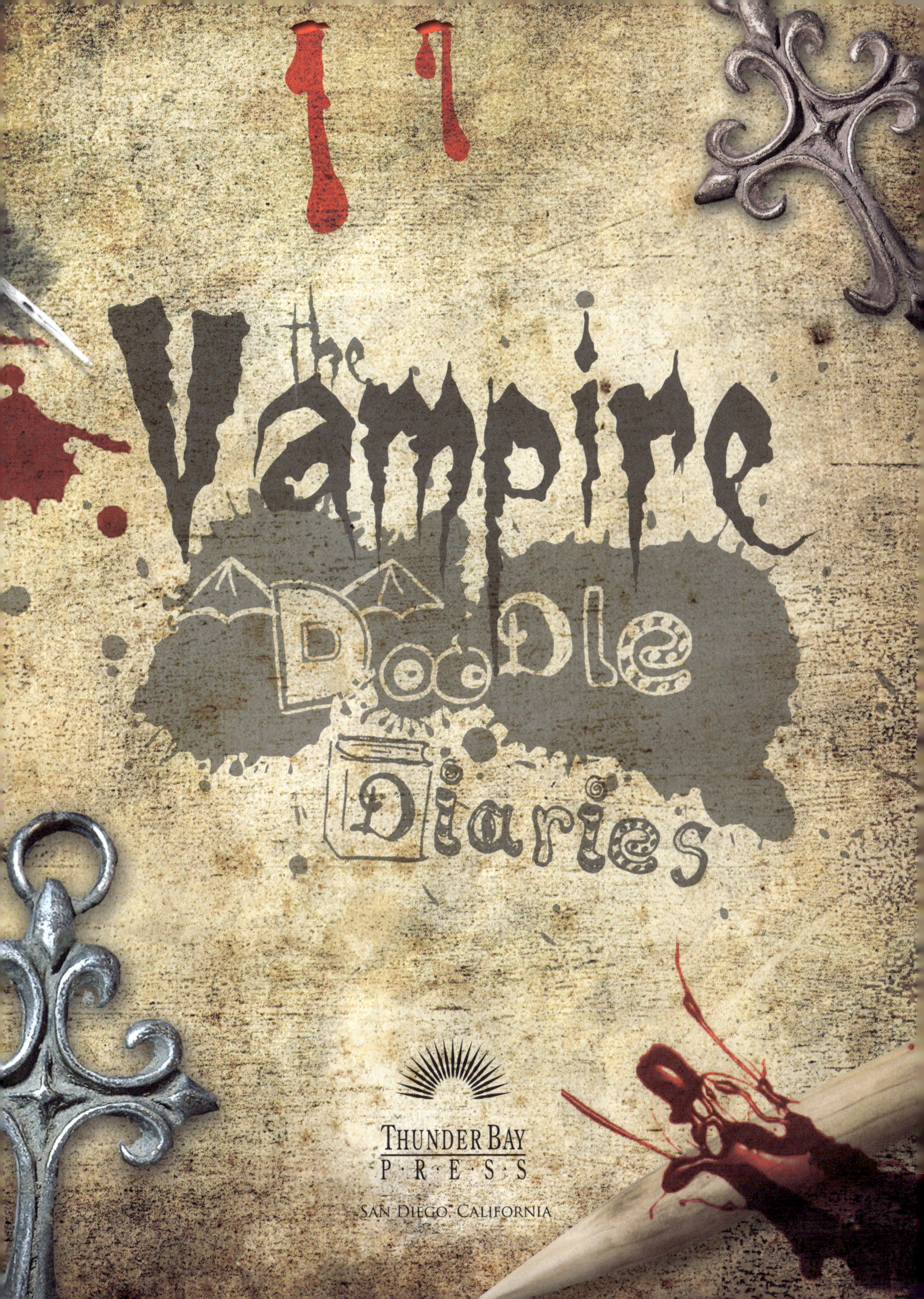

The Vampire Doodle Diaries
THUNDER BAY
P·R·E·S·S
SAN DIEGO, CALIFORNIA

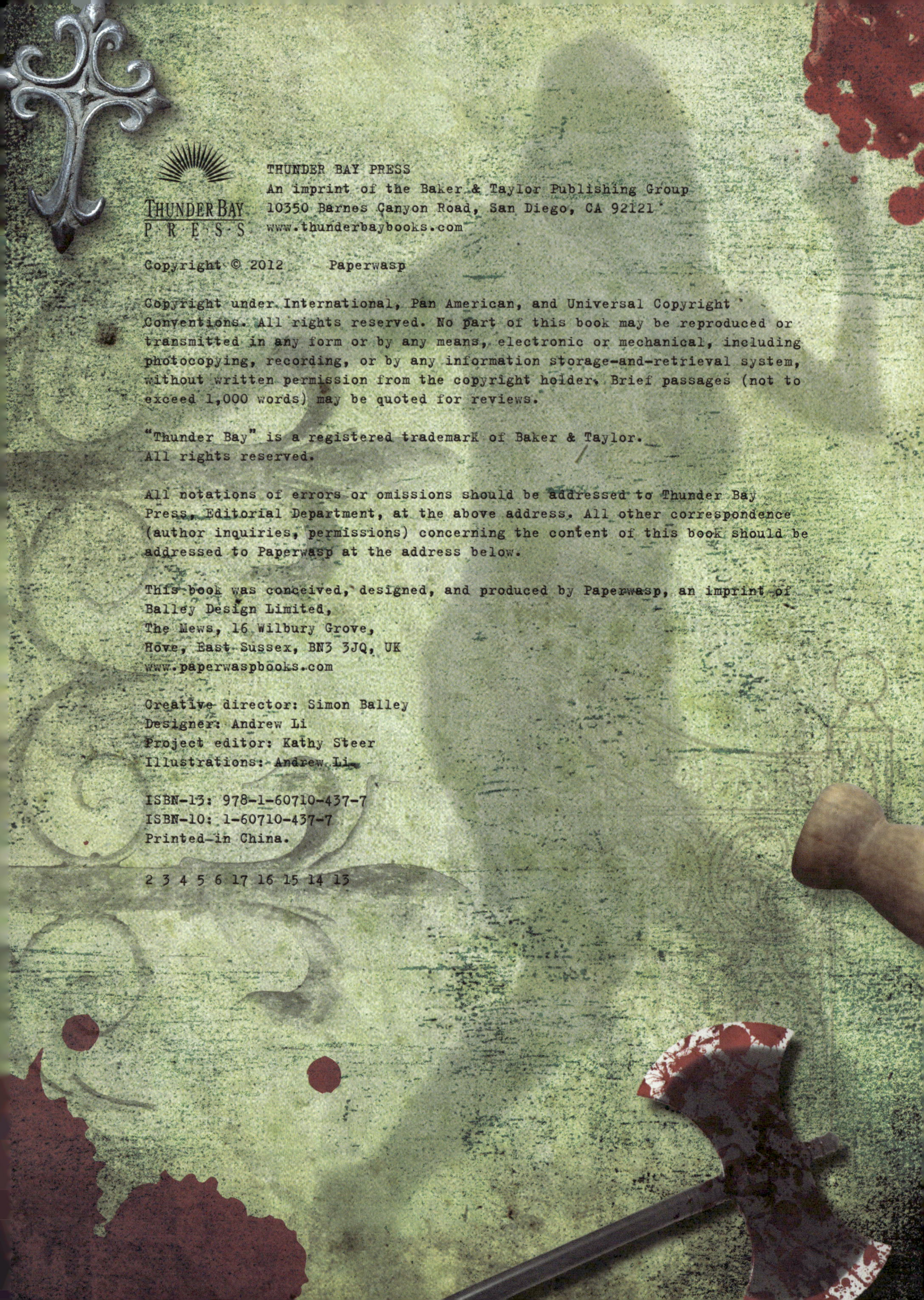

THUNDER BAY PRESS
An imprint of the Baker & Taylor Publishing Group
10350 Barnes Canyon Road, San Diego, CA 92121
www.thunderbaybooks.com

All notations of errors or omissions should be addressed to Thunder Bay Press, Editorial Department, at the above address. All other correspondence (author inquiries, permissions) concerning the content of this book should be addressed to Paperwasp at the address below.

This book was conceived, designed, and produced by Paperwasp, an imprint of Balley Design Limited,
The Mews, 16 Wilbury Grove,
Hove, East Sussex, BN3 3JQ, UK
www.paperwaspbooks.com

Creative director: Simon Balley
Designer: Andrew Li
Project editor: Kathy Steer
Illustrations: Andrew Li

ISBN-13: 978-1-60710-437-7
ISBN-10: 1-60710-437-7
Printed in China.

2 3 4 5 6 17 16 15 14 13

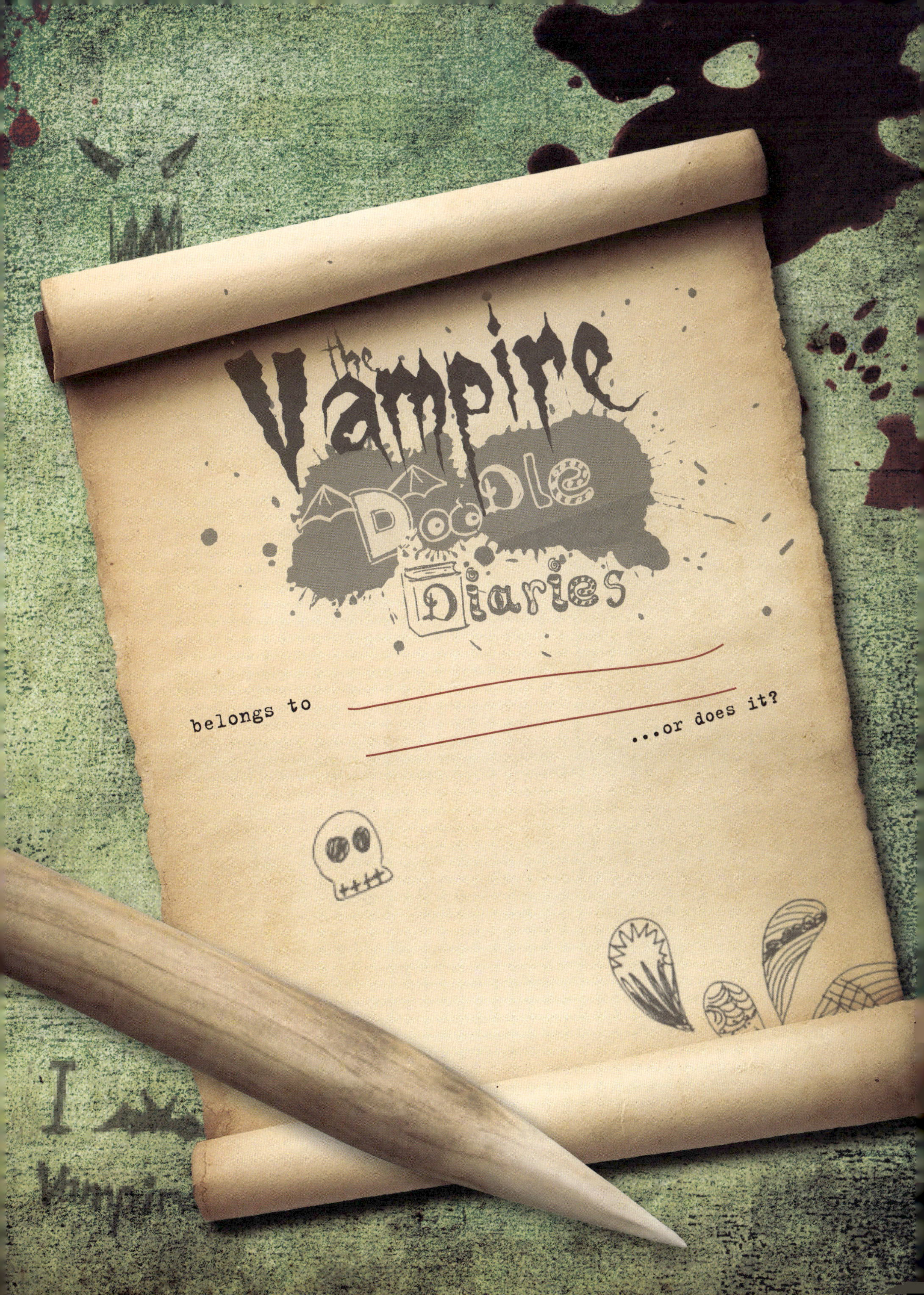
the Vampire Doodle Diaries
belongs to
...or does it?
I
Vampir

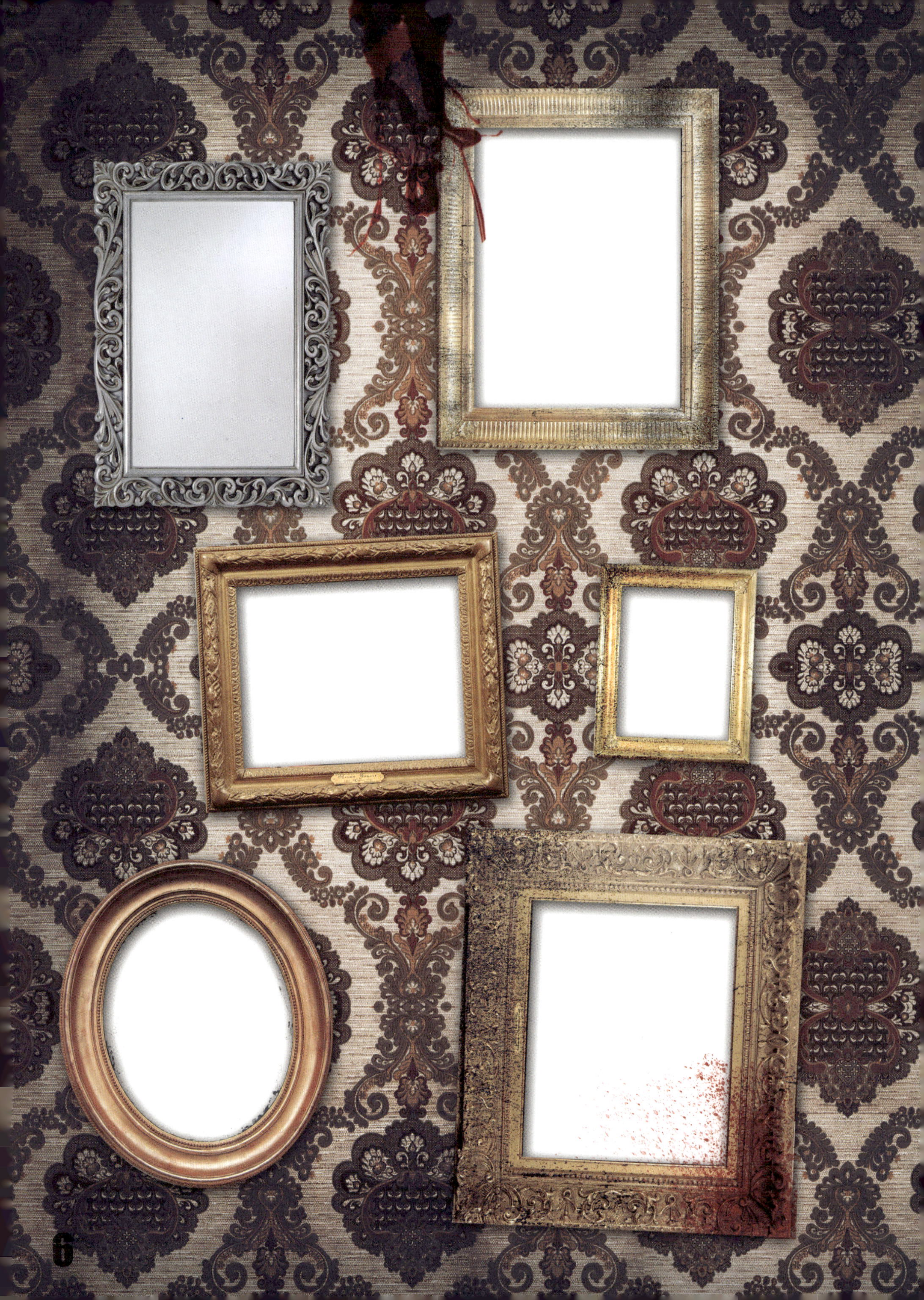

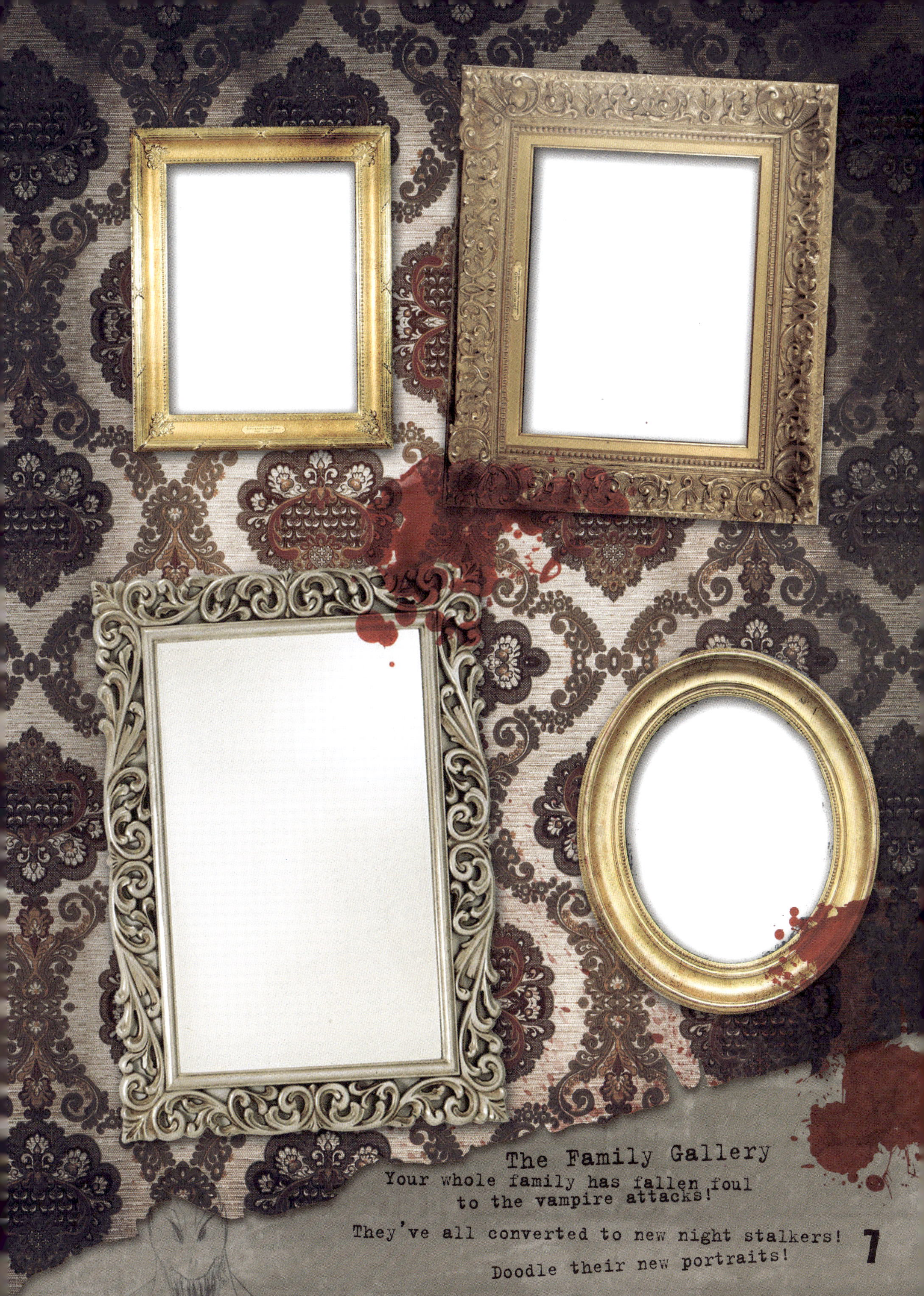

The Family Gallery

Your whole family has fallen foul to the vampire attacks!

They've all converted to new night stalkers!

Doodle their new portraits!

Word Search

T E O D D N R S L

S L A Y E R L A O

S E G N A O N R I

D E M O O R R A F

L B I I U R N M A

G L T T T O M B N

T O C C I H T O G

N O I T C U D E S

N D V A C L V N O

dead
victim
gothic
slayer
nocturnal
fangs
seduction
horror
tomb
blood

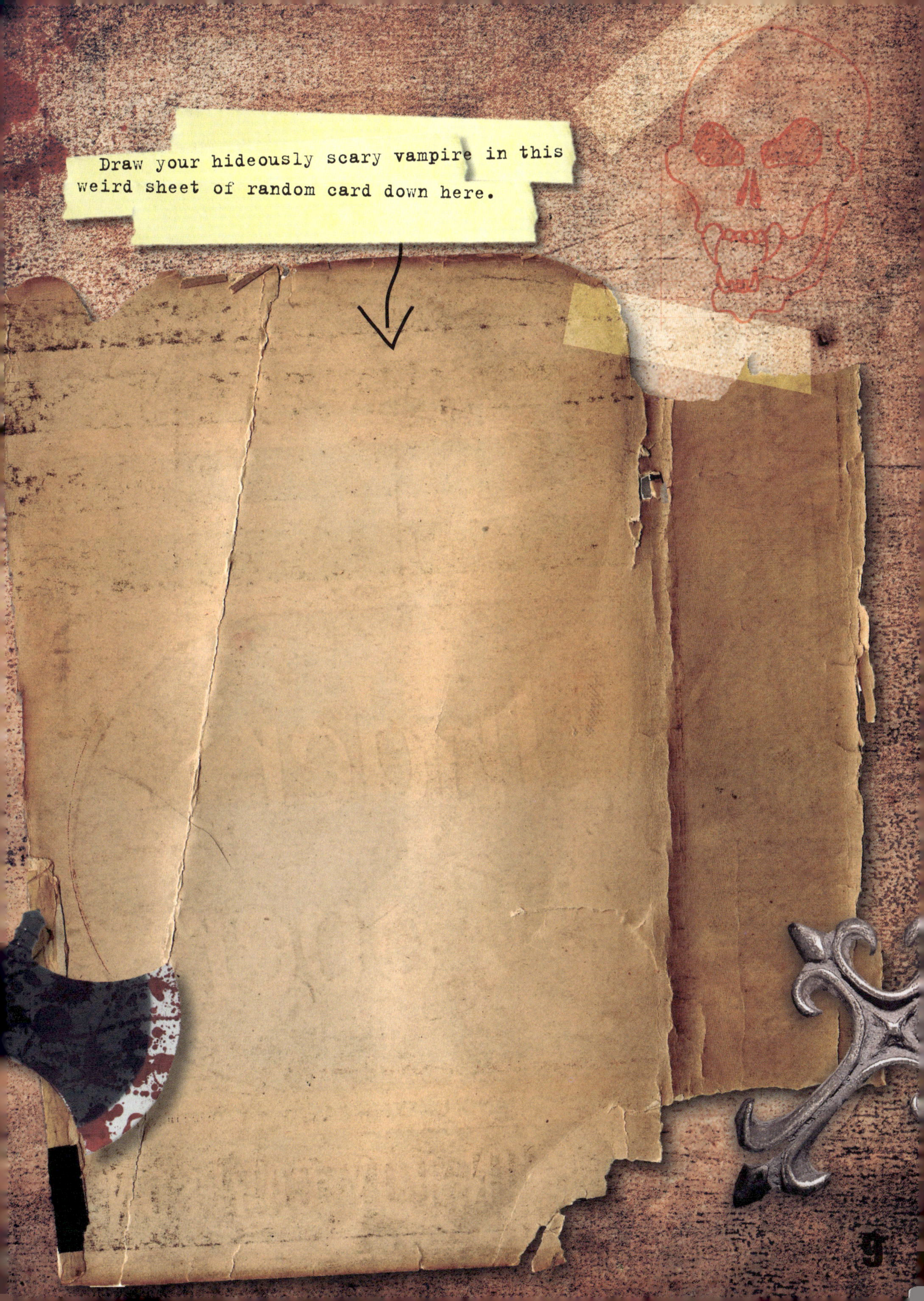
Draw your hideously scary vampire in this weird sheet of random card down here.

Vampire Tracks

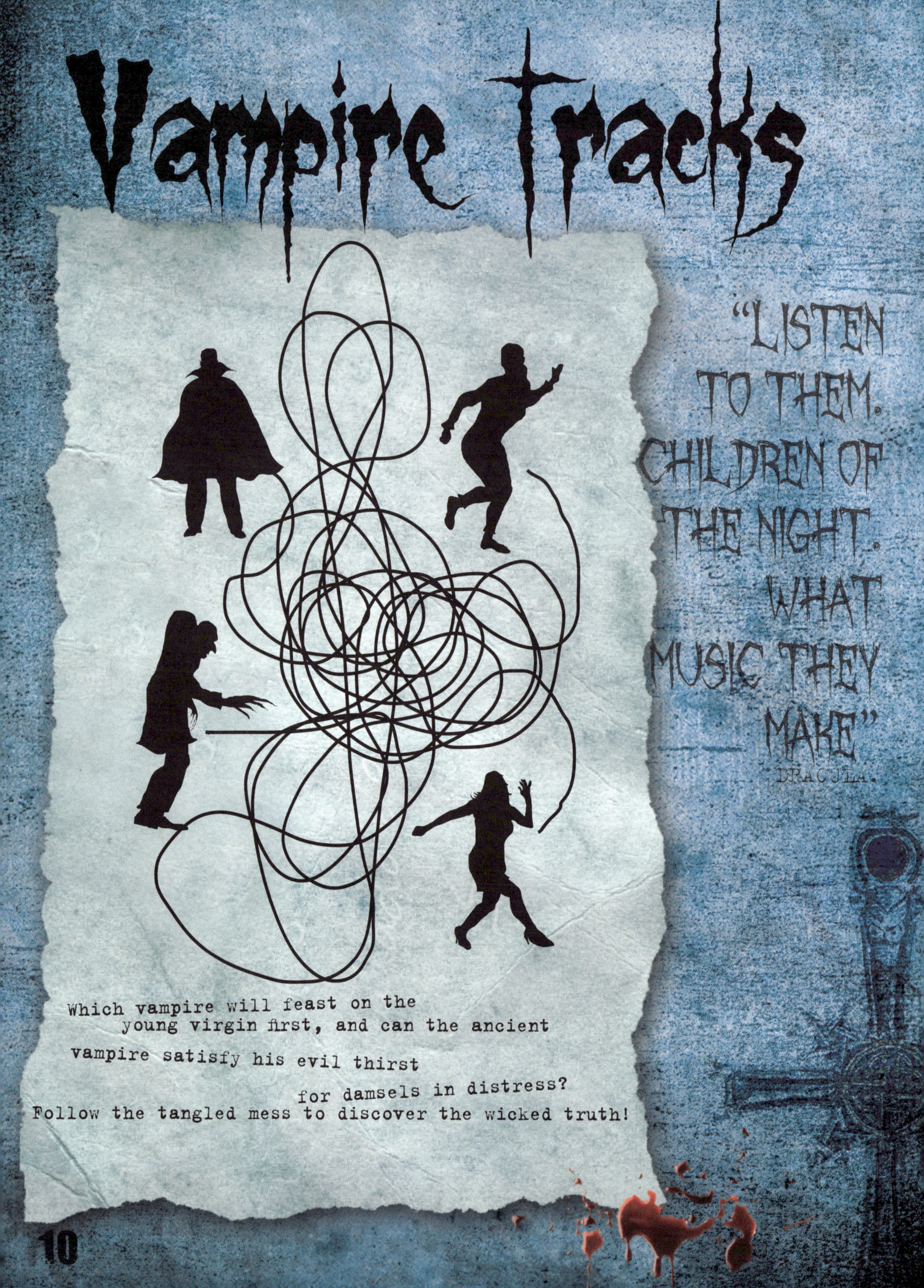

Which vampire will feast on the young virgin first, and can the ancient vampire satisfy his evil thirst for damsels in distress? Follow the tangled mess to discover the wicked truth!

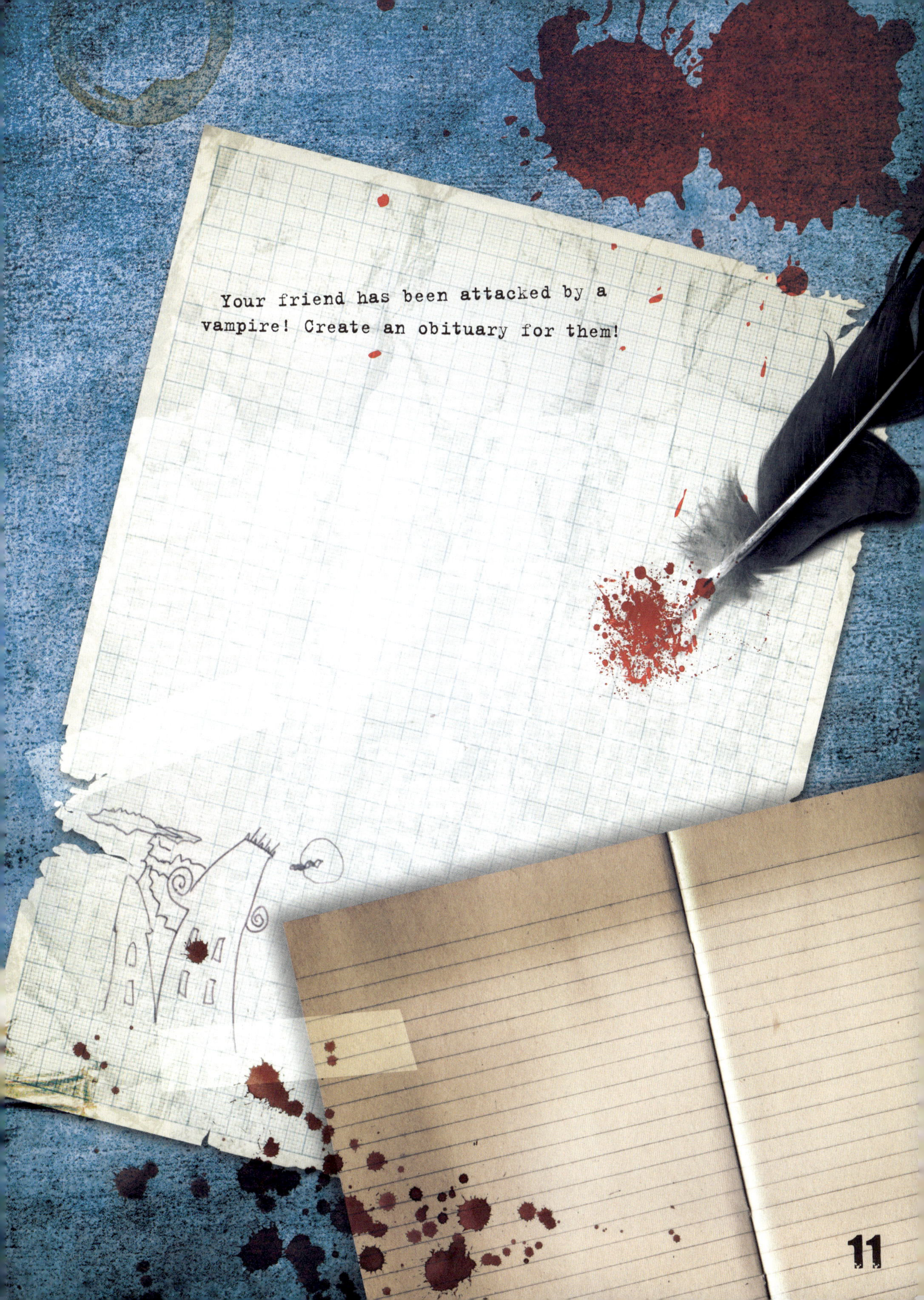

Your friend has been attacked by a vampire! Create an obituary for them!

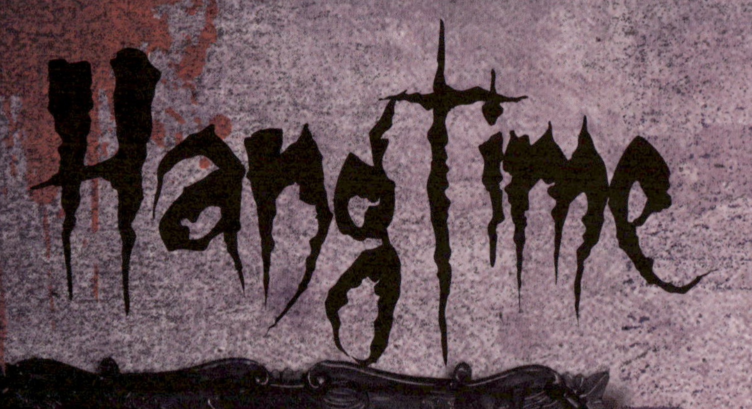

ABCDEFGHI
JKLM
NOPQRSTU
VWXYZ

Cross off the dead letters.

Draw your hangman.

hangman

Enter your blood-soaked words here.

ABCDEFG
HIJKLM
NOPQRST
UVWXYZ

It is dusk
and the vampires are waking!
Warn people of the
terror that awaits!

RUN FOR YOUR LIVES

HELP

TRANSYLVANIAN
DAILY NEWS
VAMP ATTACK!

Dot-to-Dot

Connect the dots
to reveal the horror!

34 33
35
50
51
36
32
37
53 54 31
55
38 52 30
45 49 56
60
57 29
46
28
44
39
58
47
59 27
43
40
26
3
6 48
42 41 61
5 4
2 1
62 25
9 7
8
11
10
14
63 64
12 24
13 65
22
15 17 18 23
16 21
19
20

MY BOYFRIEND IS A PAIN IN THE NECK

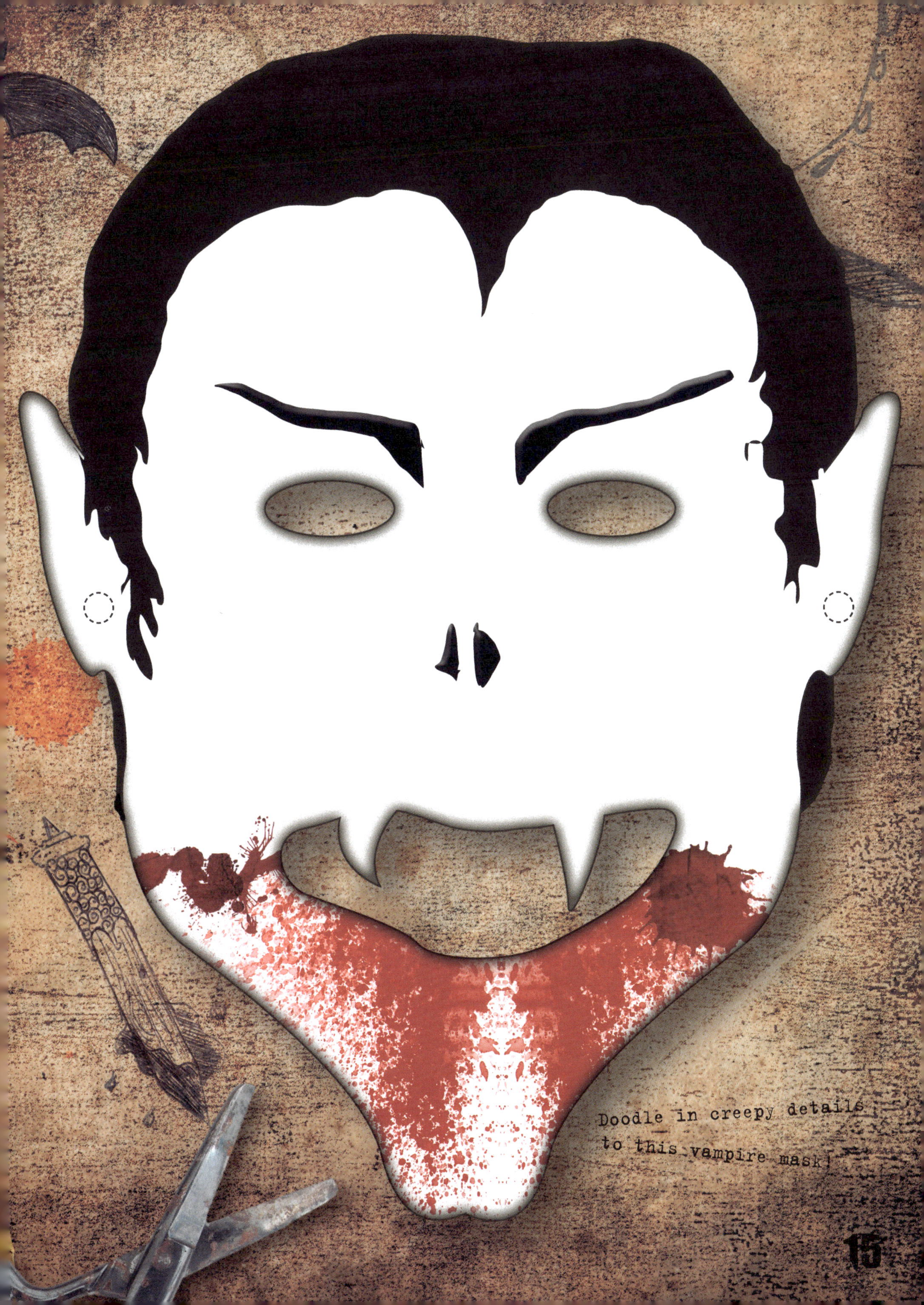
Doodle in creepy details
to this vampire mask!

Place your mirror here.

Draw in a creepy backward message on this old rotten paper.

BLOOD SUCKER

ABCDEFGHIJKLMN

OPQRSTUVWXYZ

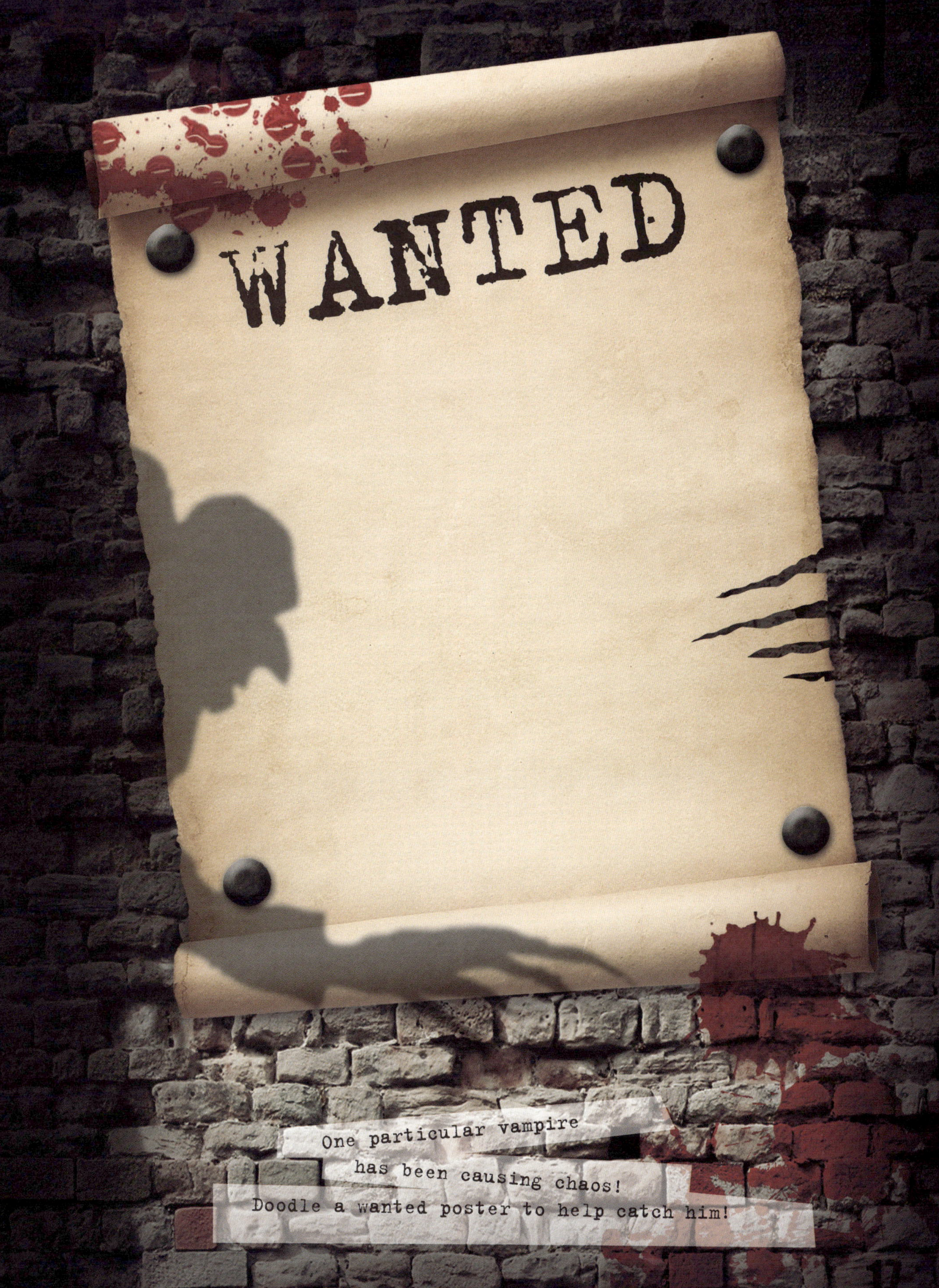

One particular vampire
has been causing chaos!
Doodle a wanted poster to help catch him!

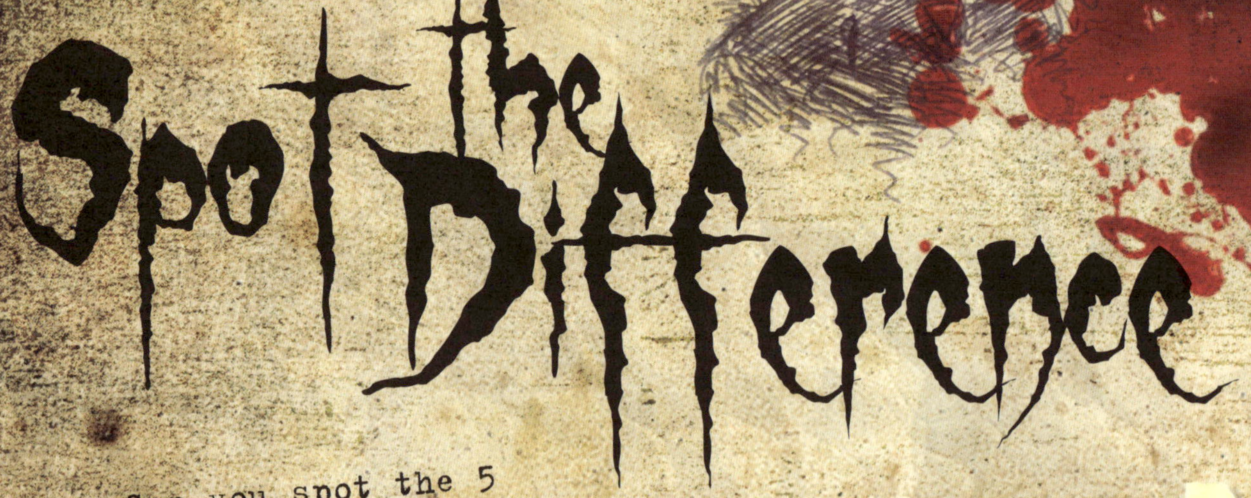

Spot the Difference

Can you spot the 5 differences between this pair of ghoulish blood suckers!

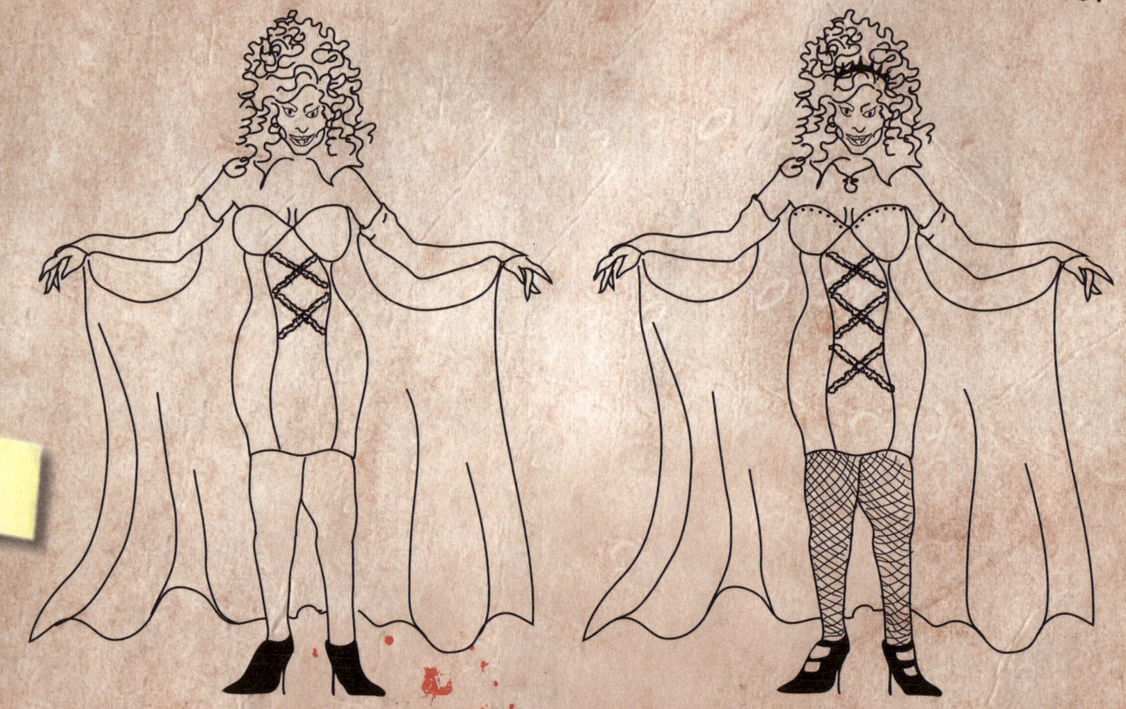

"Lisa, vampires are make-believe, like elves, gremlins, and eskimos."

Homer Simpson

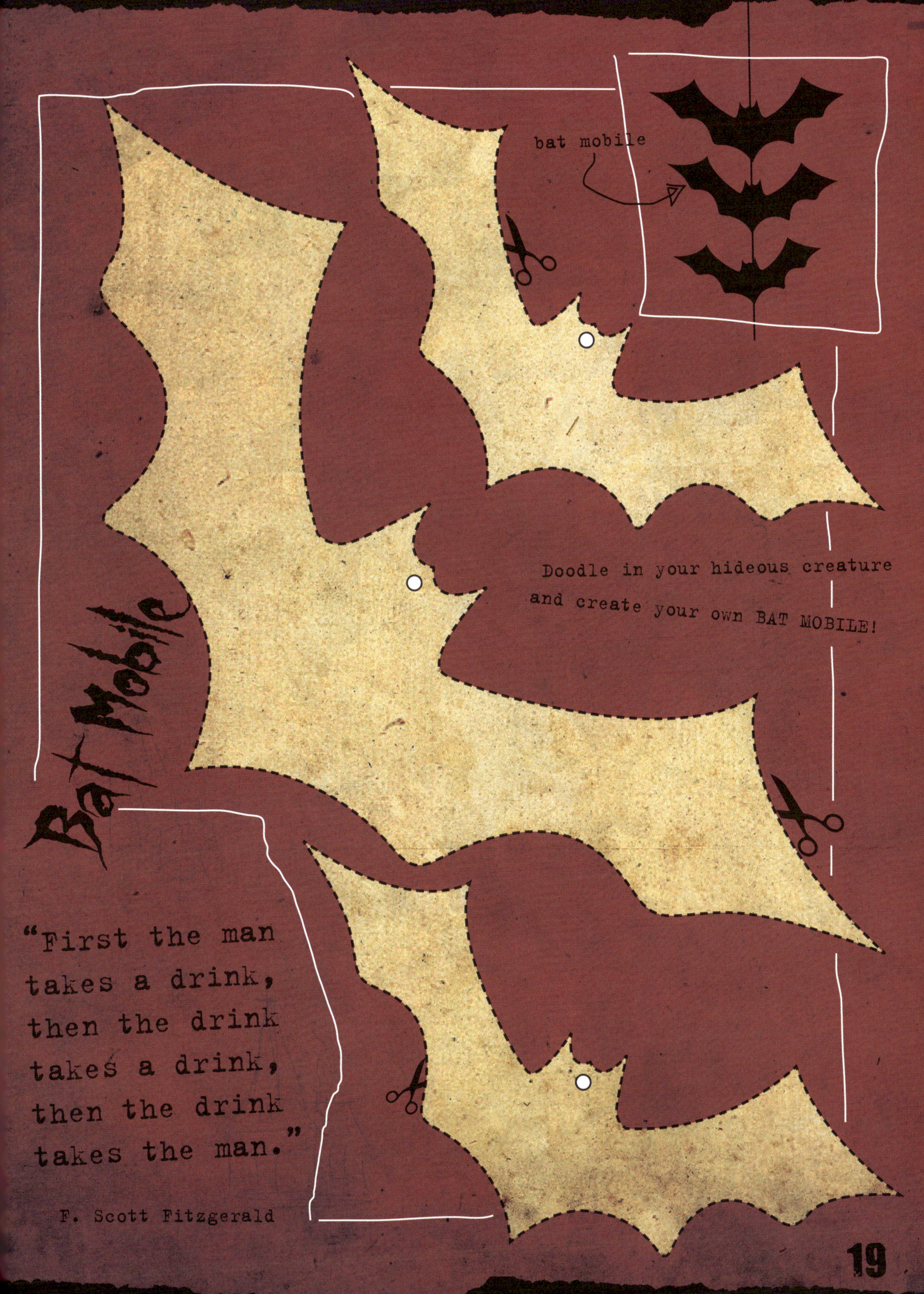

"First the man takes a drink, then the drink takes a drink, then the drink takes the man."

F. Scott Fitzgerald

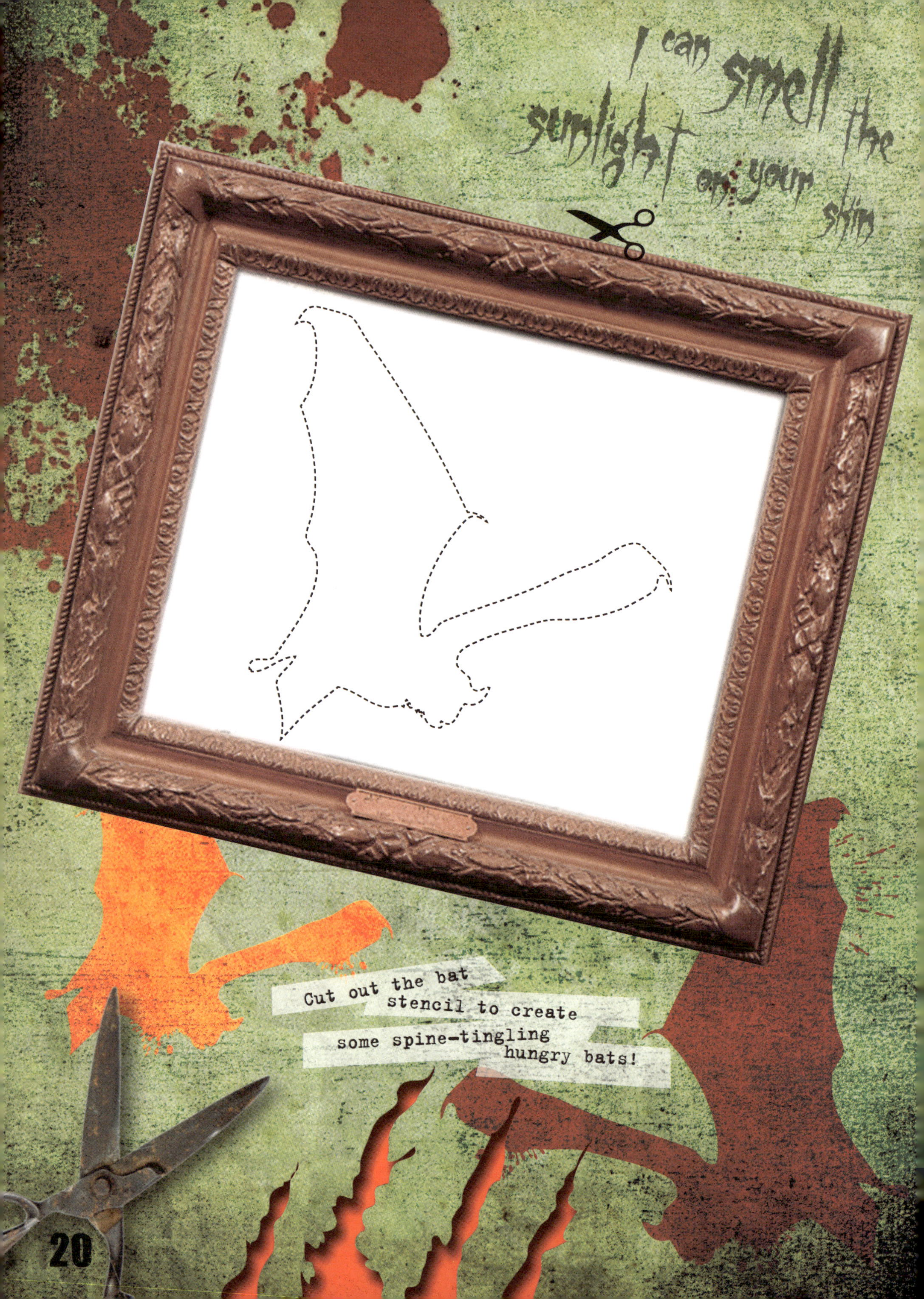
I can smell the sunlight on your skin
Cut out the bat stencil to create some spine-tingling hungry bats!

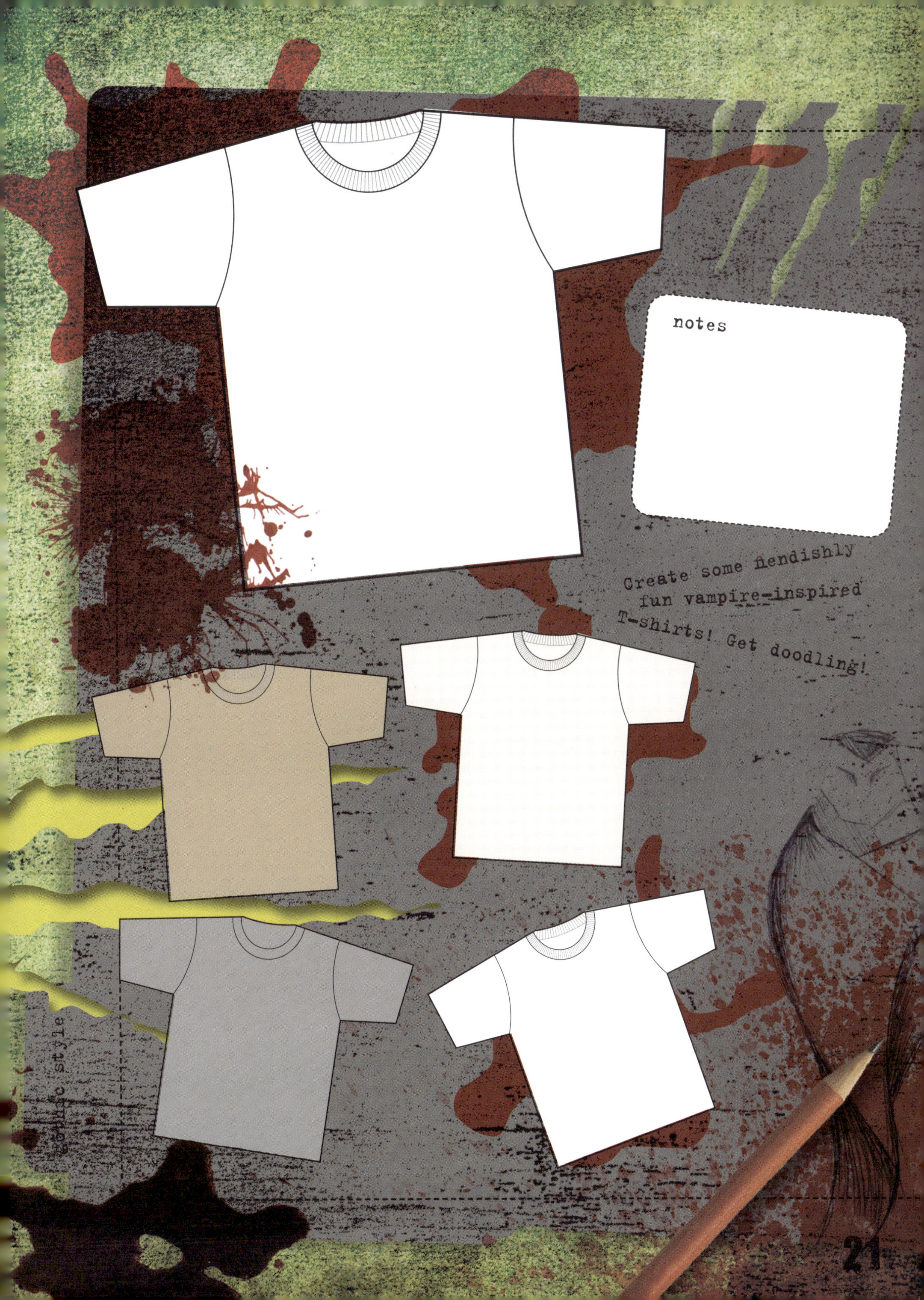
notes
Create some fiendishly fun vampire-inspired T-shirts! Get doodling!
gothic style

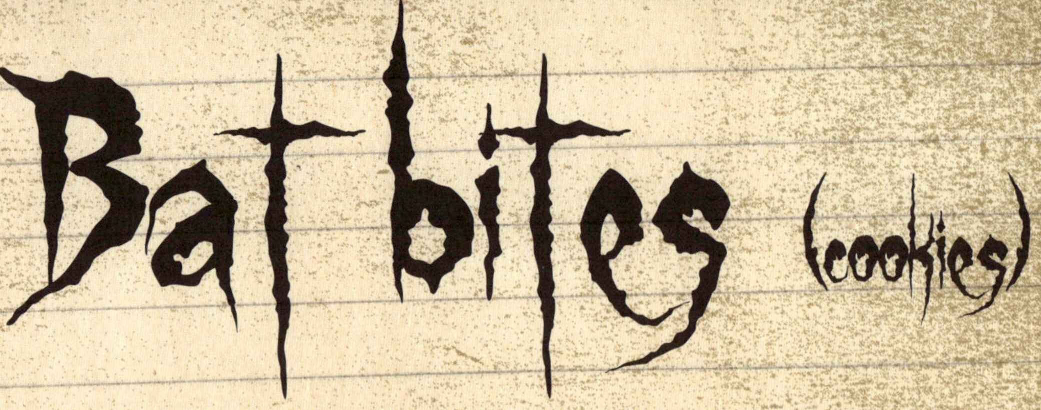

Bat bites (cookies)

Ingredients

Serves: 36

9 oz. all-purpose flour
1/4 tsp. salt
1/4 tsp. baking powder
8 oz. butter
4 oz. superfine sugar

Method

Prep: 25 mins | Cook: 15 mins

1. Preheat the oven to 325 degrees.
2. Sift together the flour, salt, and baking powder. In a large bowl, beat the butter and sugar together until light and fluffy. Add the sifted dry ingredients and mix well. Chill for 10 minutes, or until the dough is easy to handle.
3. On a lightly floured surface, roll out the dough to 1/4 inch thick. Cut into bat shapes and place on ungreased cookie sheets.
4. Bake in the oven for 10 to 15 minutes.

Use this stencil to cut out your bat shapes!

Warning
adult assistance recommended for a safe result!

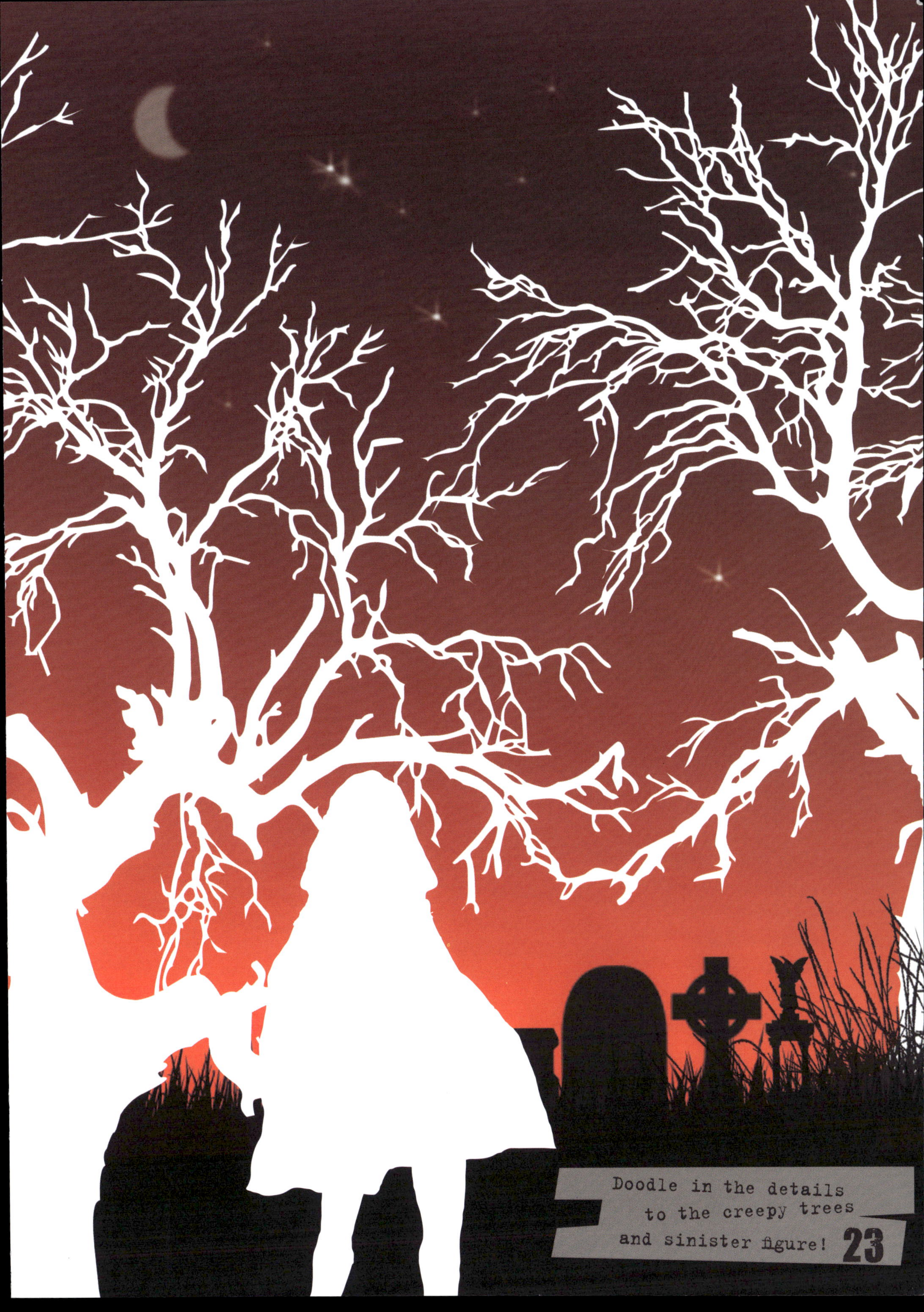
Doodle in the details
to the creepy trees
and sinister figure!

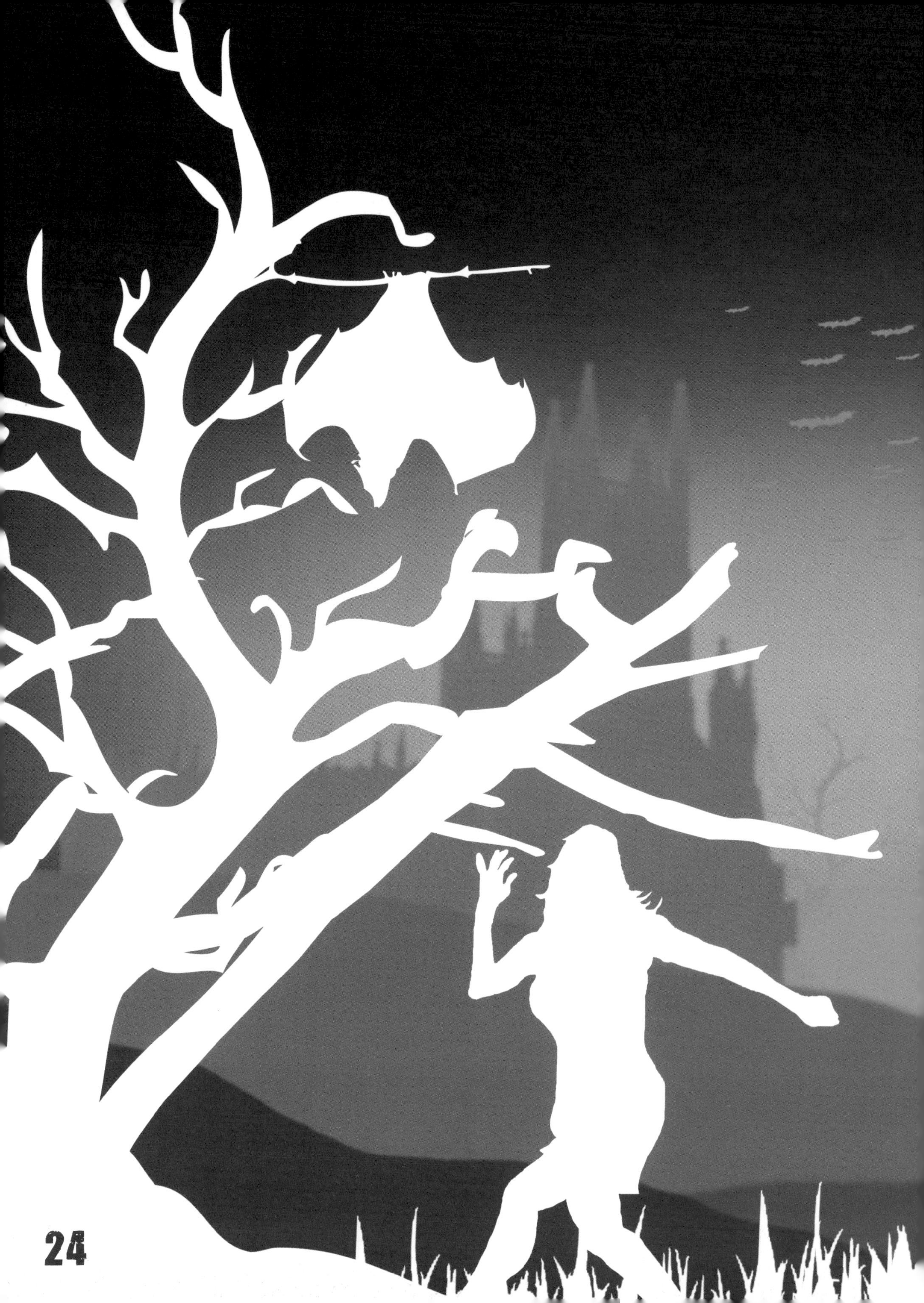

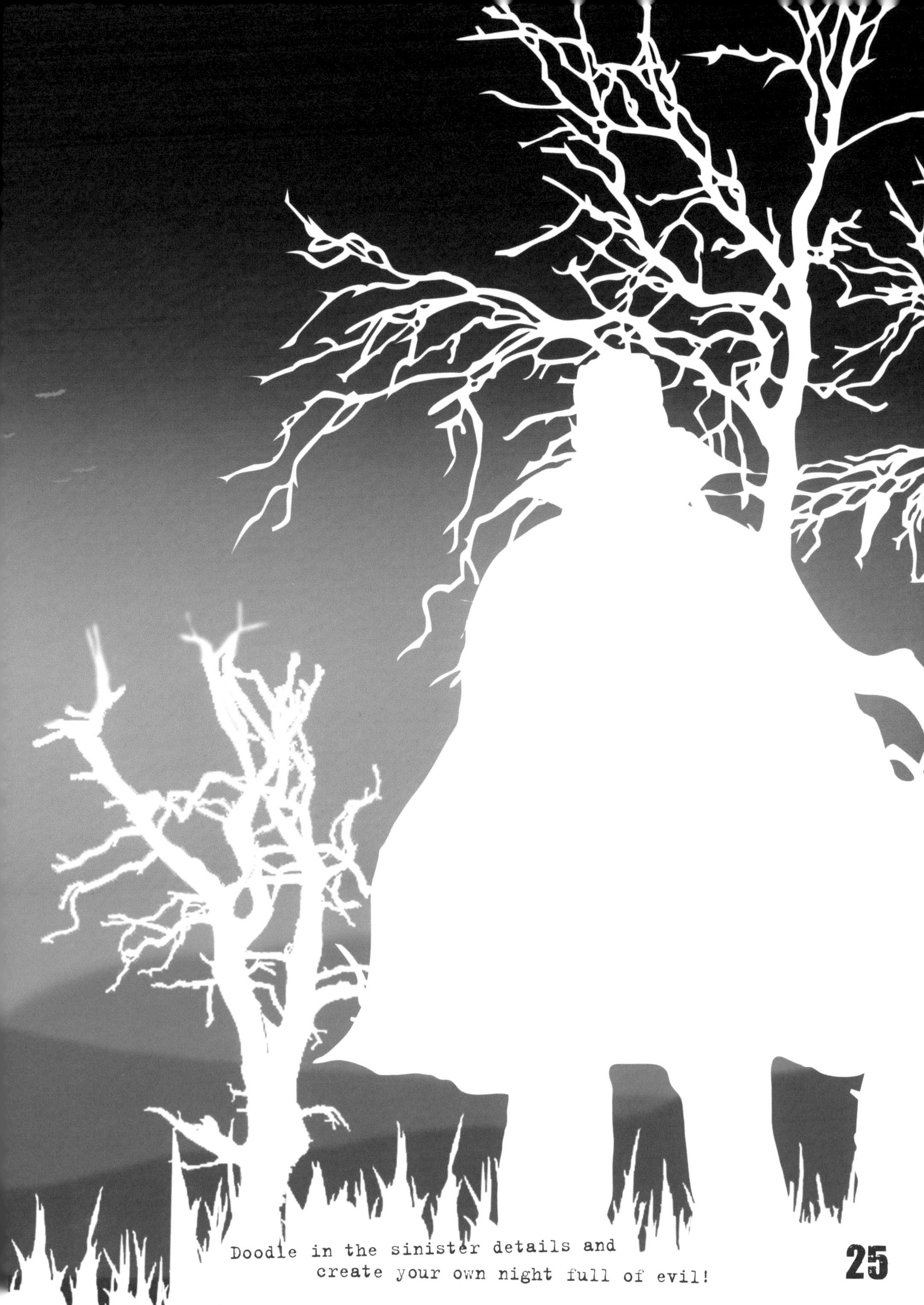
Doodle in the sinister details and
create your own night full of evil!

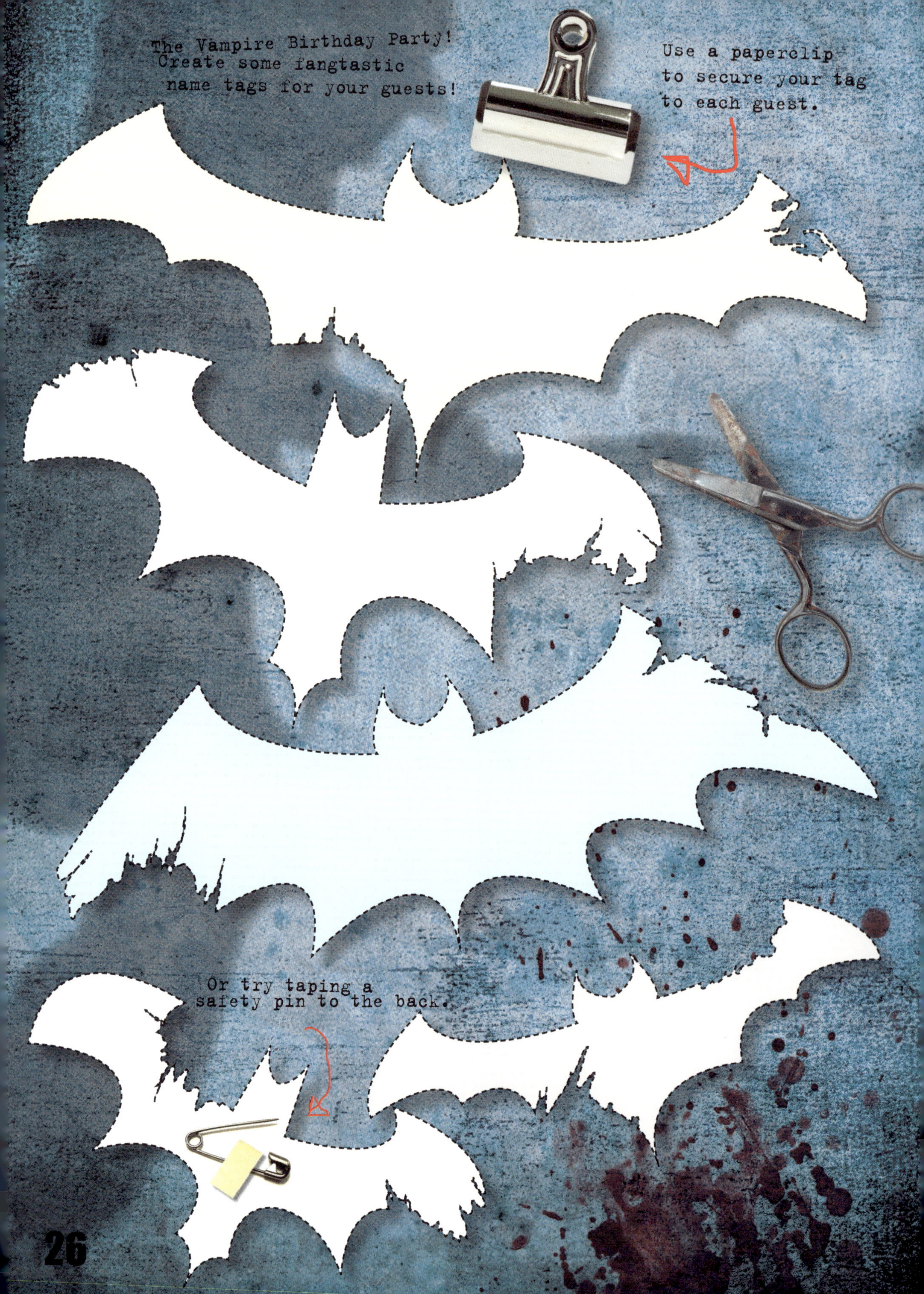
The Vampire Birthday Party!
Create some fangtastic
name tags for your guests!
Use a paperclip
to secure your tag
to each guest.
Or try taping a
safety pin to the back.

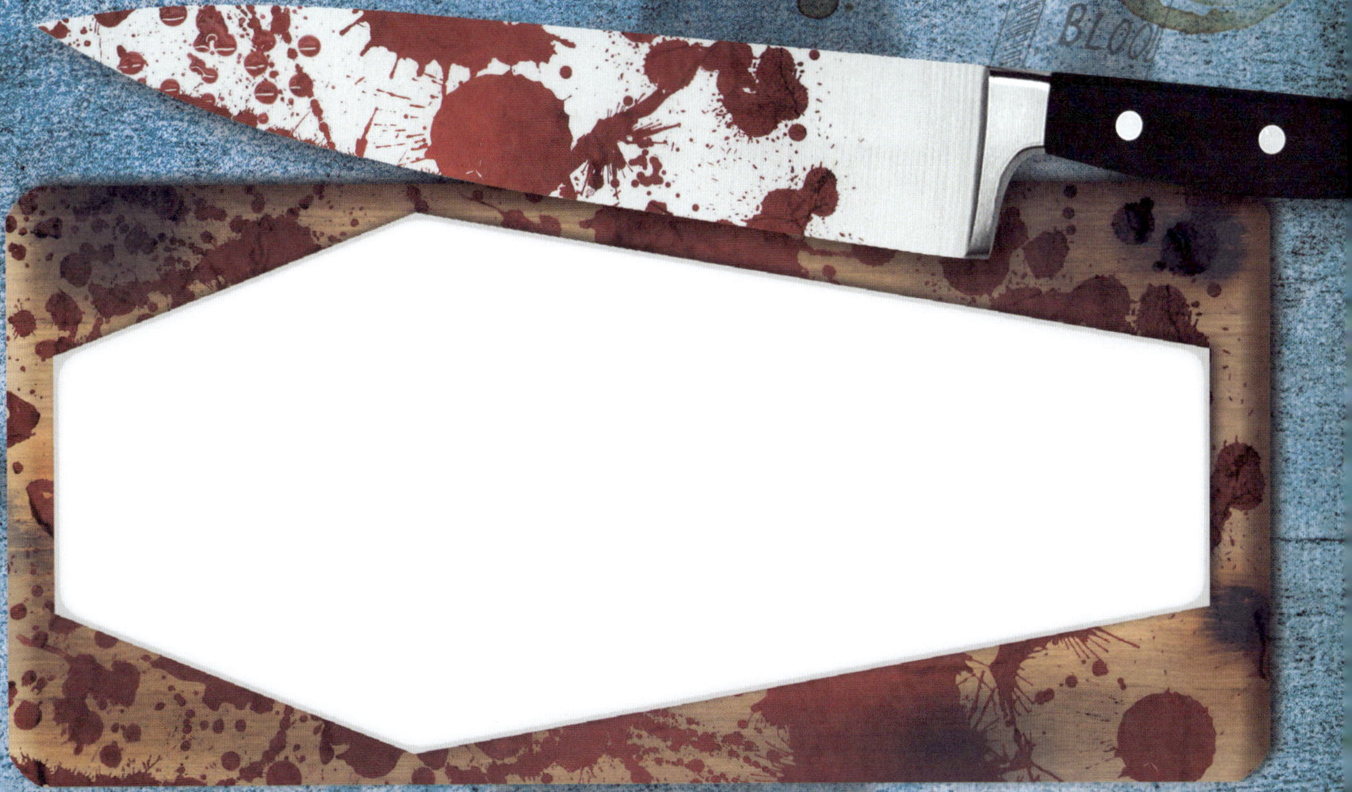

The Coffin Cake
Design some vampirish
decoration to the blood-dripping tasty party piece!

"OH, IT'S NIGHT-TIME. I WAS HAVING A DAYMARE."

DRACULA: DEAD AND LOVING IT

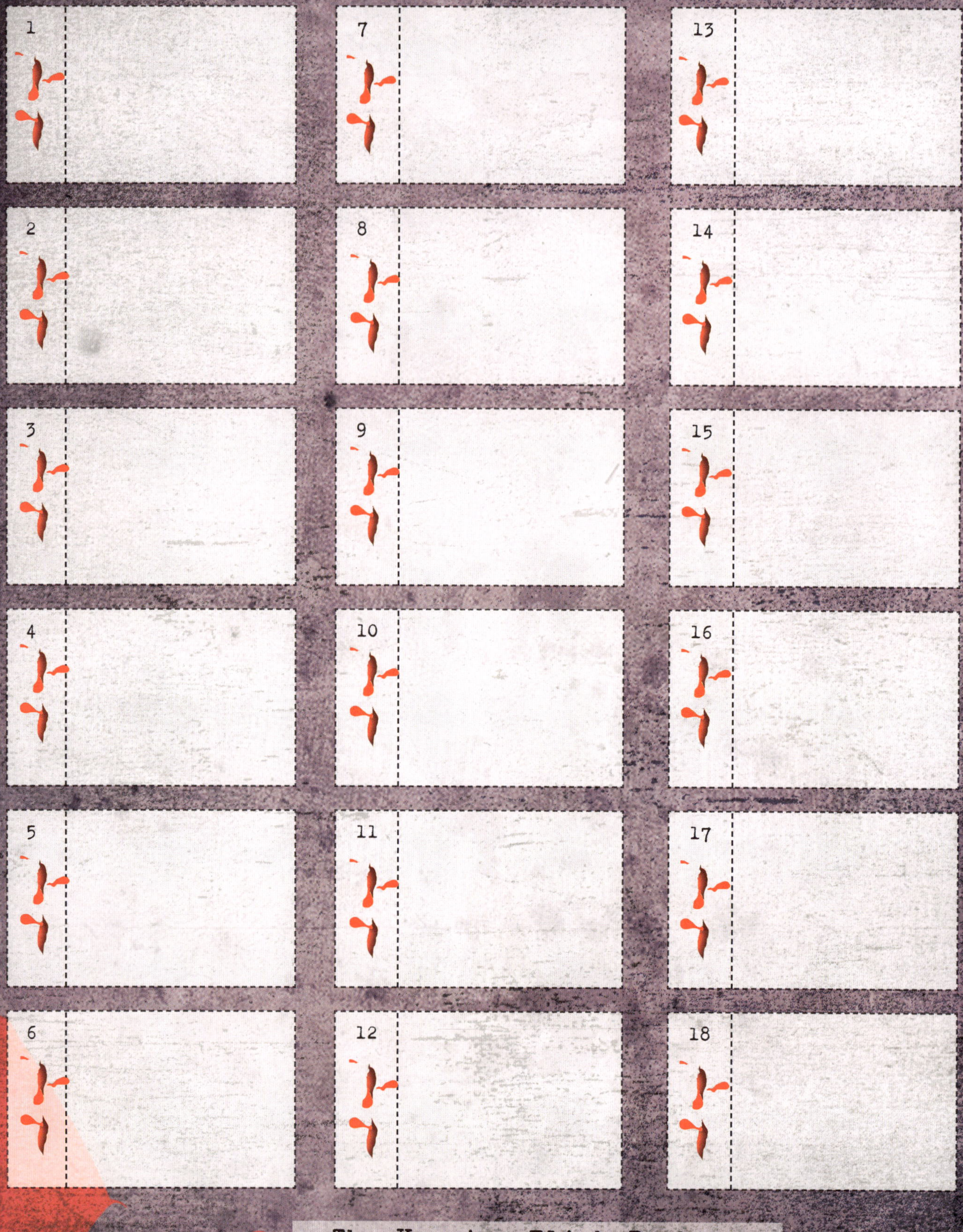

The Vampire Flick Book

You will need to copy this page four times.

Then doodle in your character, making sure that it changes slightly in each frame.

Cut all the frames out and staple together.

Watch as your creepy character comes to life!

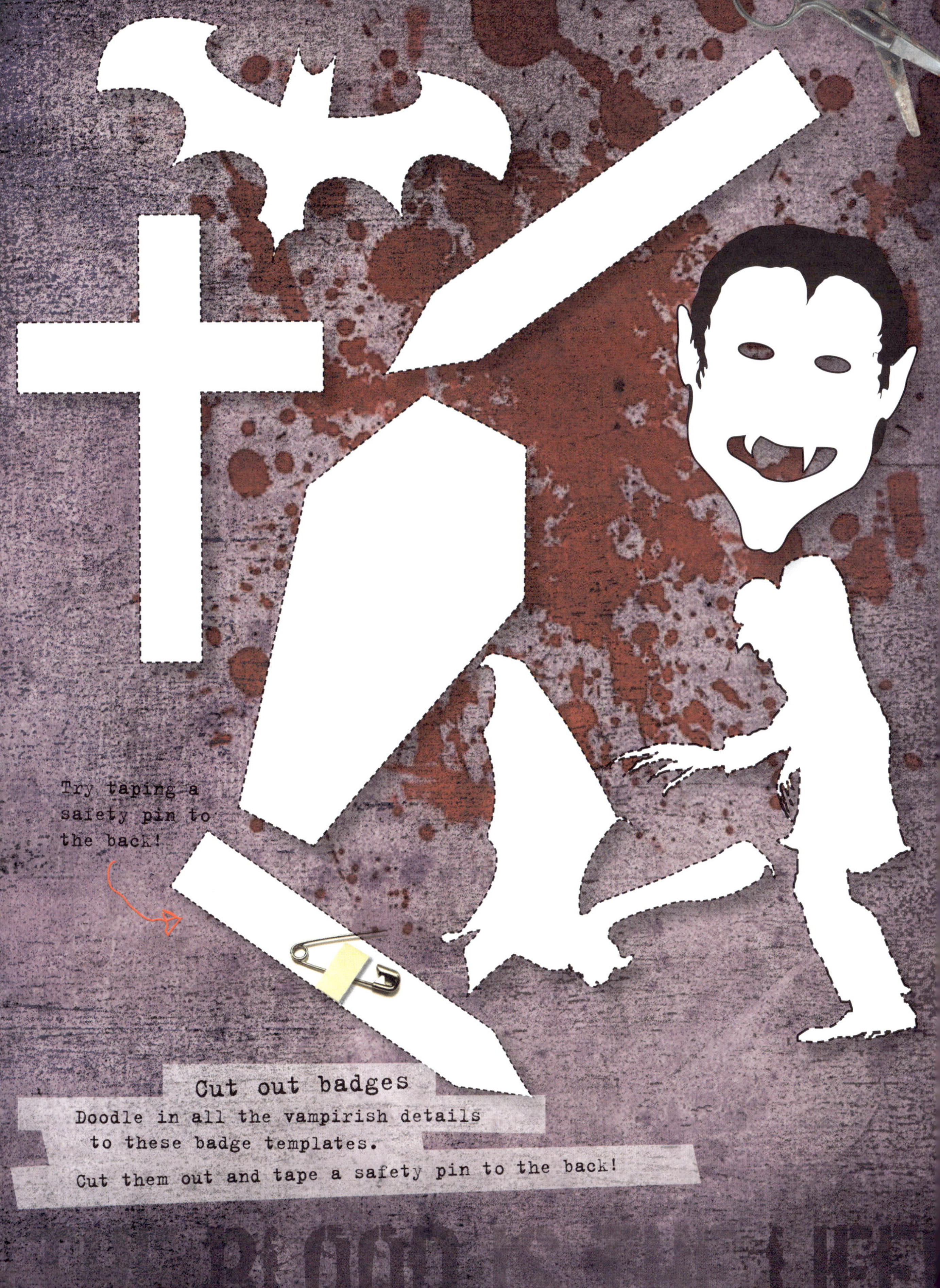
Try taping a
safety pin to
the back!
Cut out badges
Doodle in all the vampirish details
to these badge templates.
Cut them out and tape a safety pin to the back!
BLOOD
LIFE

Word Search

bat
bloodsucker
coffin
eternal
garlic
hypnotize
spooky
twilight
undead

T H G E B T L W L E T O

B Y R D S L U A A A E E

S P O O K Y I W R Y I U

K N U O A P O Y G O I N

E O U I E N N A O D O N

L T W I L I G H T D I L

A I G O W K W T A F T D

N Z O H R D S E F T D P

R E K C U S D O O L B F

E U R R F N C I L R A G

T A E H U S H E E O T S

E A F S S T O N I N N N

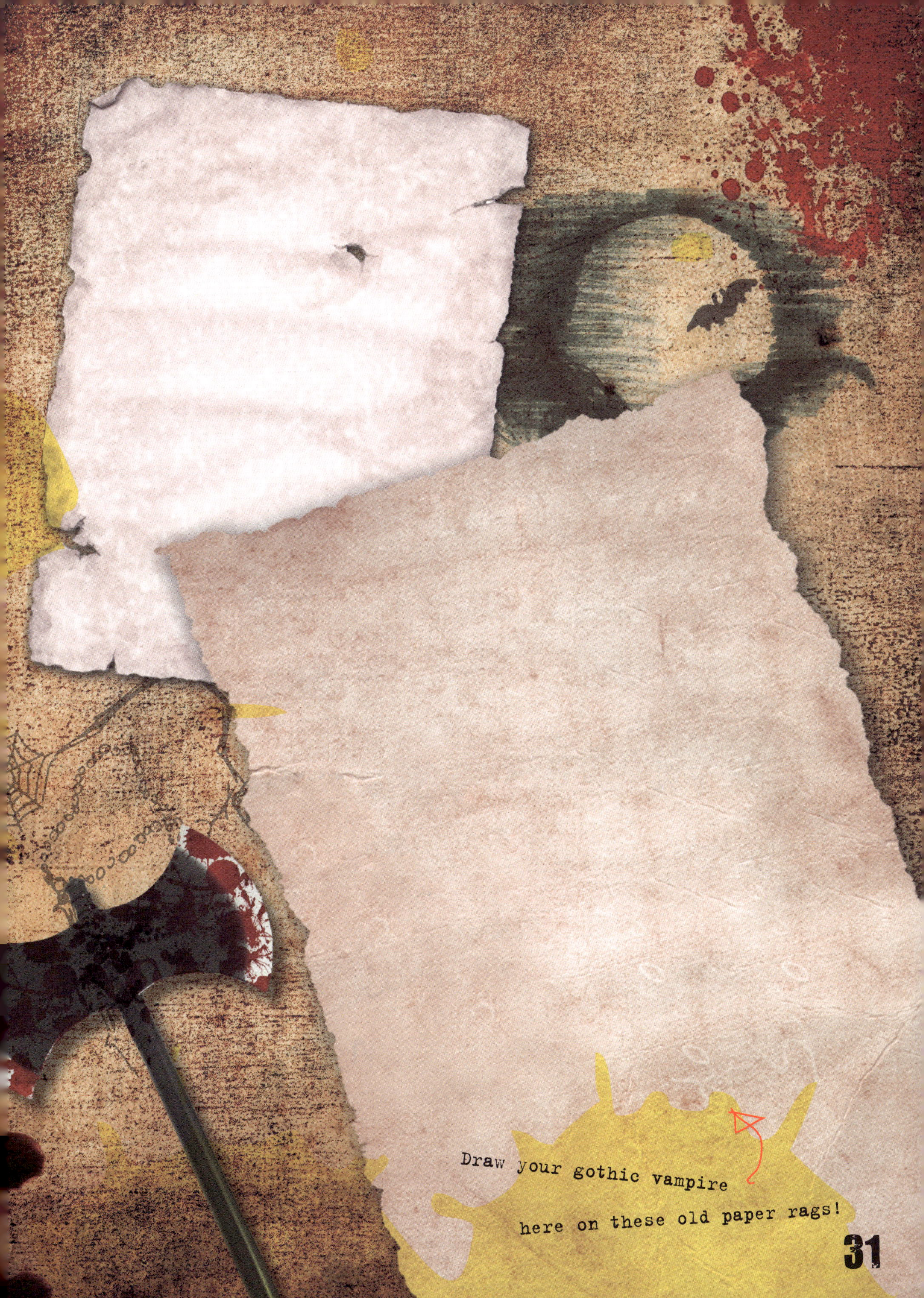
Draw your gothic vampire
here on these old paper rags!

Blood lines

Which vampire is heading for the dismal grave and does the determined vampire slayer fall foul of his task?

Unravel the tangled lines to discover their fate!

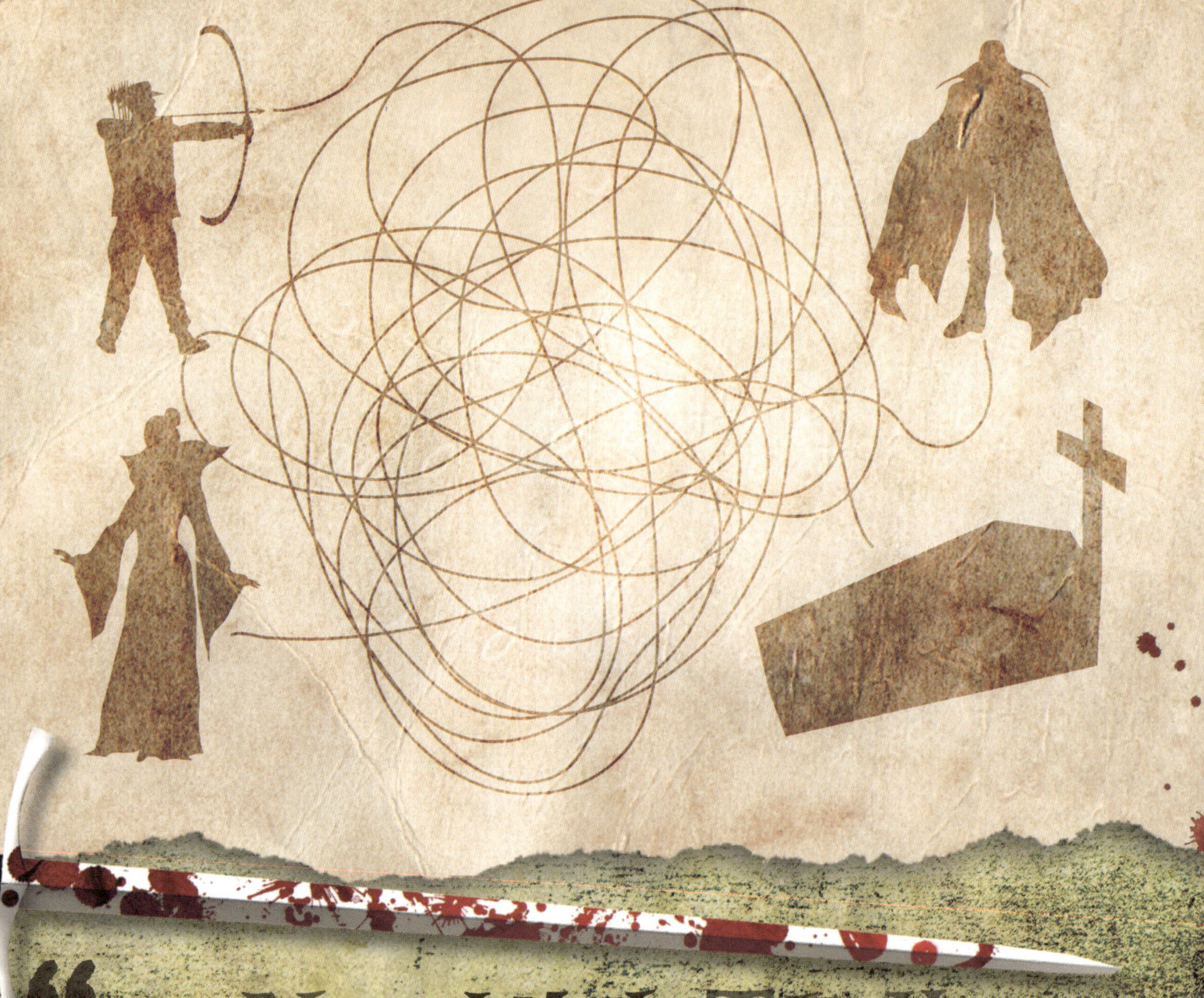

"TO WIN A WOMAN TAKE HER WITH YOU TO SEE DRACULA"

Bela Legosi

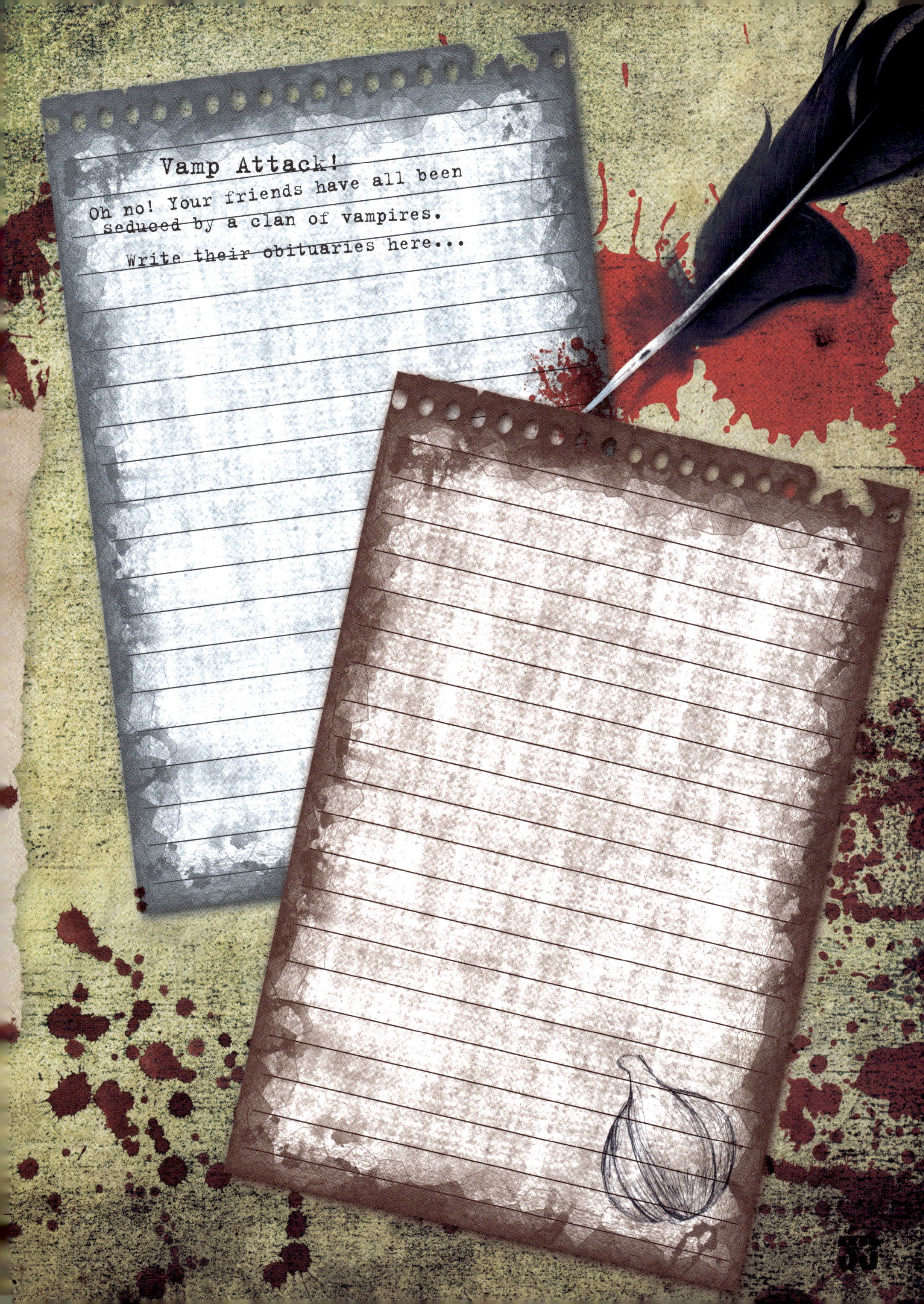
Vamp Attack!
Oh no! Your friends have all been seduced by a clan of vampires.
Write their obituaries here...

Hang in There

ABCDEFGHIJKLMNOPQRSTUVWXYZ

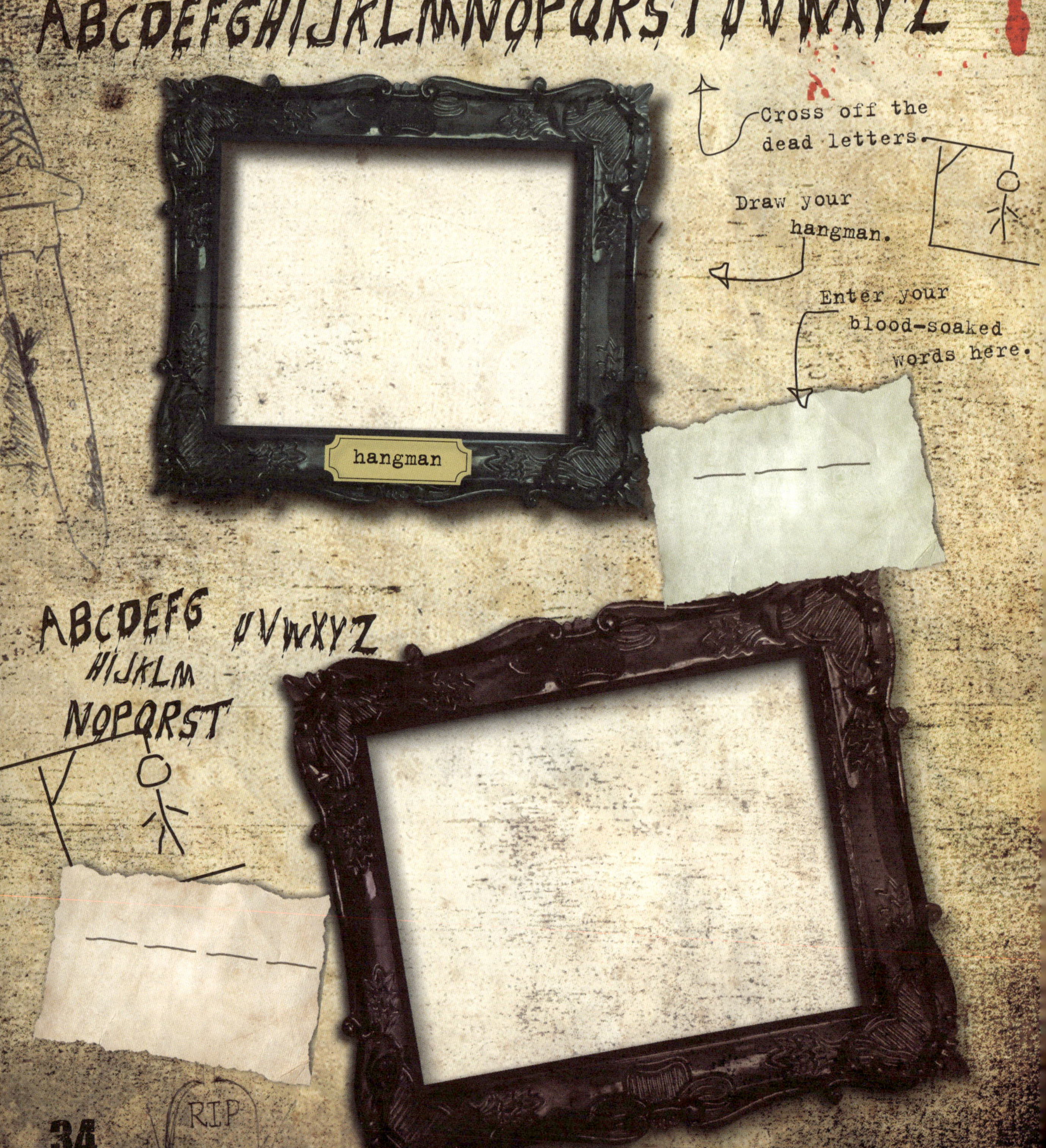

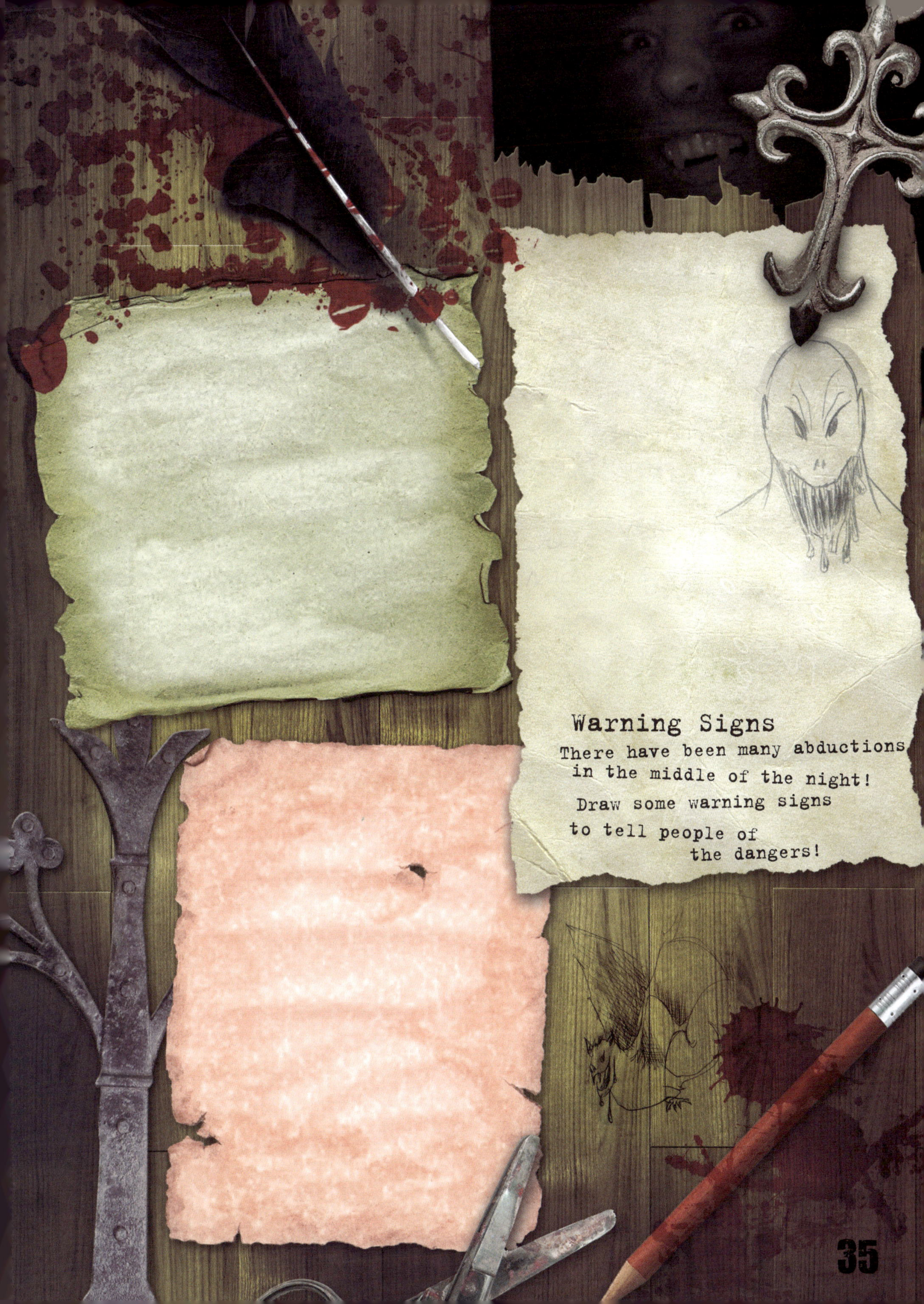

Warning Signs

There have been many abductions in the middle of the night! Draw some warning signs to tell people of the dangers!

Dot-to-Dot

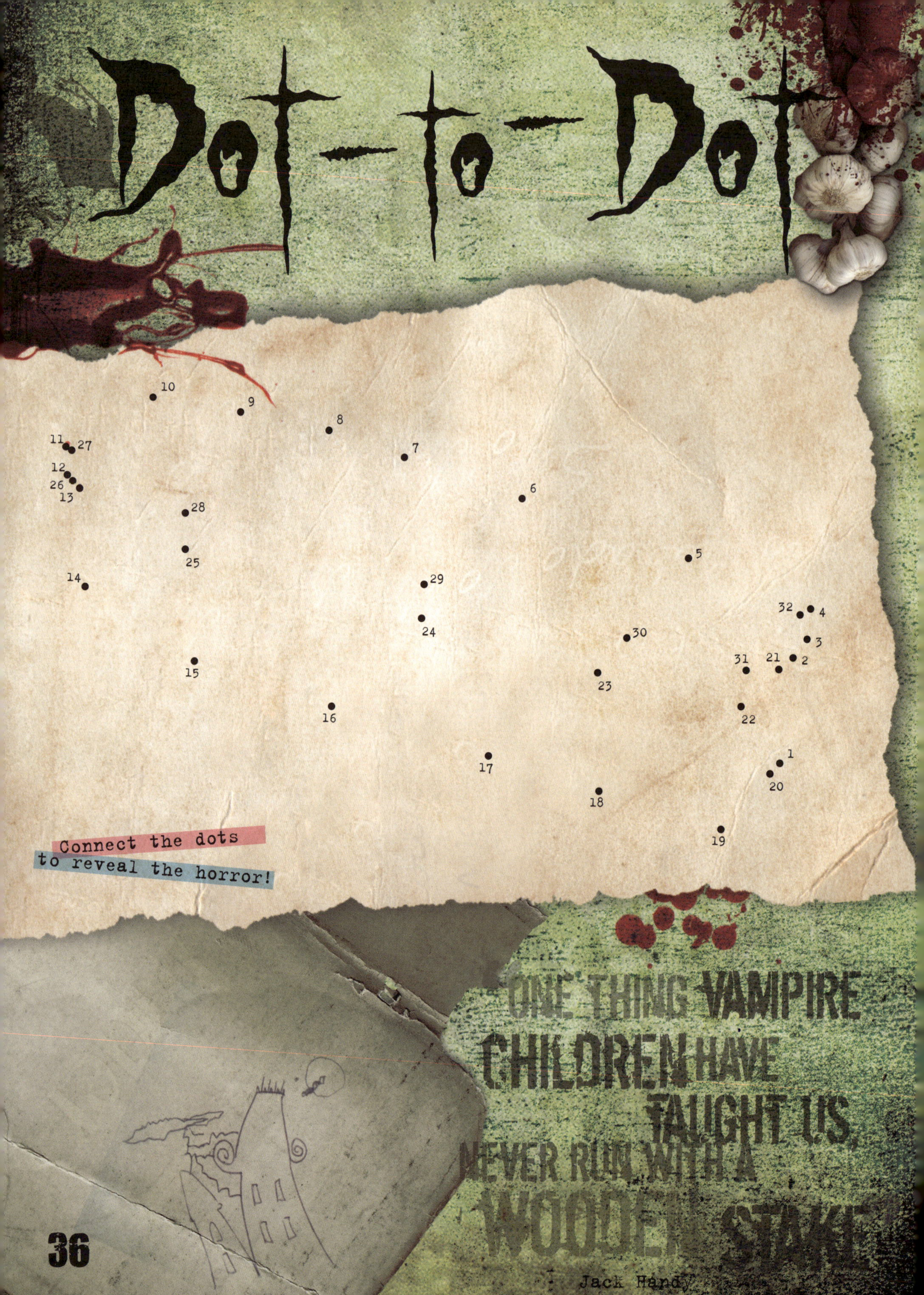

ONE THING VAMPIRE CHILDREN HAVE TAUGHT US, NEVER RUN WITH A WOODEN STAKE

Jack Handy

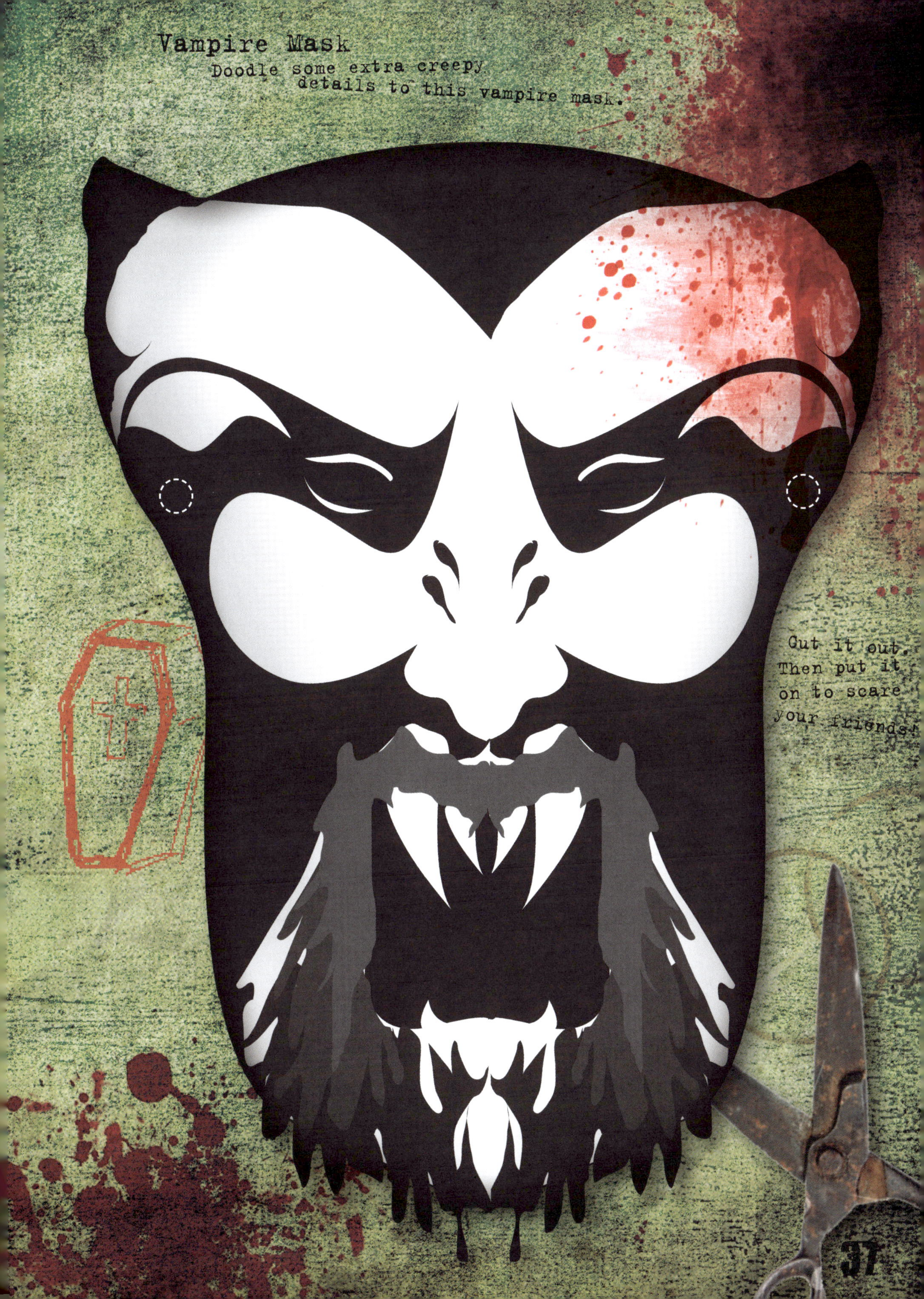
Vampire Mask
Doodle some extra creepy details to this vampire mask.
Cut it out. Then put it on to scare your friends!

Place your mirror here.

Draw in a creepy backward message on this old rotten paper.

ETERNAL LIFE

ABCDEFGH
IJKLMN
OPQRSTUVWXYZ

BLOODLIFE FILM PREMIER

Vampire Film Poster

Draw and design a fangtastic film poster to promote the latest bloodsucking blockbuster!

Spot the Difference

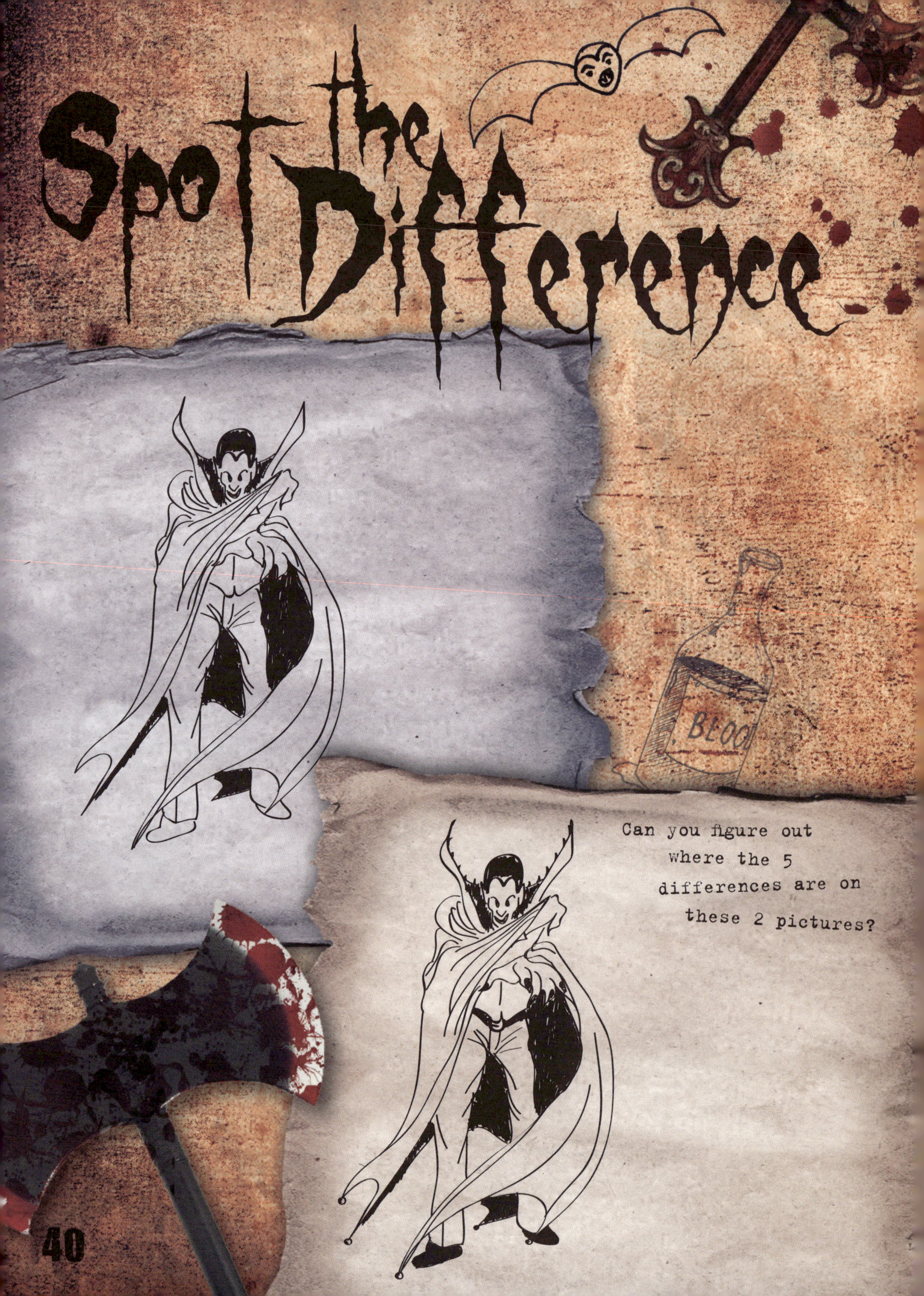

Can you figure out where the 5 differences are on these 2 pictures?

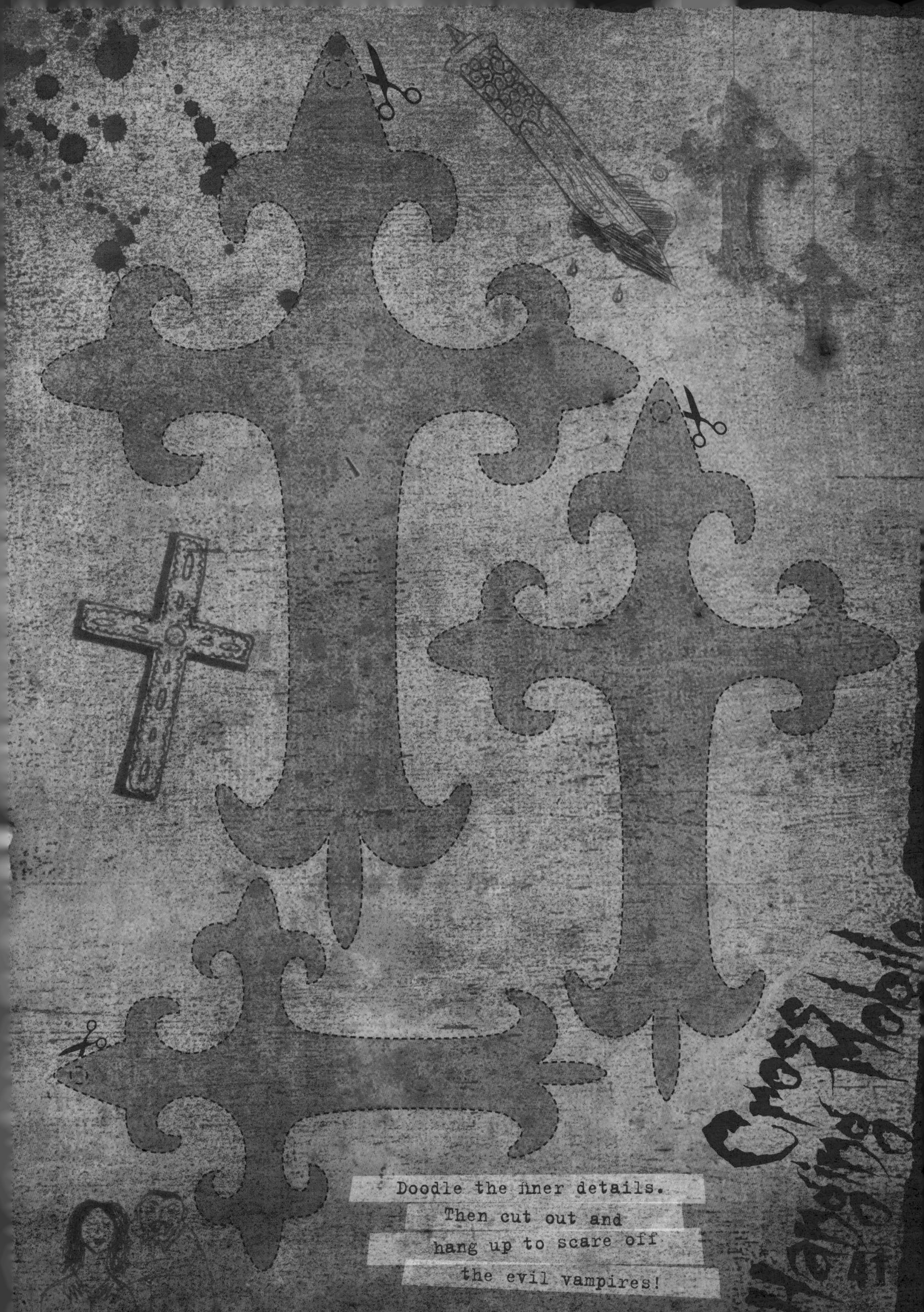
Cross
Hanging Mobile
Doodle the finer details.
Then cut out and
hang up to scare off
the evil vampires!
41

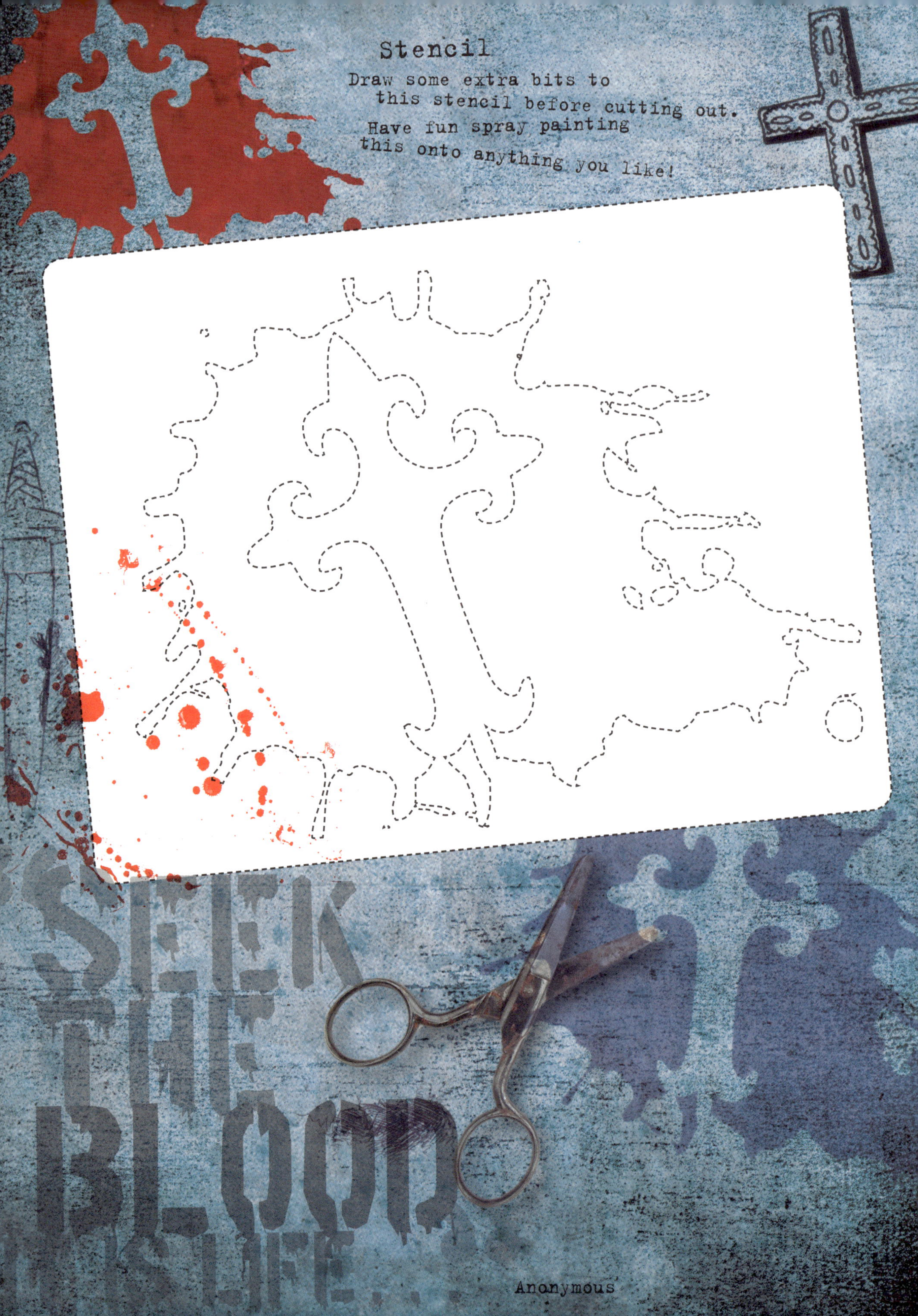
Stencil
Draw some extra bits to this stencil before cutting out.
Have fun spray painting this onto anything you like!
SEEK
THE
BLOOD
Anonymous

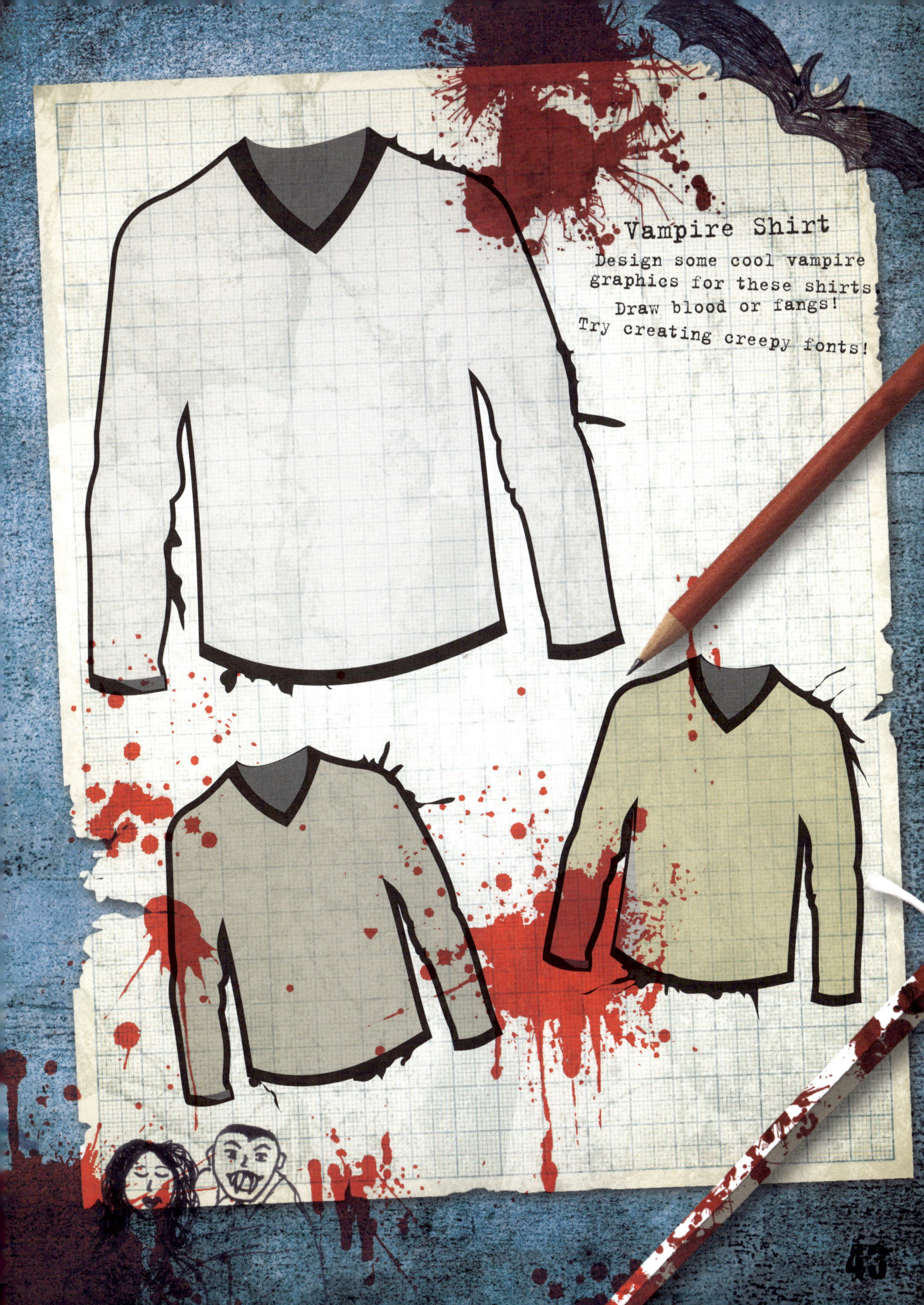

Vampire Shirt
Design some cool vampire
graphics for these shirts.
Draw blood or fangs!
Try creating creepy fonts!

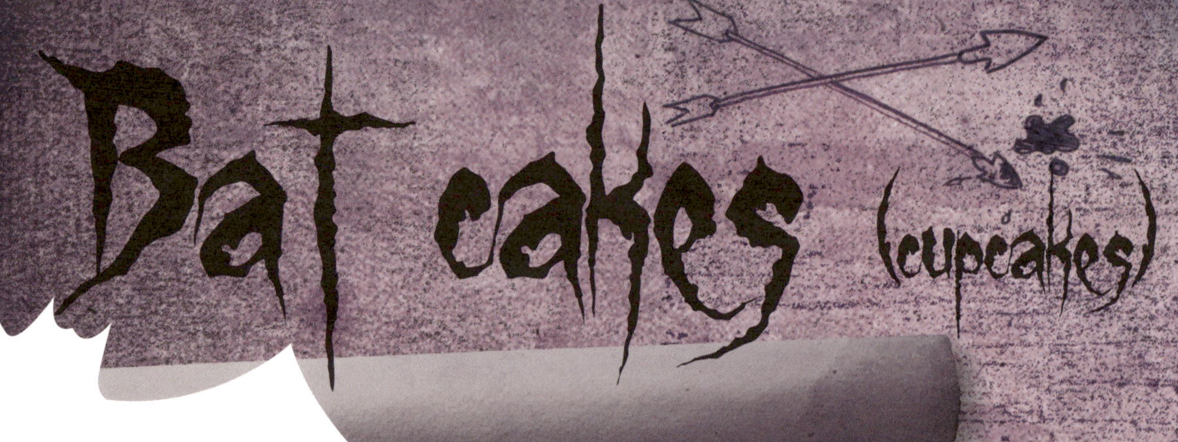

Bat cakes (cupcakes)

Use this bat stencil to add a scary element to your cupcake!

Ingredients

Serves: 12
Prep time: 15 mins
Cook time: 15 mins

4 oz. butter or margarine
4 oz. superfine sugar
2 eggs
1/2 tsp. vanilla extract (optional)
4 oz. self-rising flour, sifted
1/4 tsp. baking powder (optional)

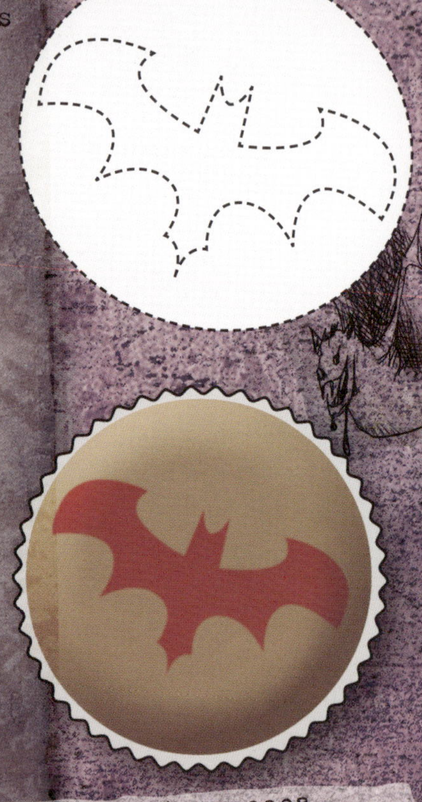

Method

1. Preheat the oven to 350 degrees and place 12 paper cases into a 12-hole muffin pan.
2. Using an electric blender, food processor, or wooden spoon, beat the butter and sugar. until very light and fluffy.
3. Add the eggs one at a time, beating each one in well before adding the next. Add the vanilla extract, if using.
4. Carefully fold in the flour and baking powder if using.
5. Bake in the oven for 10 to 20 minutes. After 10 minutes, check to see if the cupcakes are ready by inserting a toothpick into one of the cupcakes. Lift the cupcakes out of the muffin pan and let cool on a wire rack.

Try using cocoa powder or dark cinnamon!

Warning
adult assistance recommended for a safe result!

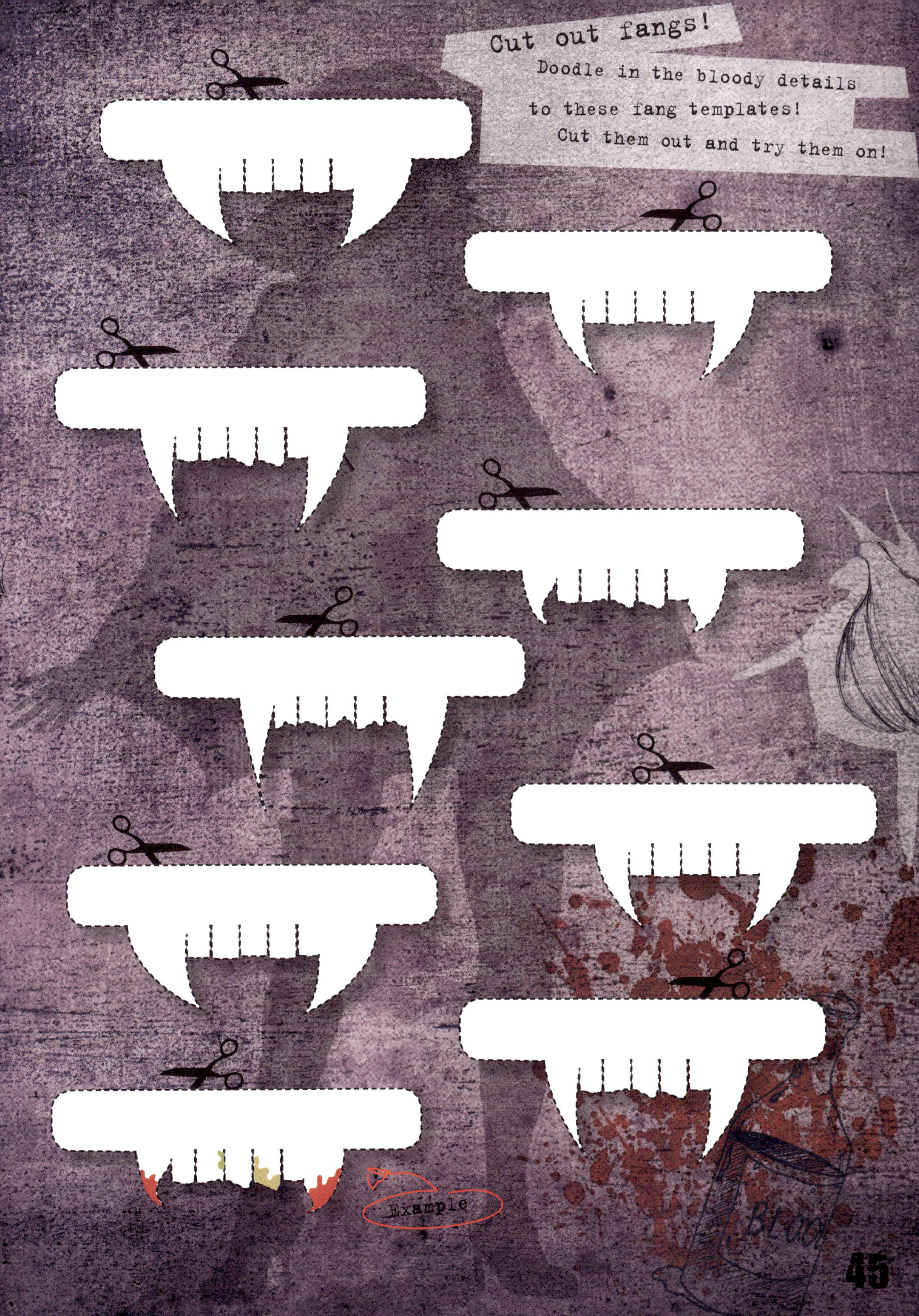
Cut out fangs!
Doodle in the bloody details
to these fang templates!
Cut them out and try them on!
Example
Blood

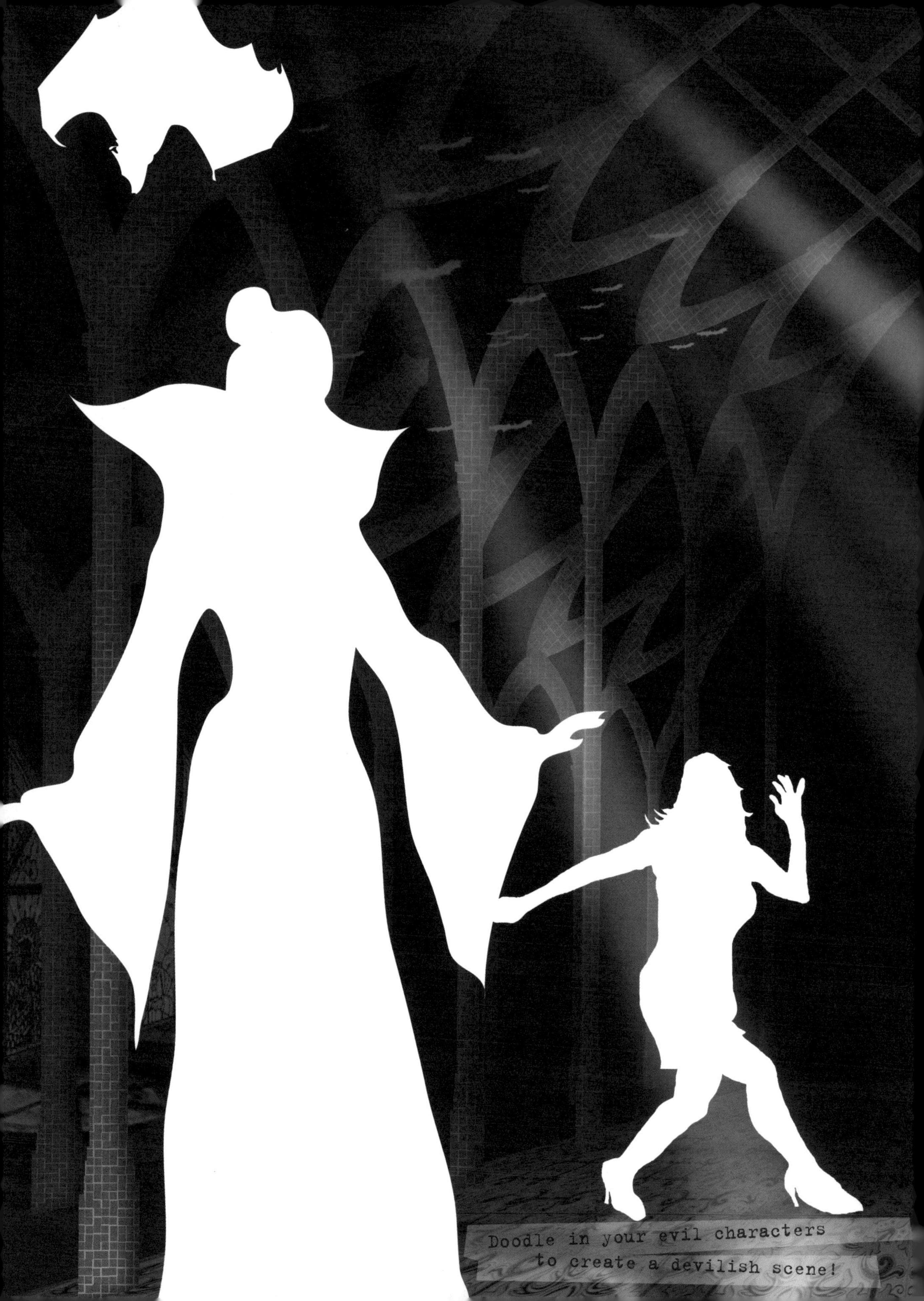
Doodle in your evil characters
to create a devilish scene!

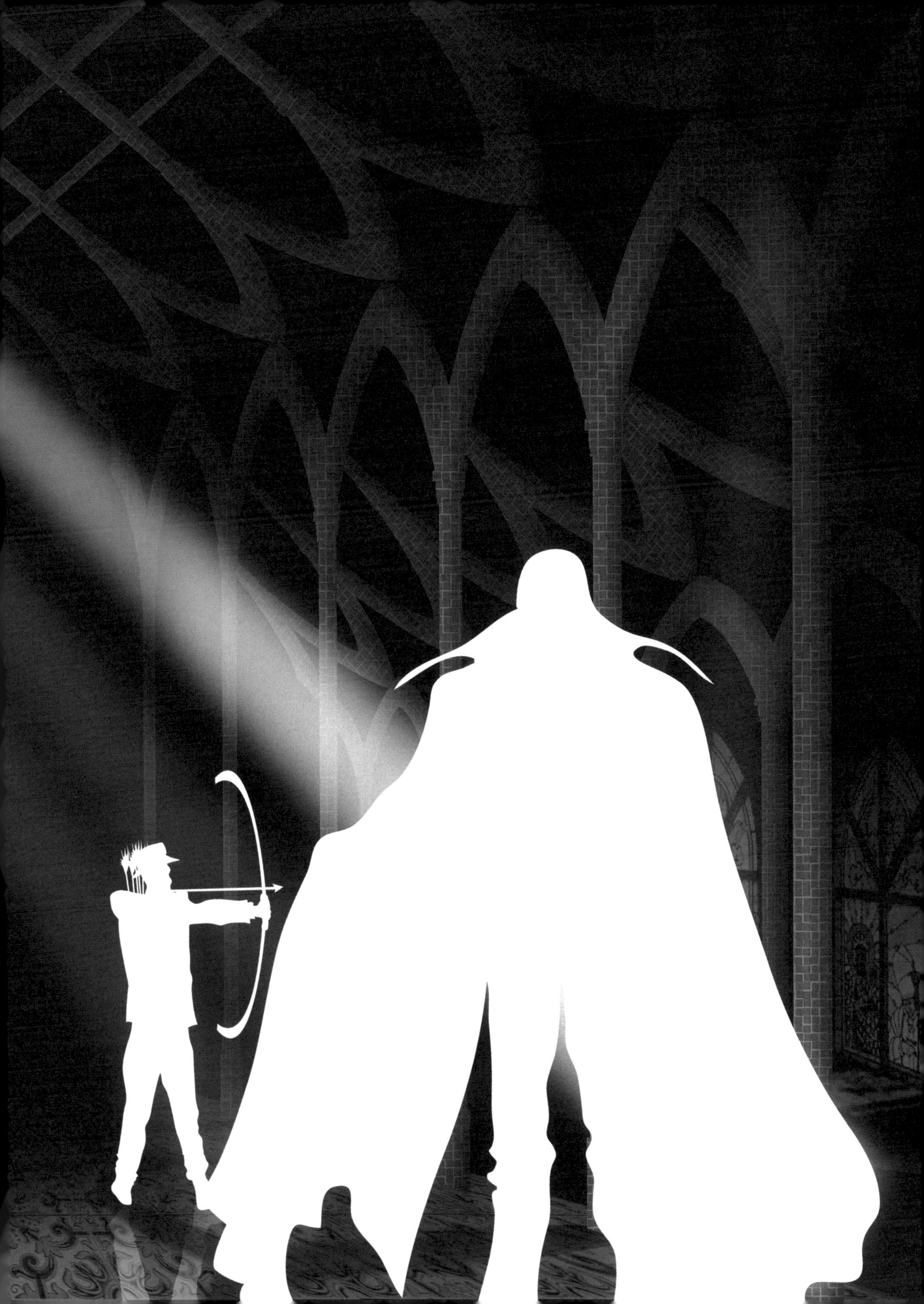

Vamp tattoo

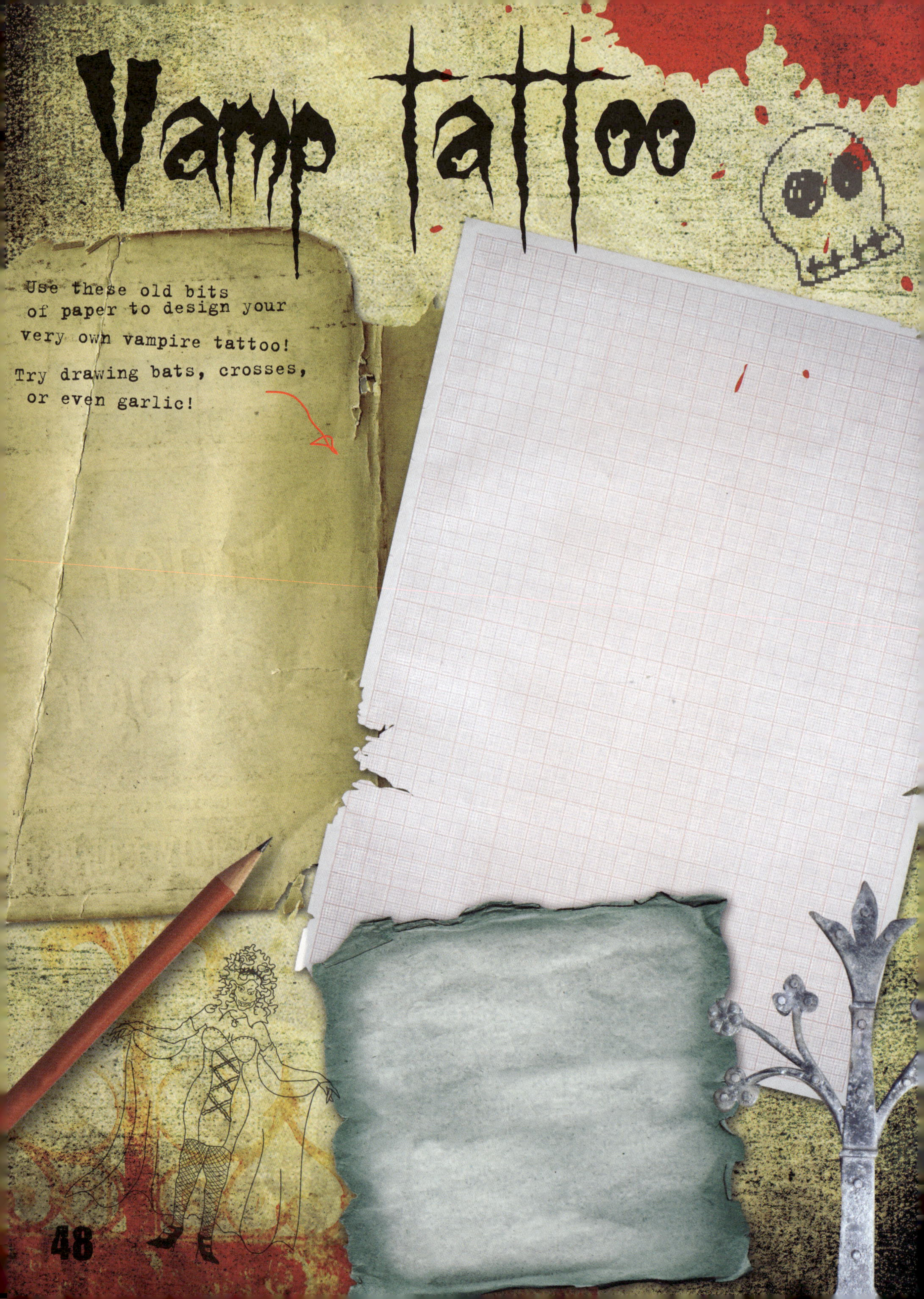

Use these old bits of paper to design your very own vampire tattoo! Try drawing bats, crosses, or even garlic!

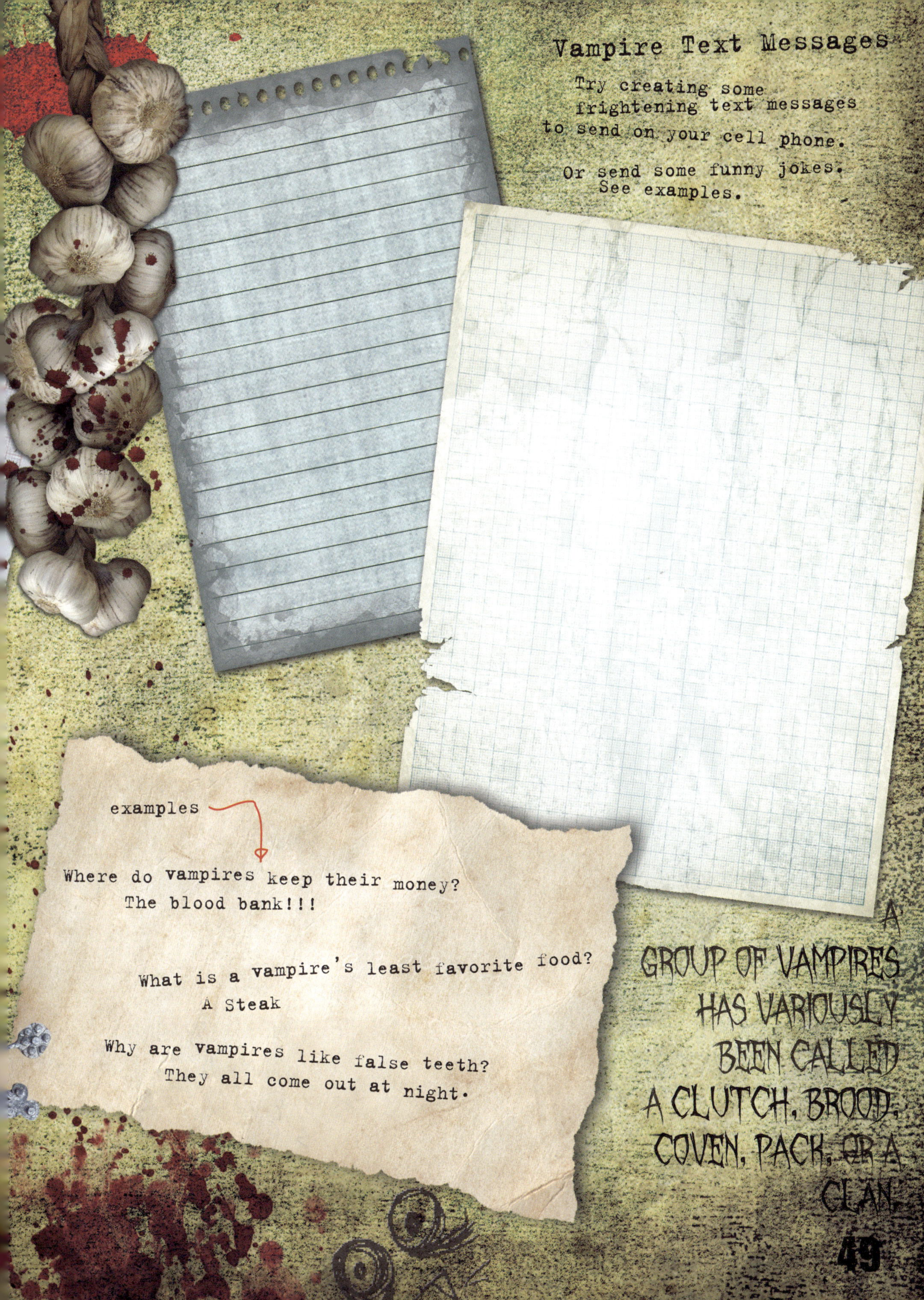

Vampire Text Messages

Try creating some frightening text messages to send on your cell phone.

Or send some funny jokes. See examples.

examples

Where do vampires keep their money?
The blood bank!!!

What is a vampire's least favorite food?
A Steak

Why are vampires like false teeth?
They all come out at night.

A GROUP OF VAMPIRES HAS VARIOUSLY BEEN CALLED A CLUTCH, BROOD, COVEN, PACK, OR A CLAN.

The Vampire

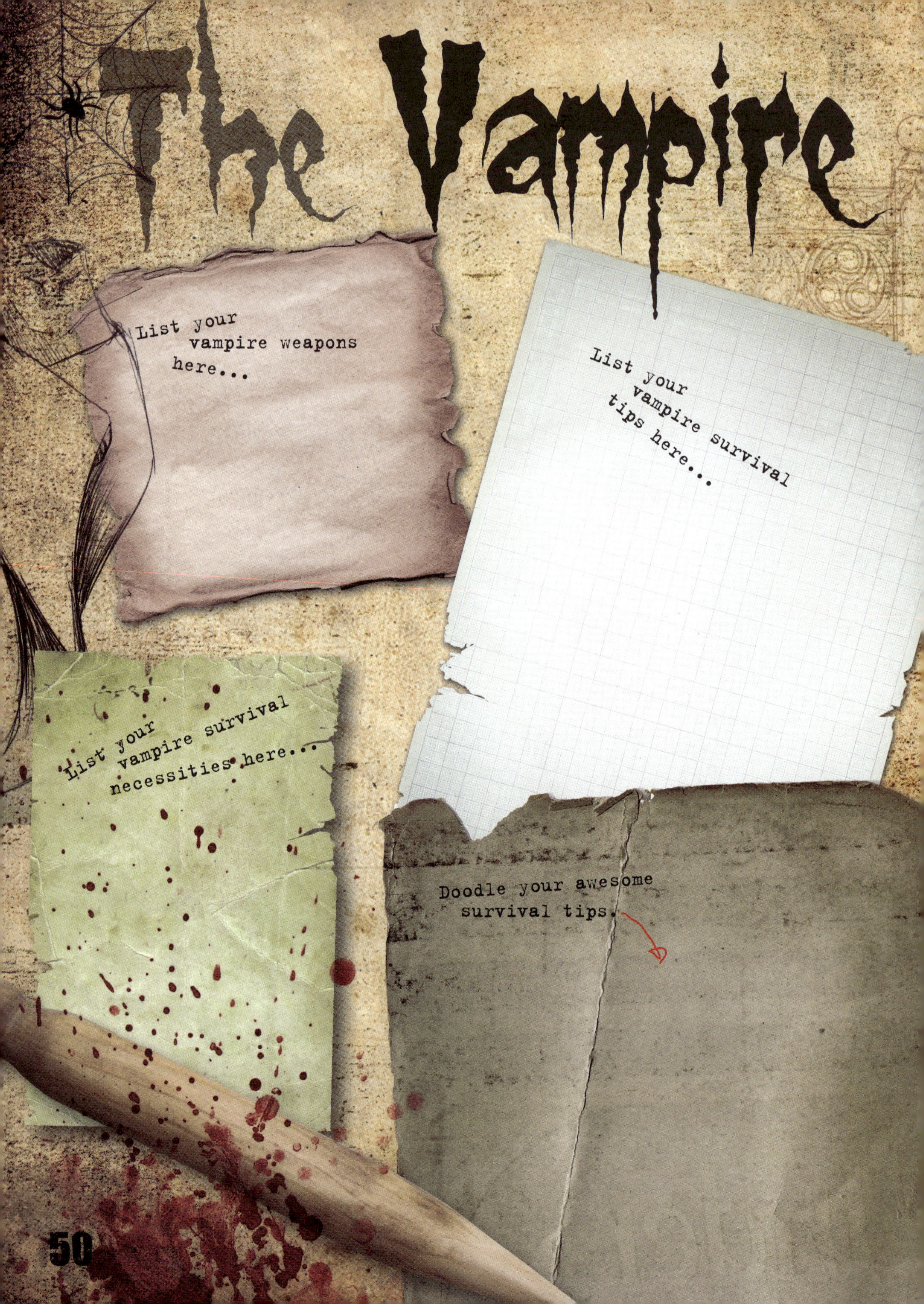
List your
vampire weapons
here...
List your
vampire survival
tips here...
List your
vampire survival
necessities here...
Doodle your awesome
survival tips.

Survival Kit

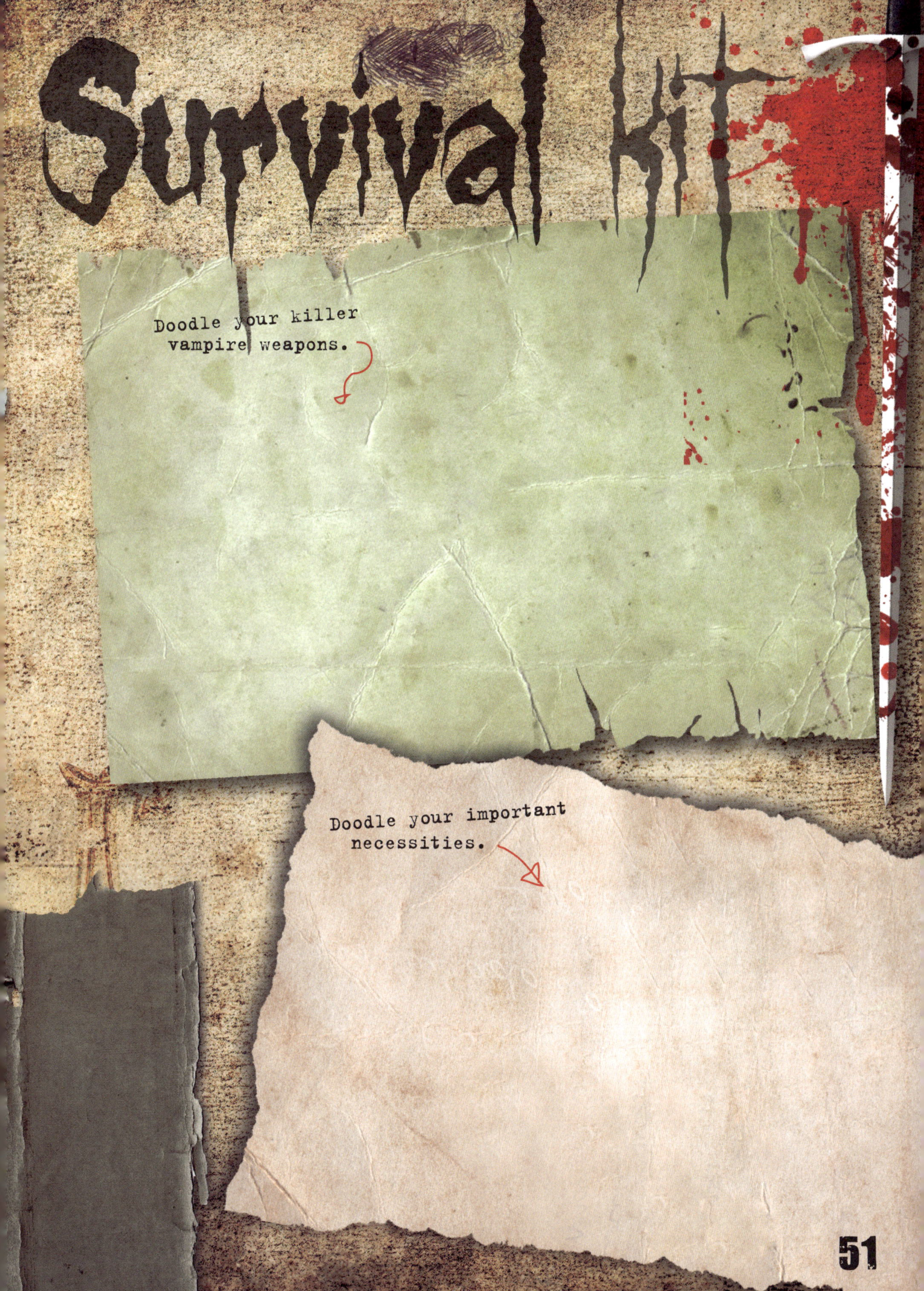

Doodle your killer vampire weapons.

Doodle your important necessities.

Your Vampire

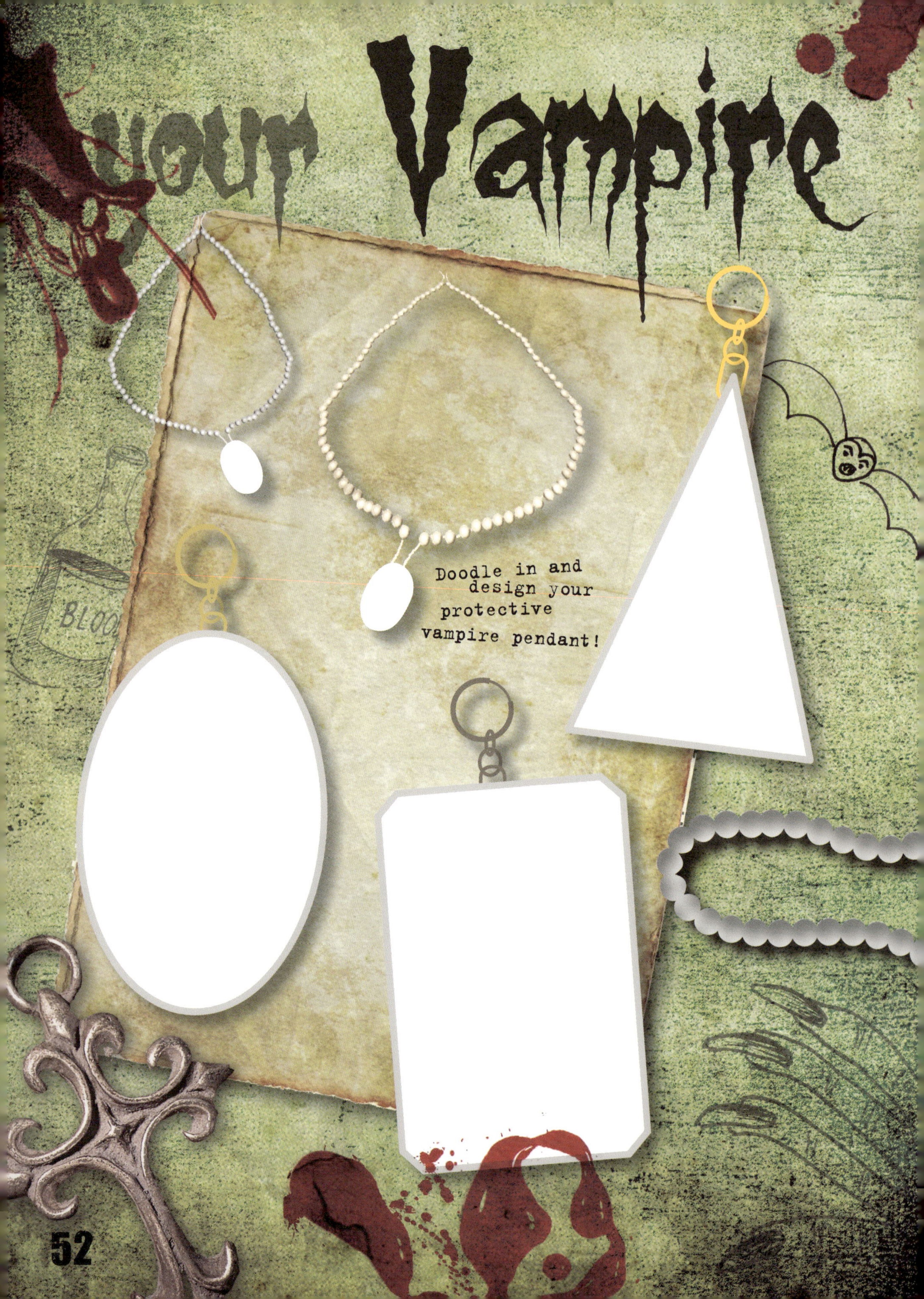

Doodle in and design your protective vampire pendant!

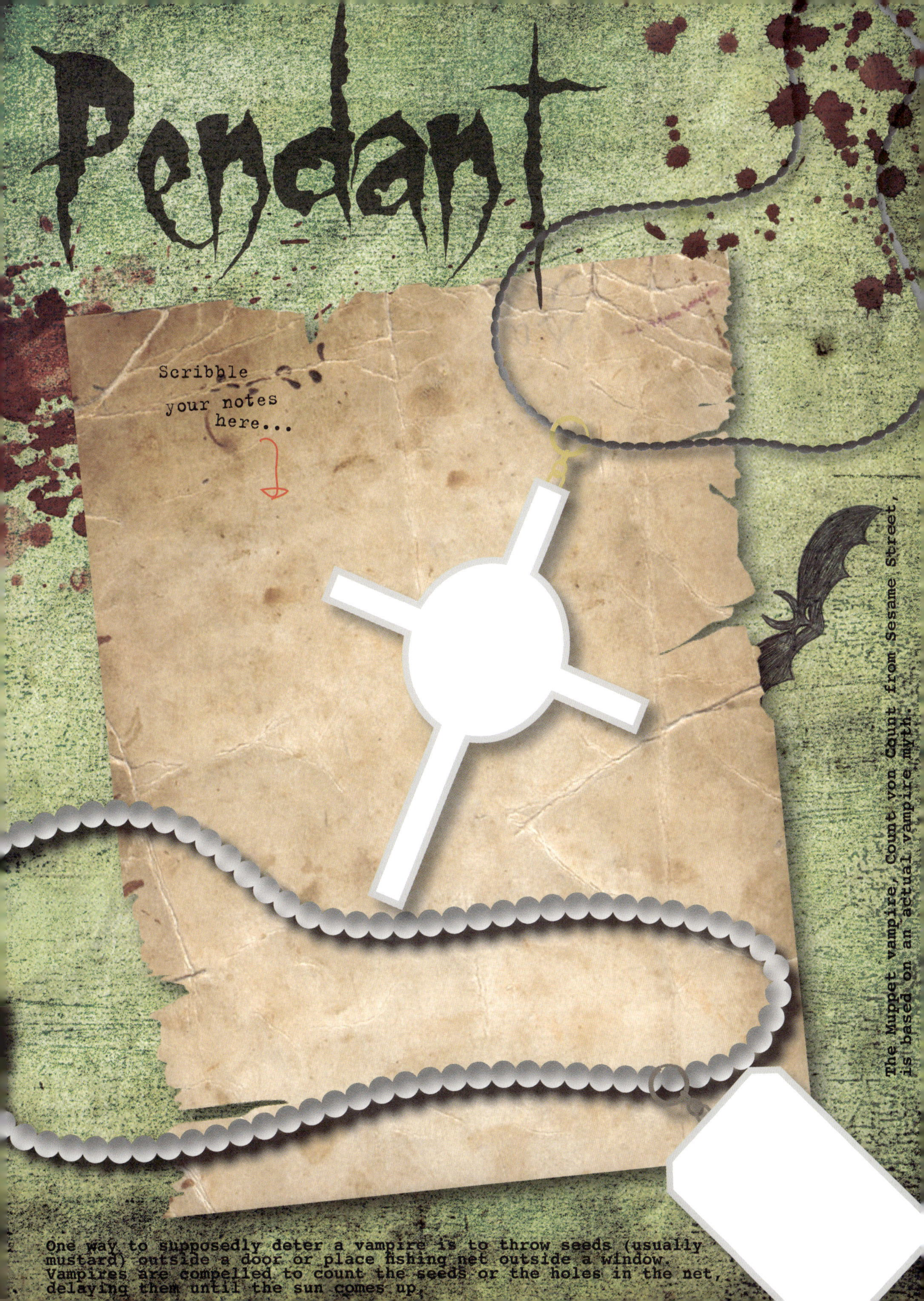
Pendant
Scribble your notes here...
The Muppet vampire, Count von Count from Sesame Street, is based on an actual vampire myth.
One way to supposedly deter a vampire is to throw seeds (usually mustard) outside a door or place fishing net outside a window. Vampires are compelled to count the seeds or the holes in the net, delaying them until the sun comes up.

Word Search

cape
cemetery
crucifix
lifeless
mirror
sunrise
terror
thirst
vampire

r m i s r c s s l y
r i t l u o h o s r
m s e s x n r c r e
e s n r r o r r e t
t e r t e u n i i e
t l a h c a p e s m
i e r i p m a v e e
t f f r s r u e i c
r i m s a f s i s i
x l t t r v i s o r

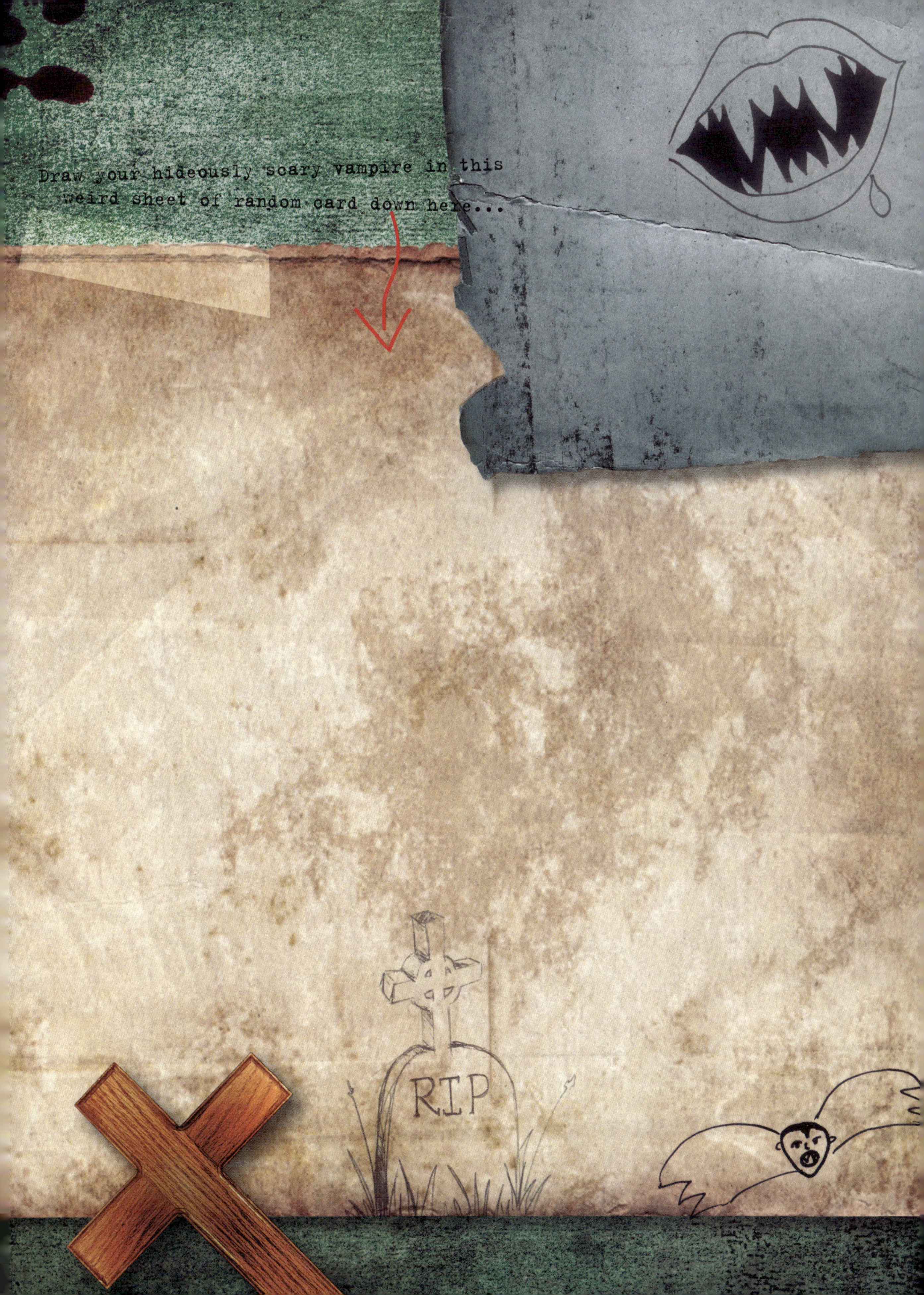
Draw your hideously scary vampire in this weird sheet of random card down here...
RIP

Vampire Tracks

The man has been seduced by the beautiful vampire; help her find her next victim!

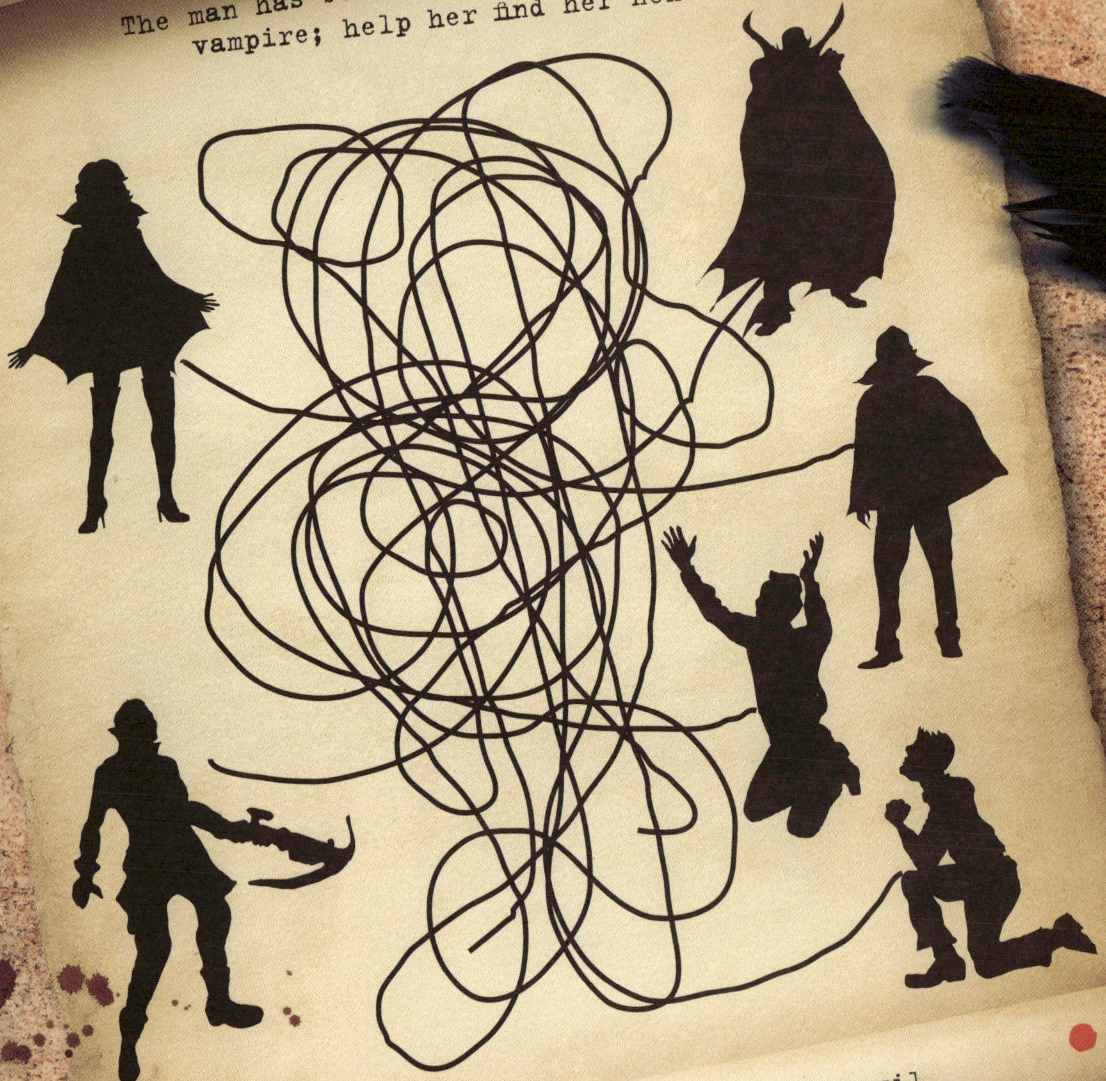

Help the vampire slayer find the evil vampire, otherwise more will be bitten!

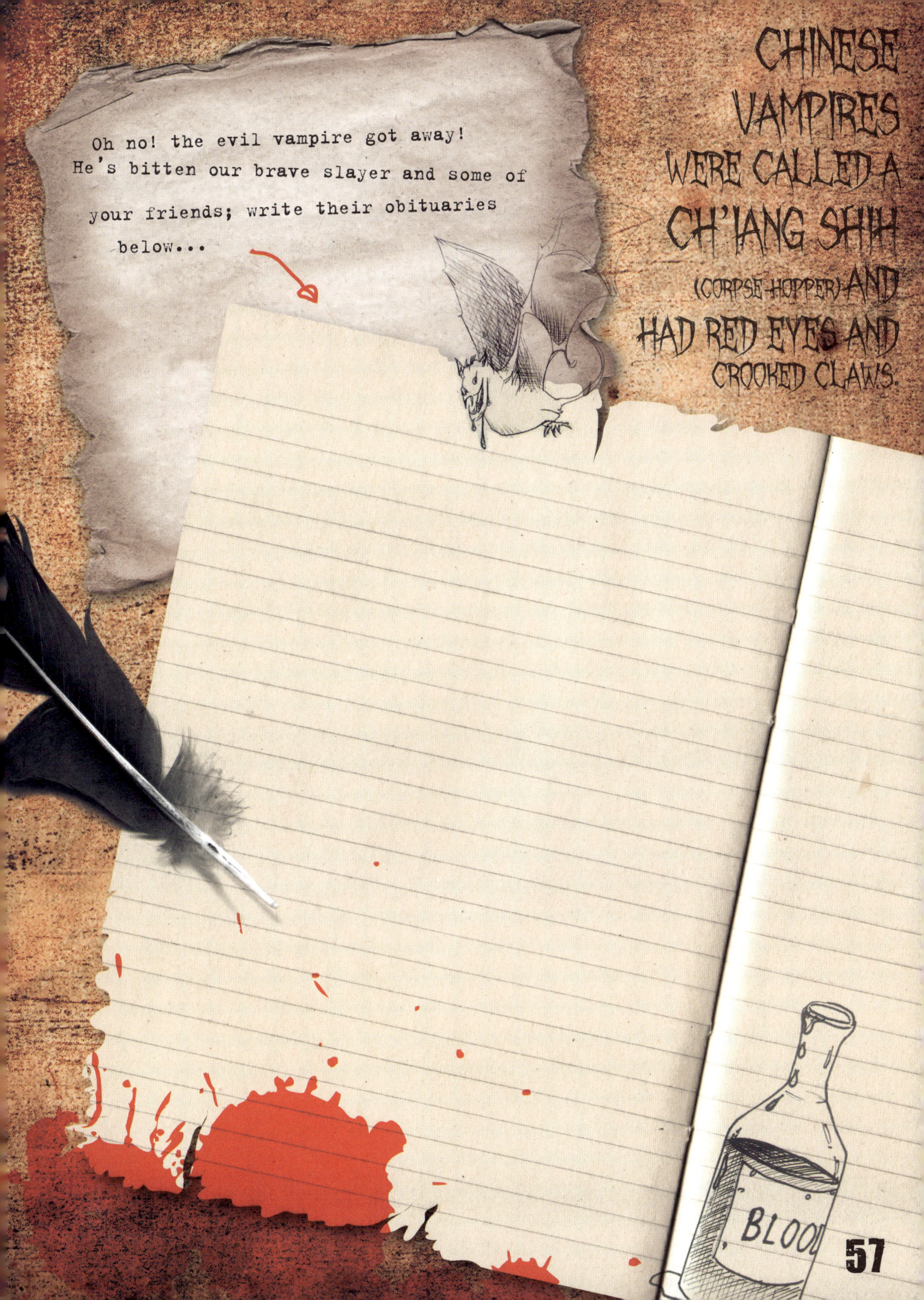
Oh no! the evil vampire got away! He's bitten our brave slayer and some of your friends; write their obituaries below...
CHINESE VAMPIRES WERE CALLED A CH'IANG SHIH (CORPSE-HOPPER) AND HAD RED EYES AND CROOKED CLAWS.
BLOO

Hangover

Cross off the dead letters.

ABCDEFGHIJKLM
NOPQRSTUVWXYZ

Draw your hangman.

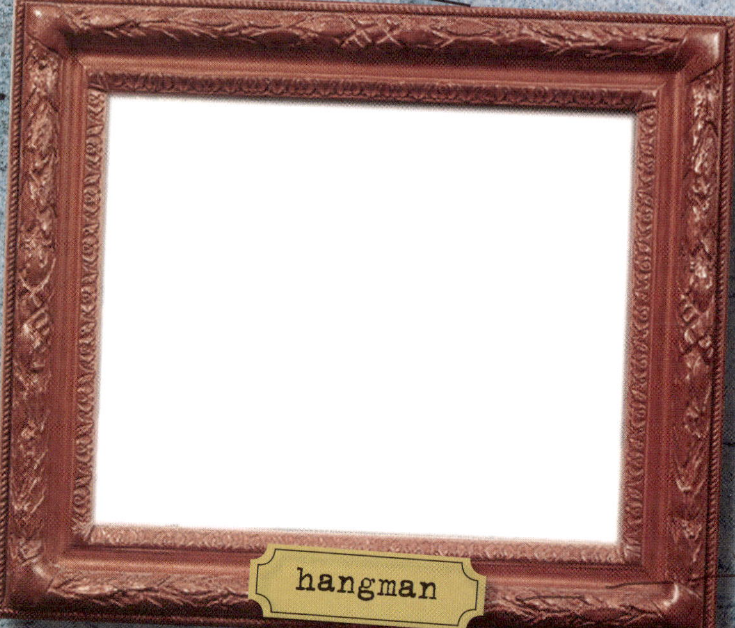

Enter your blood-soaked words here.

ABCDEFG UVWXYZ
HIJKLM
NOPQRST

Enter your blood-soaked words here.

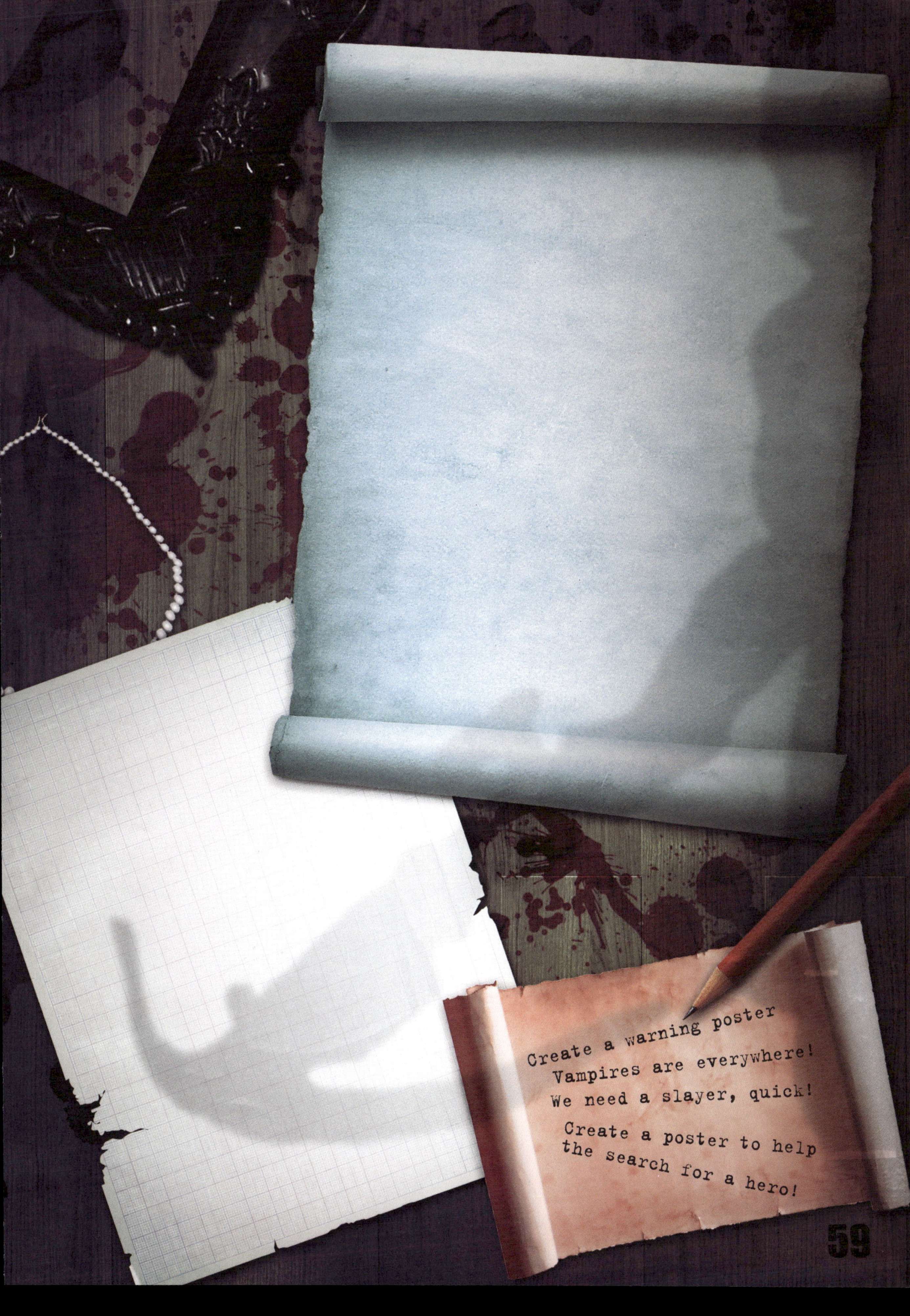
Create a warning poster
Vampires are everywhere!
We need a slayer, quick!
Create a poster to help the search for a hero!

Dot-to-Dot

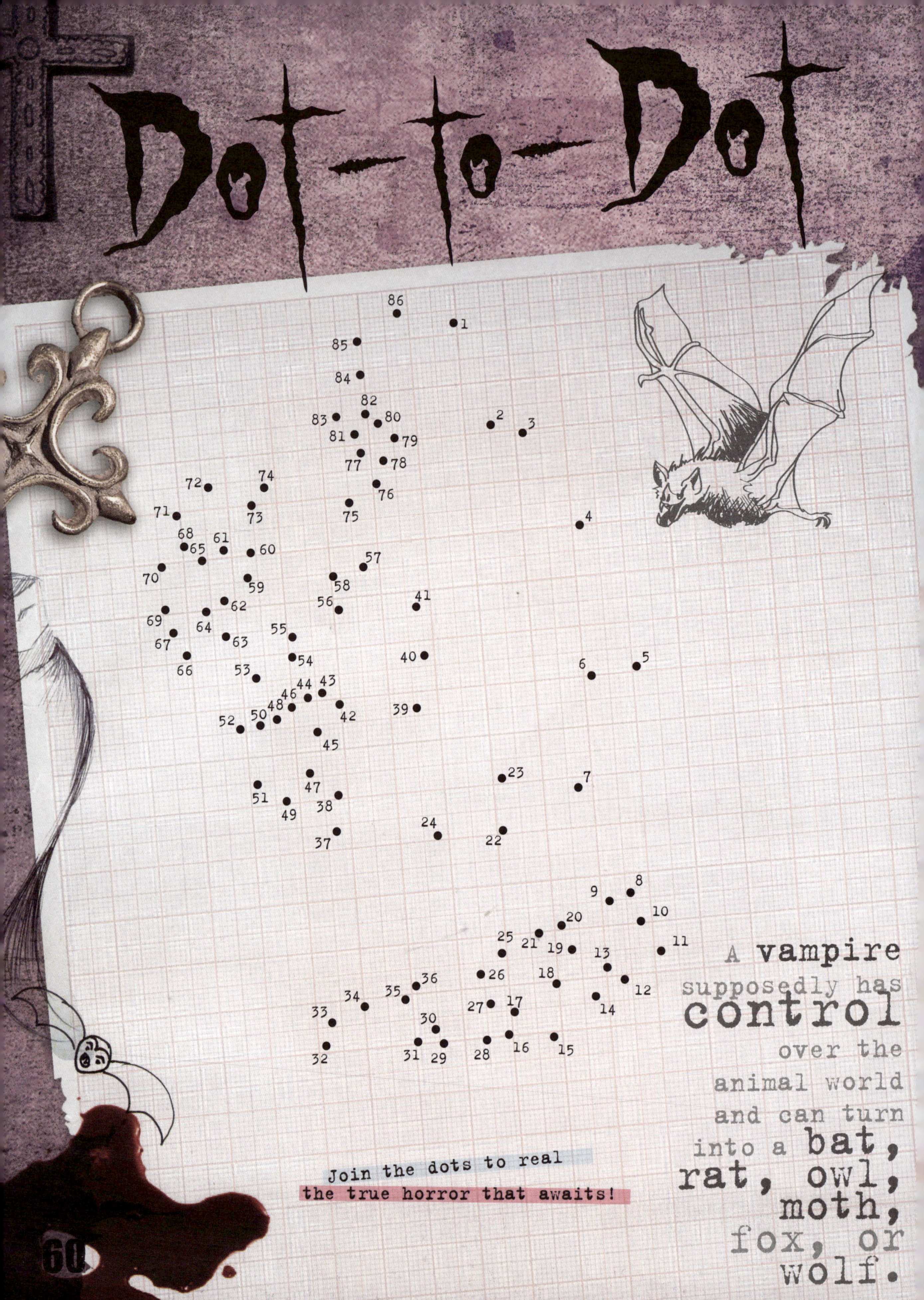

Join the dots to real the true horror that awaits!

A **vampire** supposedly has **control** over the animal world and can turn into a **bat**, **rat**, **owl**, **moth**, fox, or wolf.

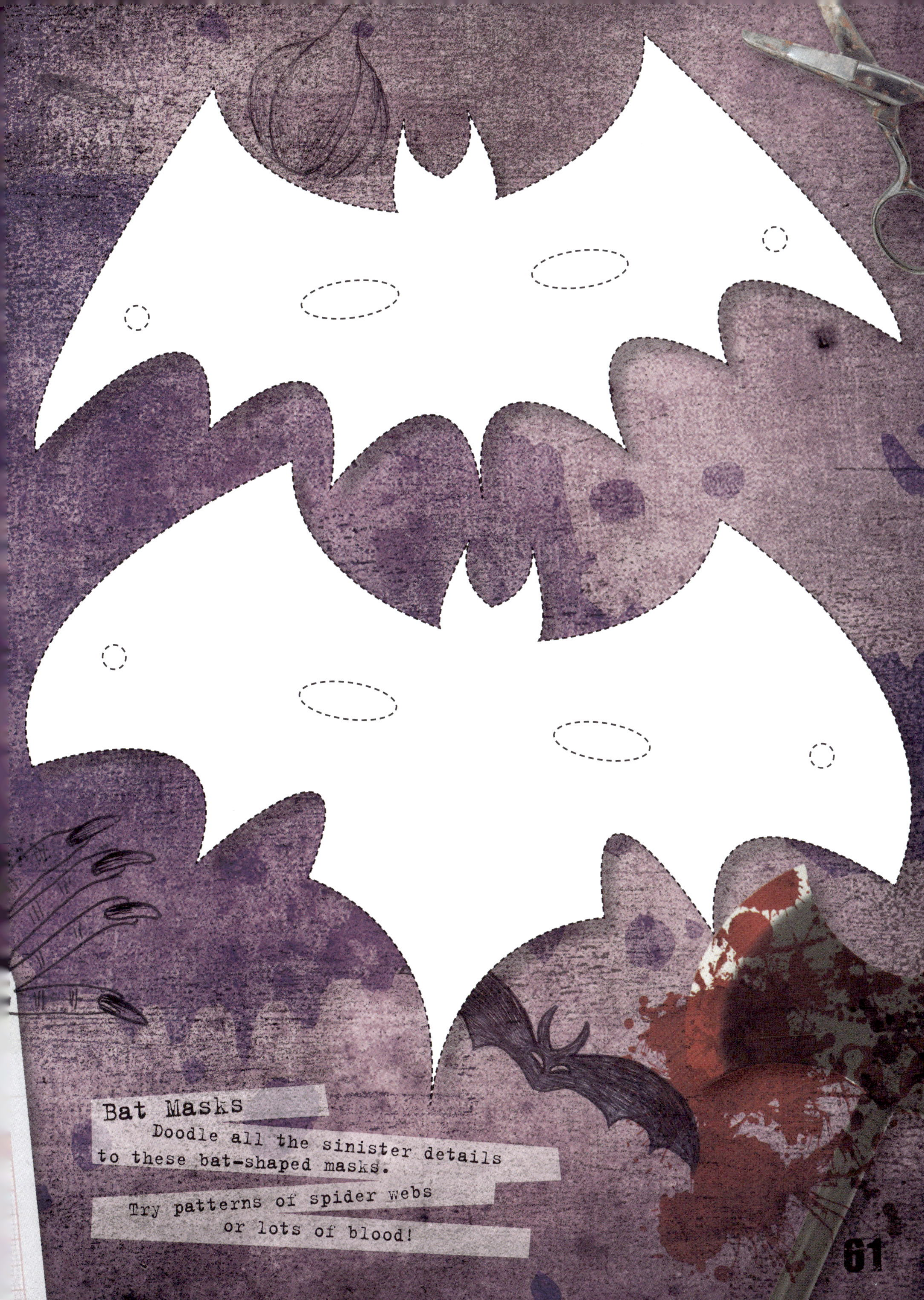

Bat Masks

Doodle all the sinister details to these bat-shaped masks.

Try patterns of spider webs or lots of blood!

Place your mirror here.

ABCDEFGHIJKLMN
OPQRSTU
VWXYZ

I HATE
GARLIC

Draw in a creepy
backward message
on this old rotten paper.

Create an iconic vampire poster for the ultimate fan.

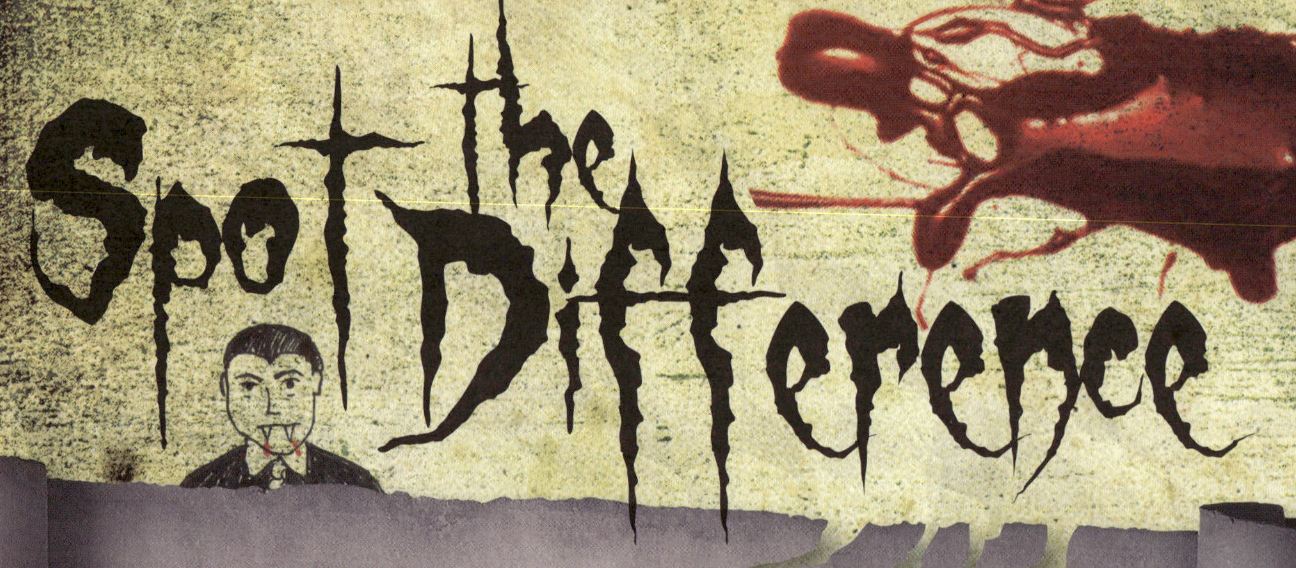

Spot the Difference

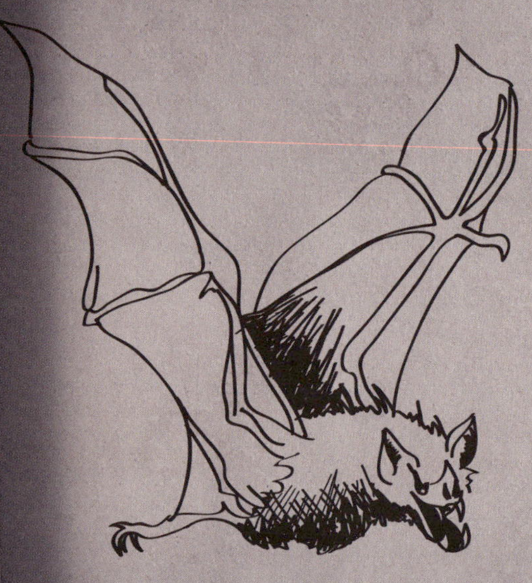

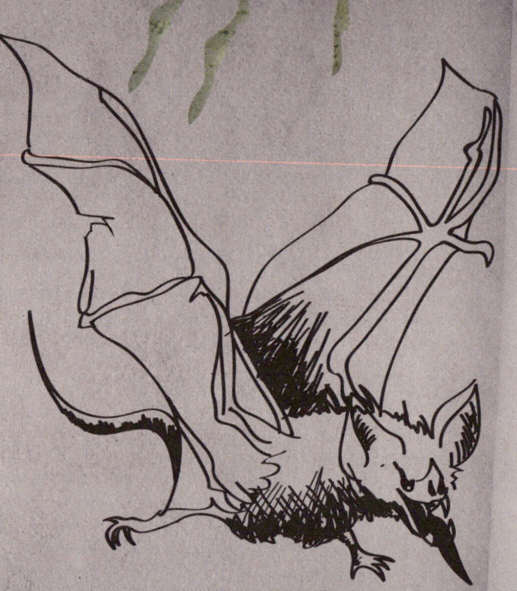

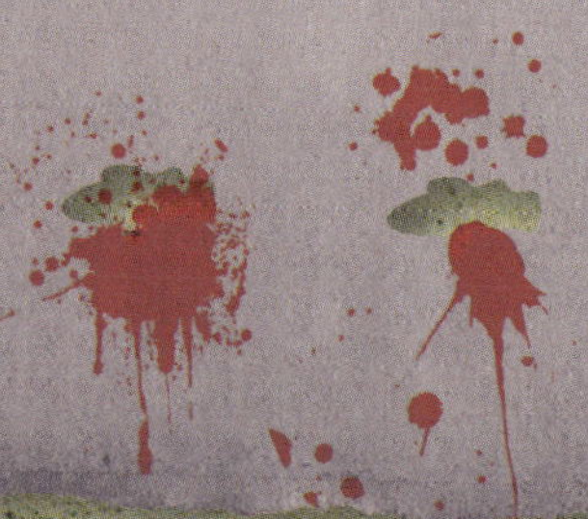

Can you spot the 5 differences between these chilling and creepy pictures?

According to several legends, if someone was bitten by a suspected vampire, he or she should drink the ashes of a burned vampire.

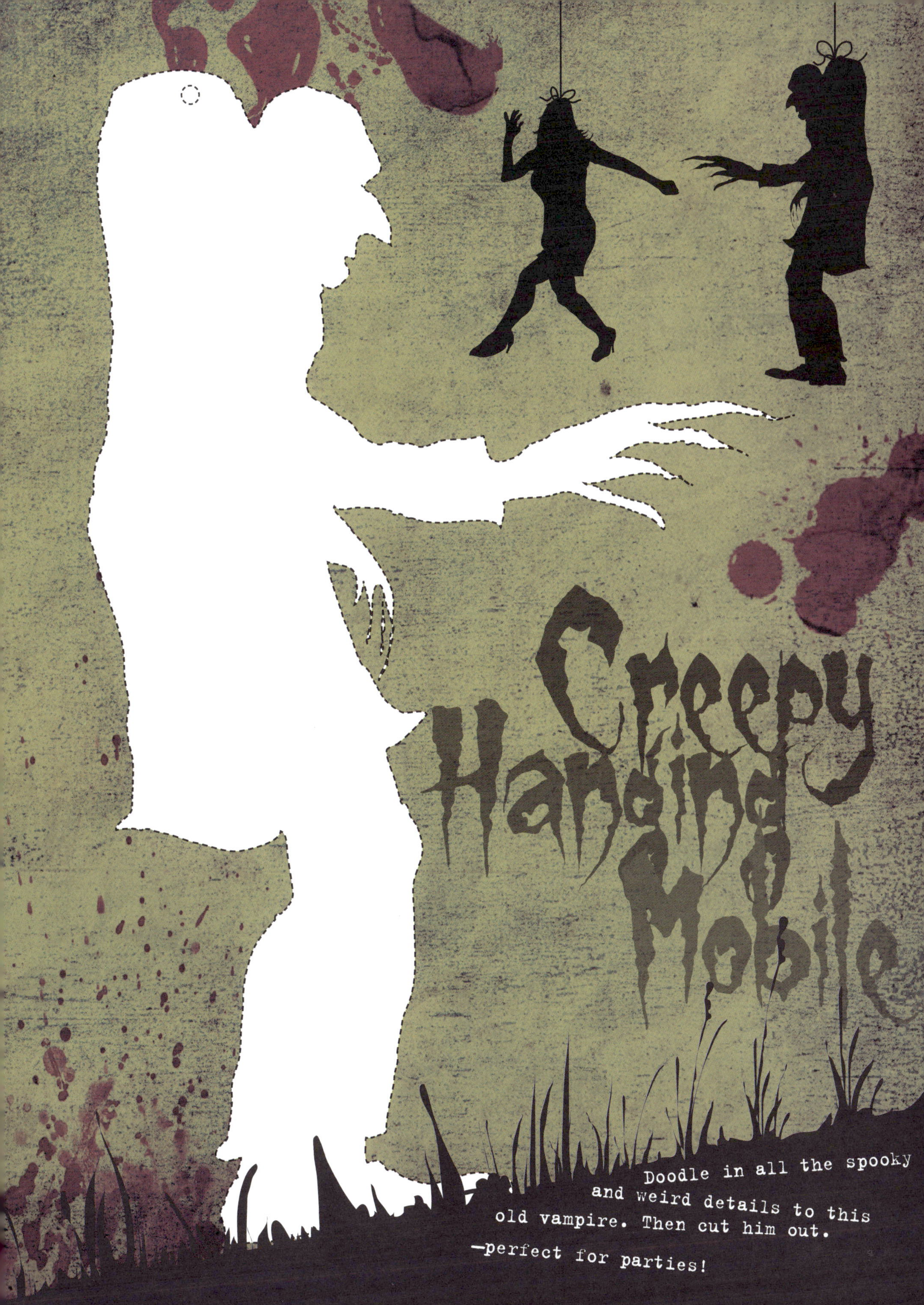
Creepy Hanging Mobile
Doodle in all the spooky
and weird details to this
old vampire. Then cut him out.
—perfect for parties!

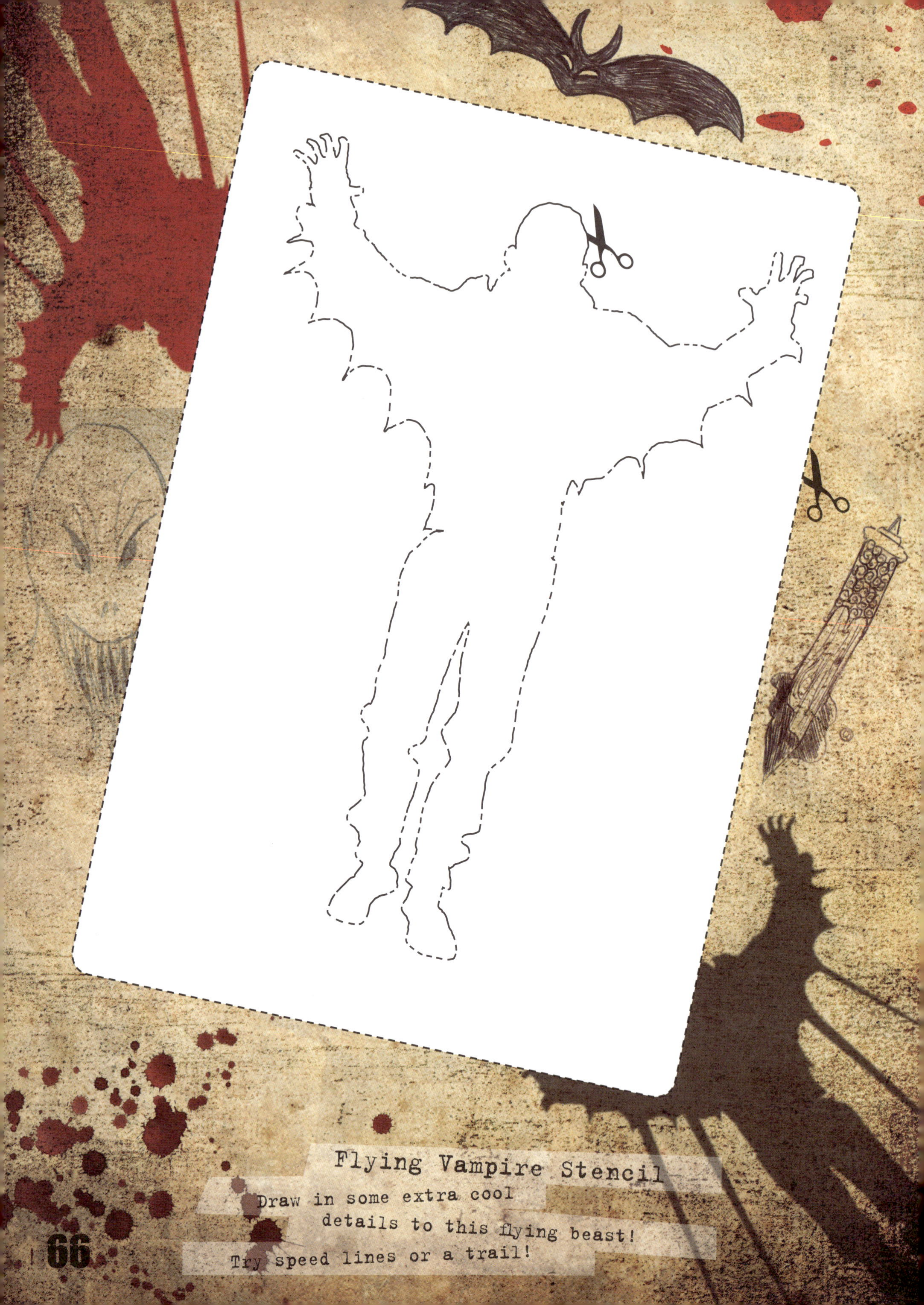

Flying Vampire Stencil

Draw in some extra cool details to this flying beast! Try speed lines or a trail!

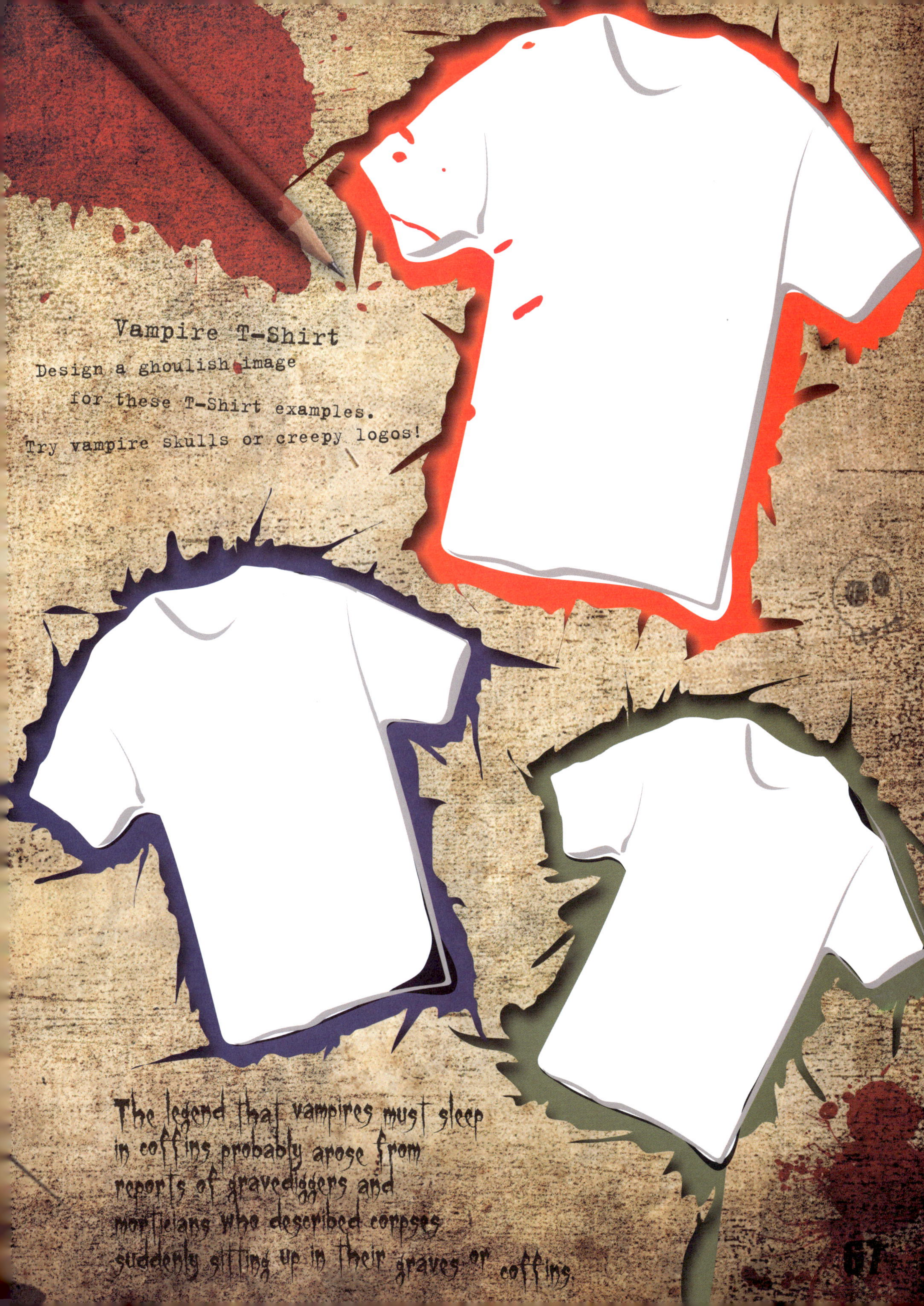

Vampire T-Shirt

Design a ghoulish image for these T-Shirt examples. Try vampire skulls or creepy logos!

The legend that vampires must sleep in coffins probably arose from reports of gravediggers and morticians who described corpses suddenly sitting up in their graves or coffins.

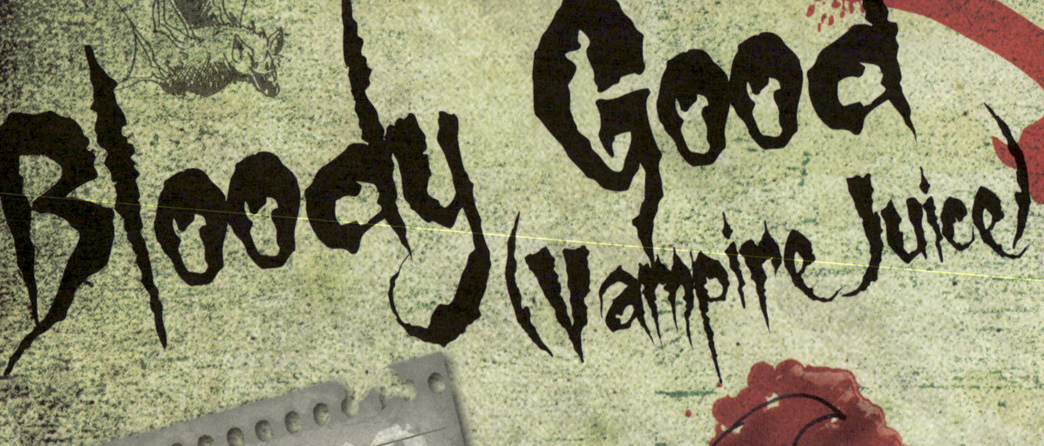

Bloody Good (Vampire Juice)

Ingredients

4 oz. tomato juice
$^1/_4$ tsp. horseradish
splash of Tabasco sauce
2-3 dashes lemon juice

Method

Put all the ingredients into a highball glass and stir well. I prefer to serve this without ice as the tomato juice ensures that the cocktail is quite a thick blood-like consistency, but this is up to you.

Warning
adult assistance recommended for a safe result!

Bloody glasses

You will need

$^1/_2$ cup corn or maple syrup
few drops of red food coloring

What to do

In a shallow bowl, mix the corn syrup with enough red food coloring until combined and the corn syrup turns red. Dip your glasses (glass or plastic is best for the look) and give it a gentle twirl before taking the glass out and propping it right side-up on a sheet of waxed paper. Let the mixture run down the side of the glass like drops of blood. Let the mixture set a little before serving with your favorite drink.

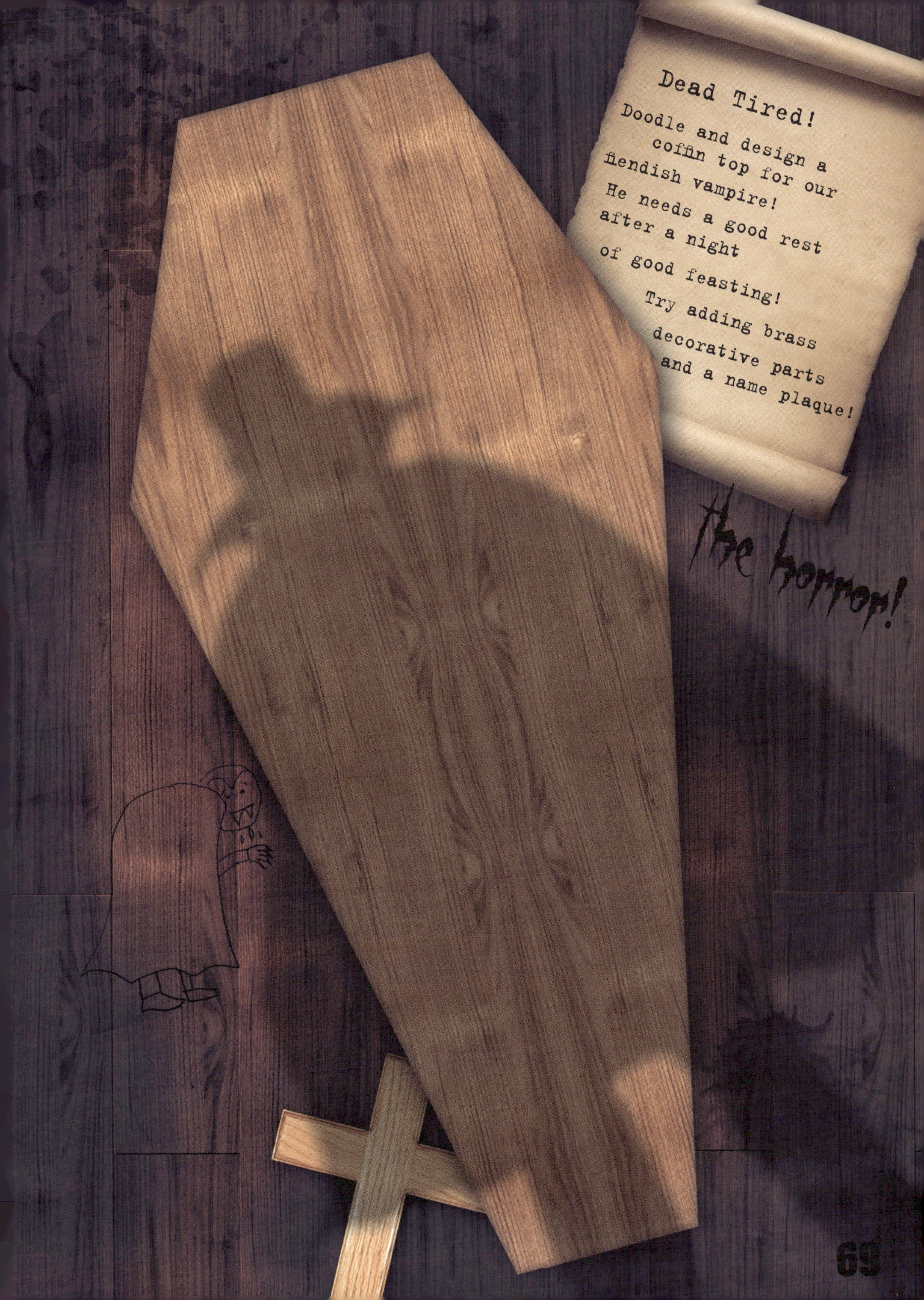
Dead Tired!
Doodle and design a coffin top for our fiendish vampire!
He needs a good rest after a night of good feasting!
Try adding brass decorative parts and a name plaque!
the horror!

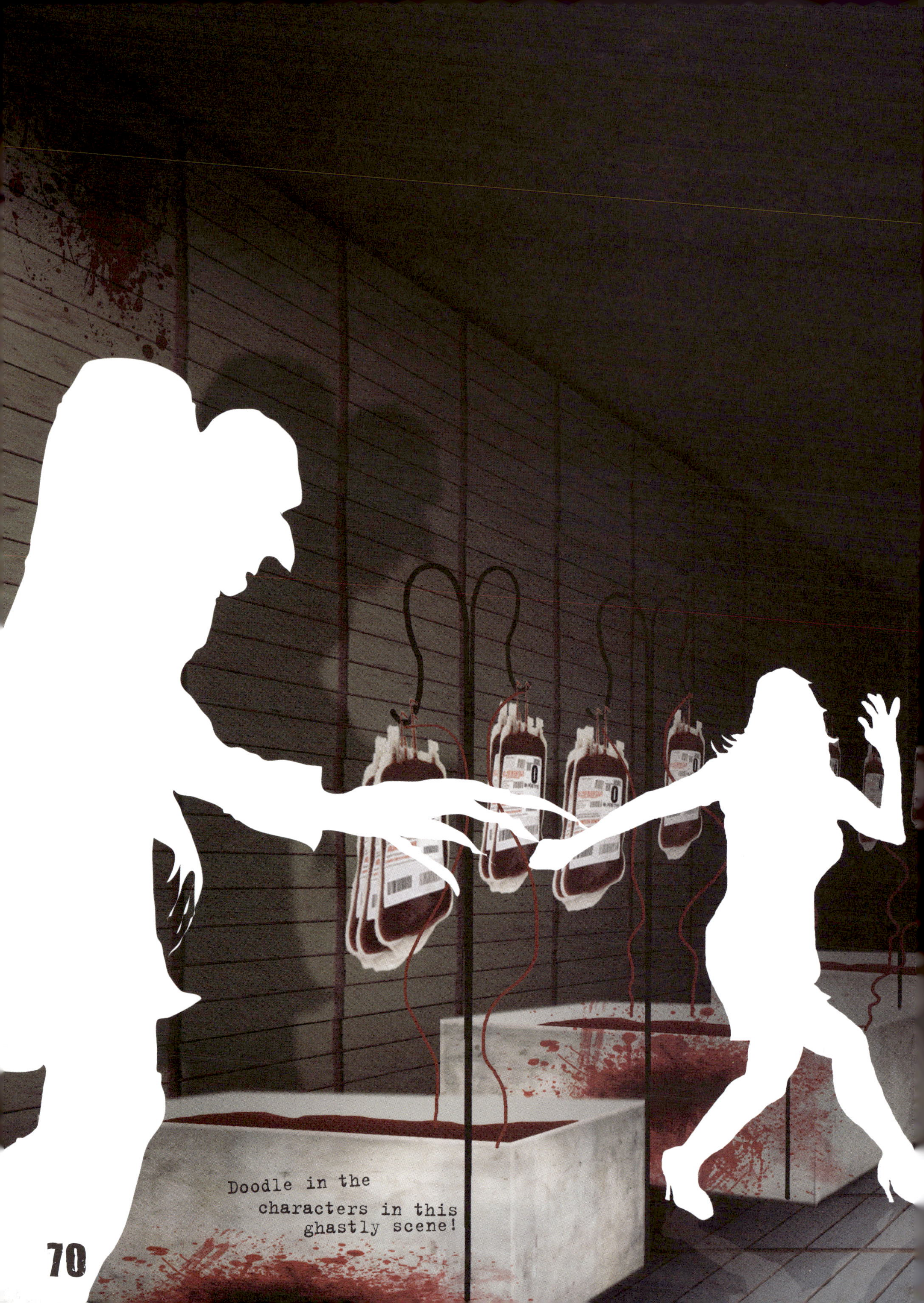
Doodle in the
characters in this
ghastly scene!

the Halloween

Guest List

Food and drink list

THE FIRST VAMPIRE FILM IS SUPPOSEDLY SECRETS OF HOUSE NO. 5 IN 1912

Party Planner

Costume ideas

Decoration ideas

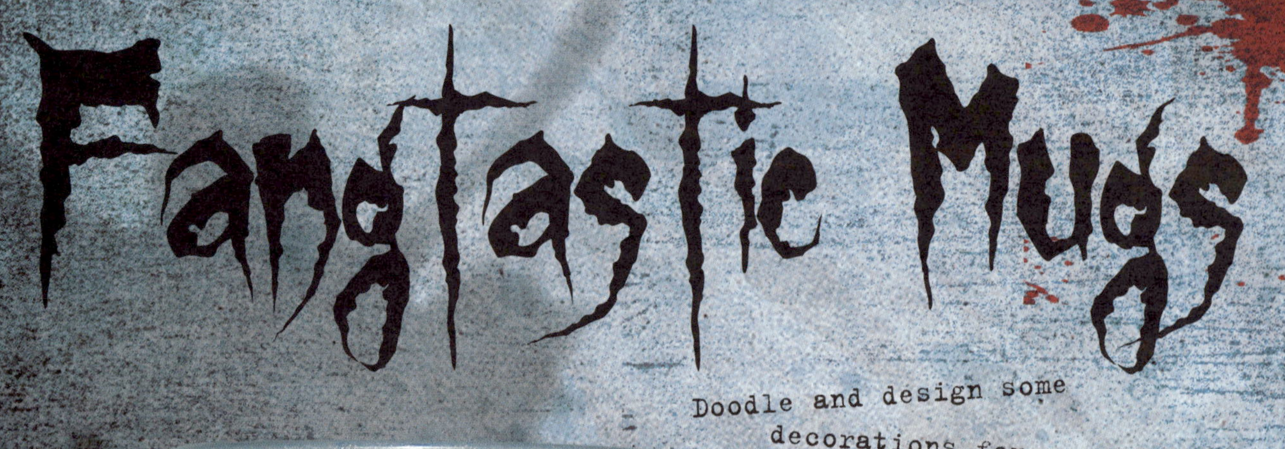

Doodle and design some decorations for your mug!

Try doodling cartoons or design a vampire logo!

ONE OF THE MOST FAMOUS 'TRUE VAMPIRES' WAS COUNTESS ELIZABETH BATHORY (1560-1614) WHO WAS ACCUSED OF BITING THE FLESH OF GIRLS WHILE TORTURING THEM AND BATHING IN THEIR BLOOD TO RETAIN HER YOUTHFUL BEAUTY. SHE WAS BY ALL ACCOUNTS A VERY ATTRACTIVE WOMAN.

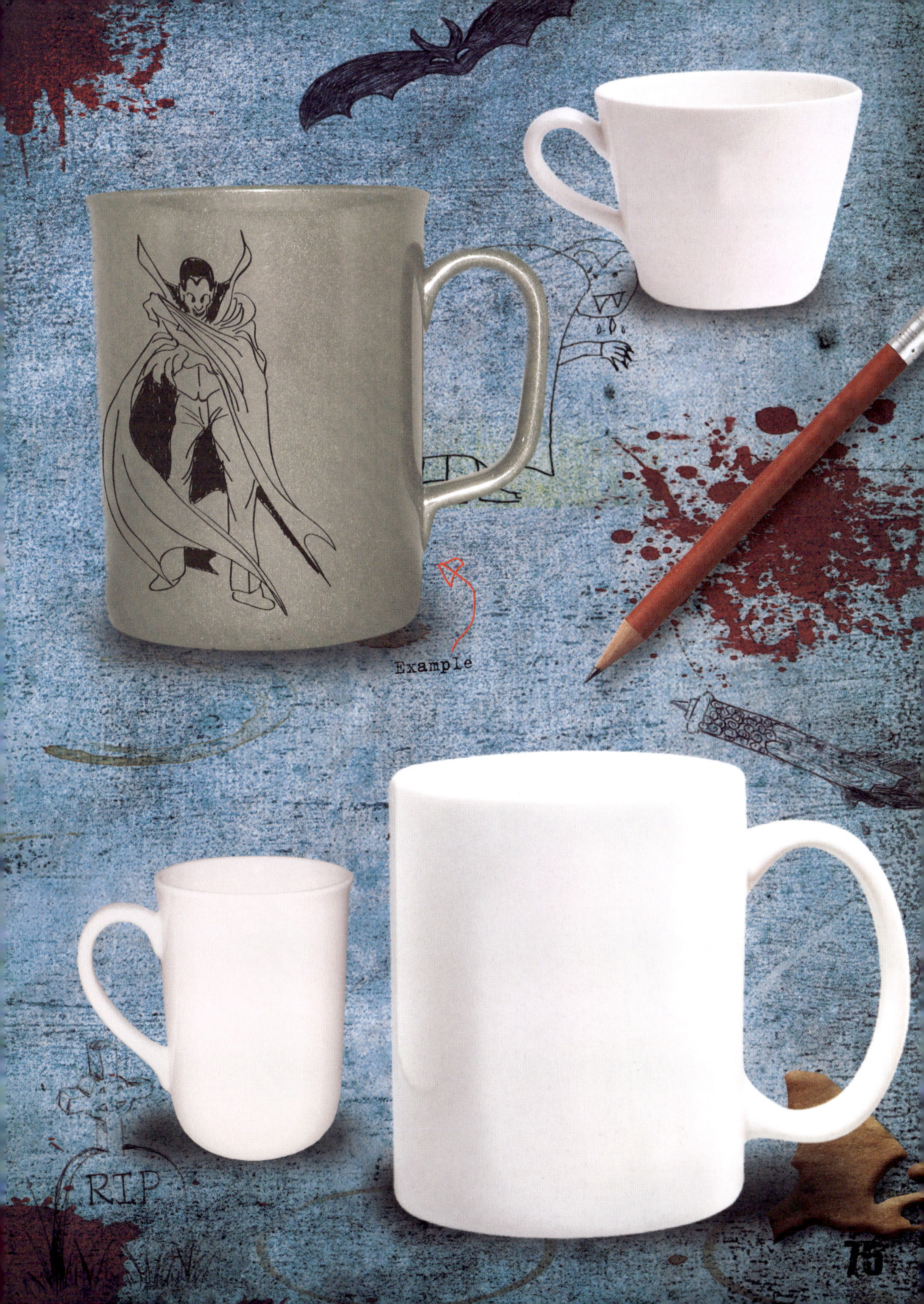
Example
R.I.P

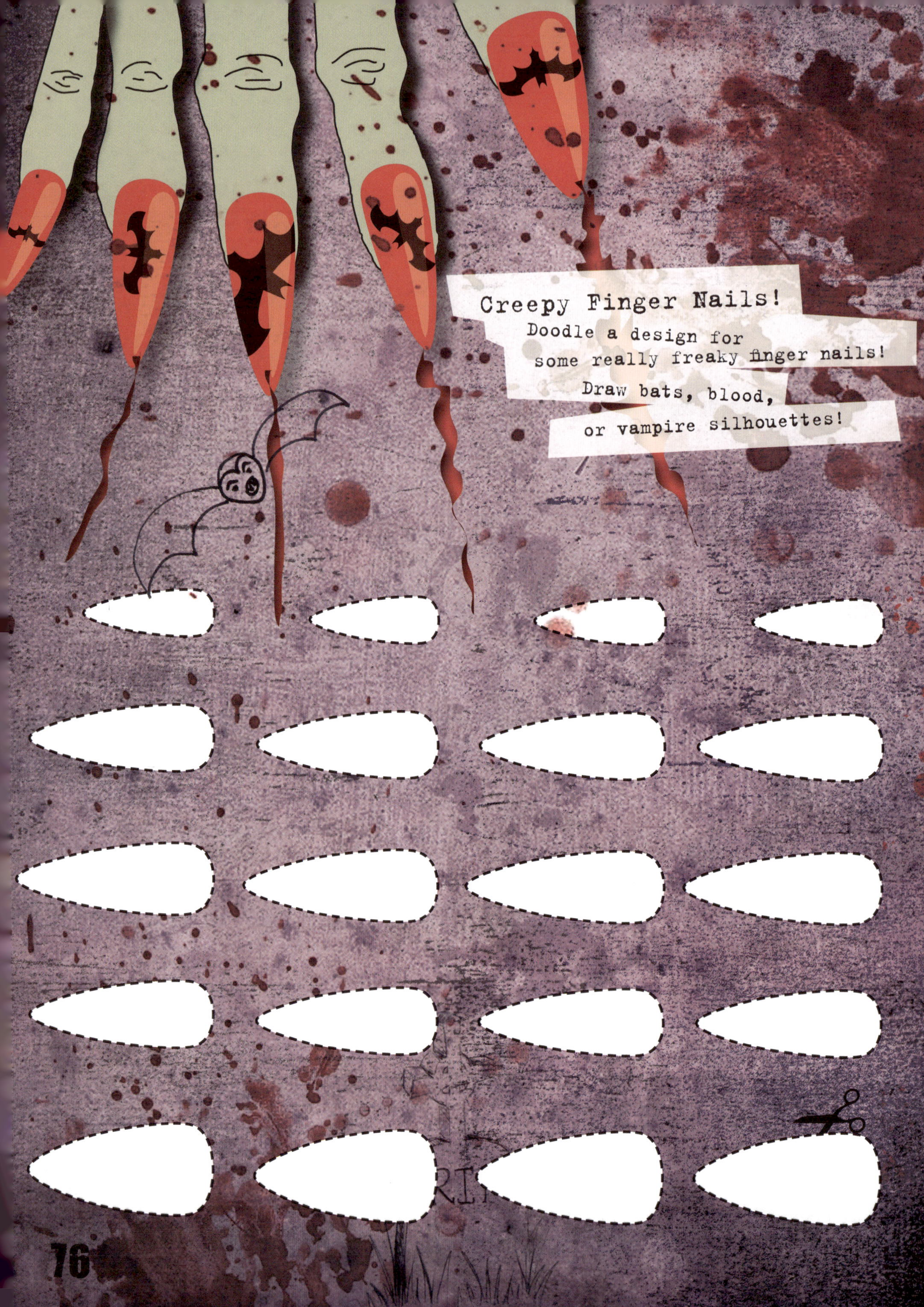
Creepy Finger Nails!
Doodle a design for
some really freaky finger nails!
Draw bats, blood,
or vampire silhouettes!

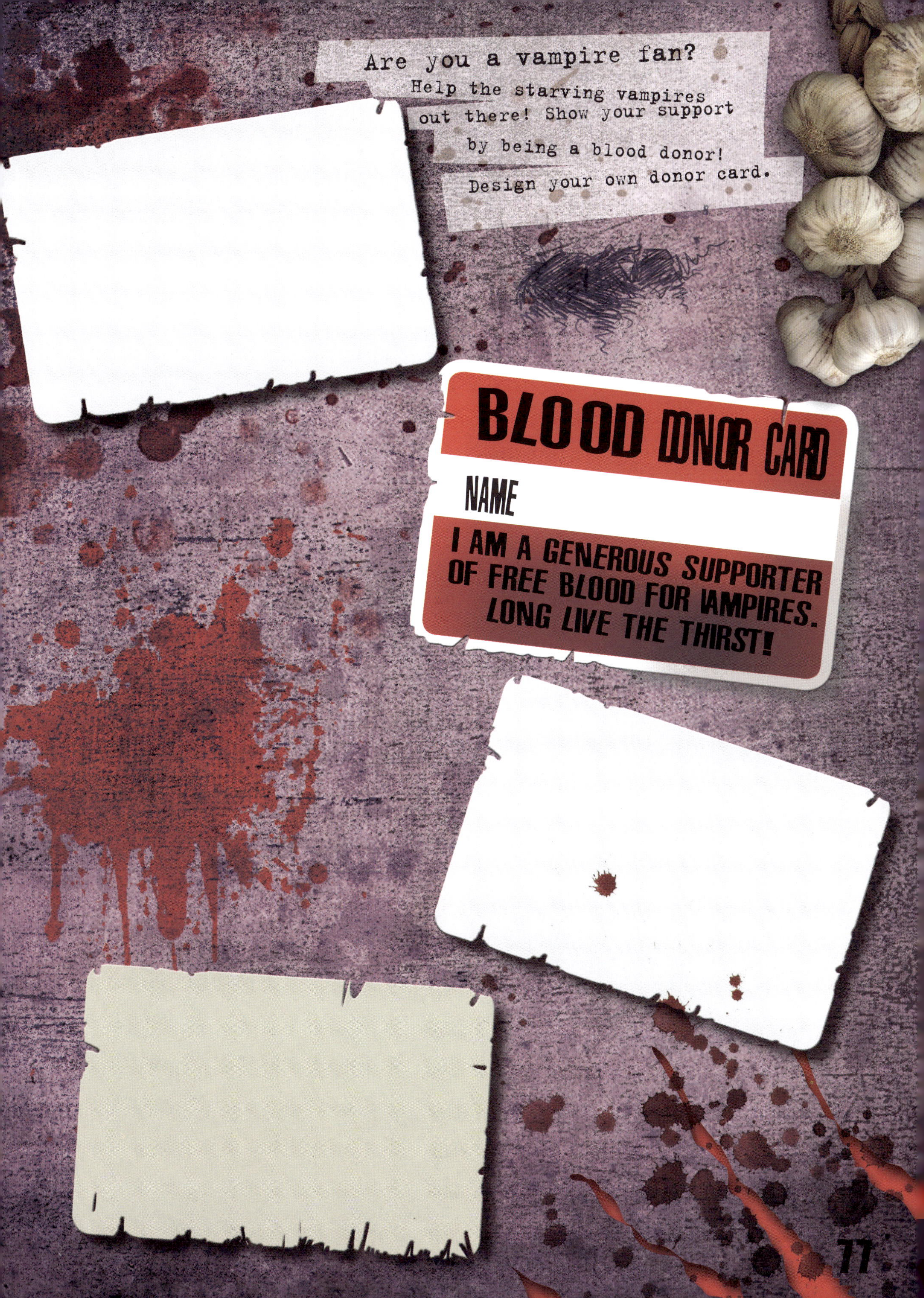
Are you a vampire fan?
Help the starving vampires out there! Show your support by being a blood donor!
Design your own donor card.
BLOOD DONOR CARD
NAME
I AM A GENEROUS SUPPORTER OF FREE BLOOD FOR VAMPIRES. LONG LIVE THE THIRST!

Word Search

E R A T O T S K D L
T R D R A C U L A Y
N O I T C E L F E R
K B E R A R K R D T
S I U S C R E A M S
C M L R R U M E T L
A S E L I S I R M S
R S I R E E A S L R
Y S E L S R D R I E
L S I E A E U U L A

buried
damsel
dracula
killer
reflection
resurrect
scary
screams
stake

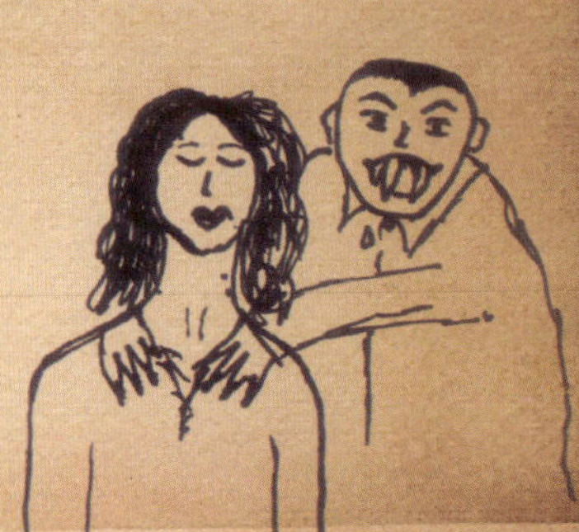

Draw your hideously scary vampire in this weird sheet of random card down here...

Vampire Tracks

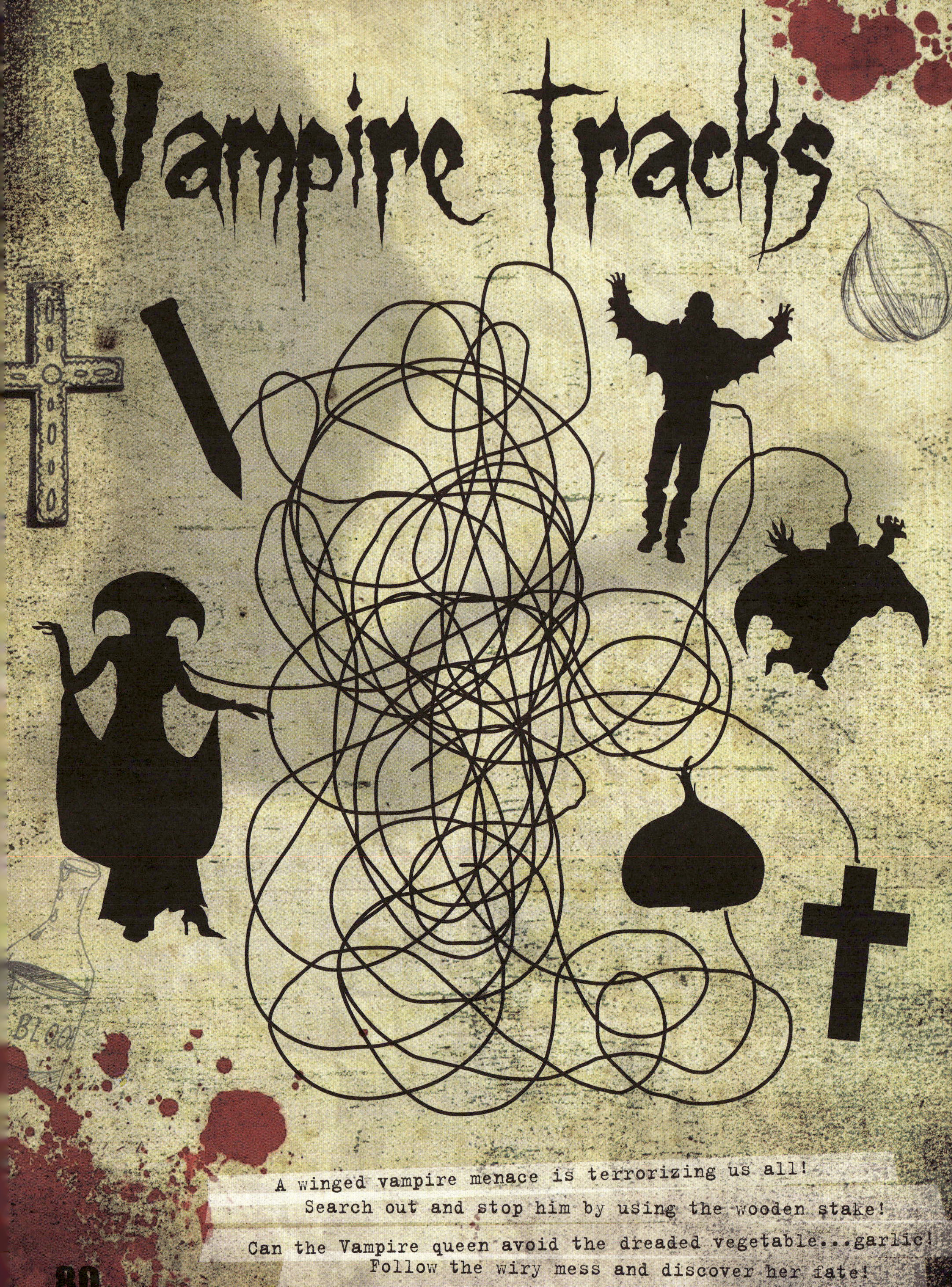

A winged vampire menace is terrorizing us all!
Search out and stop him by using the wooden stake!

Can the Vampire queen avoid the dreaded vegetable...garlic!
Follow the wiry mess and discover her fate!

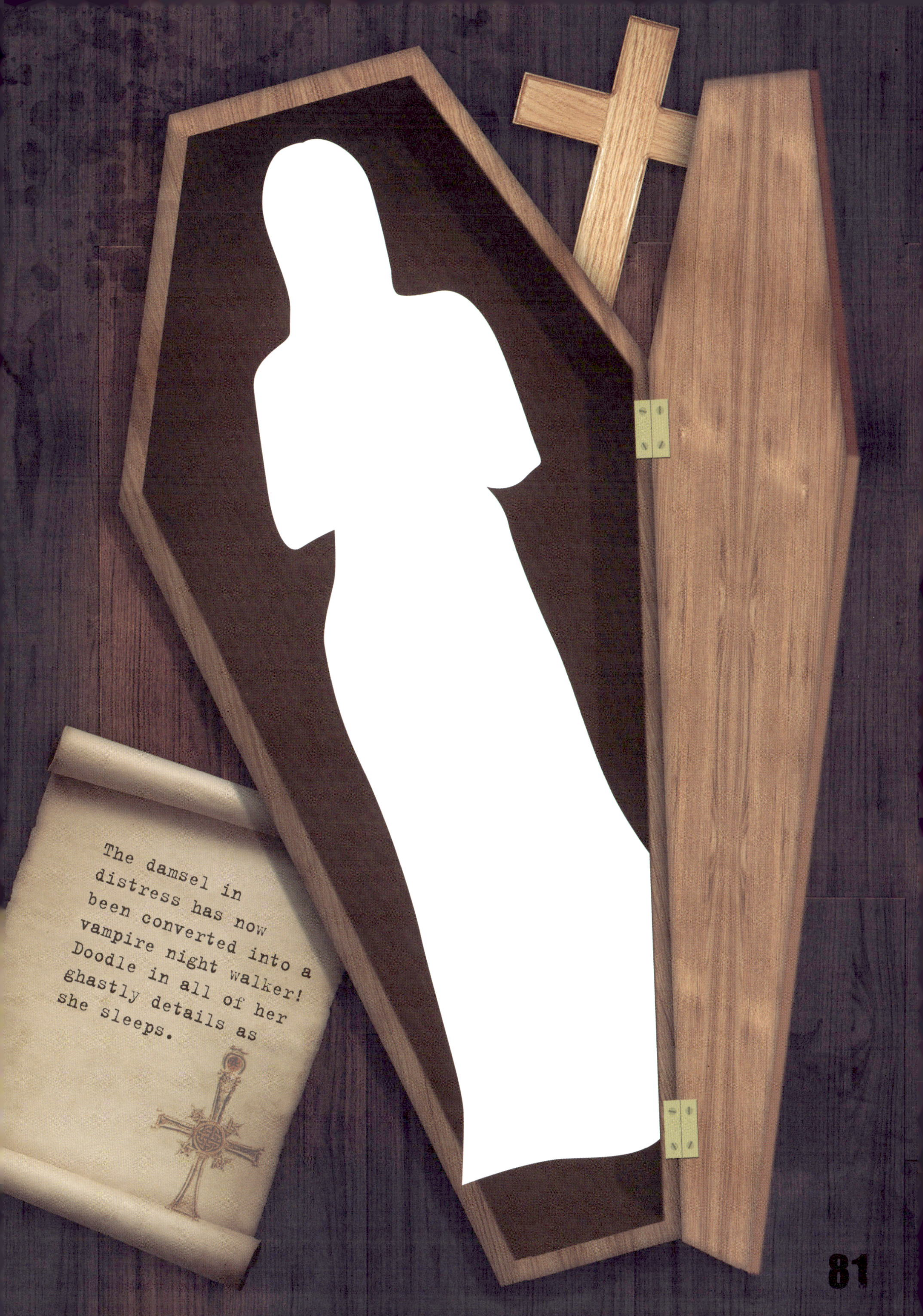
The damsel in
distress has now
been converted into a
vampire night walker!
Doodle in all of her
ghastly details as
she sleeps.

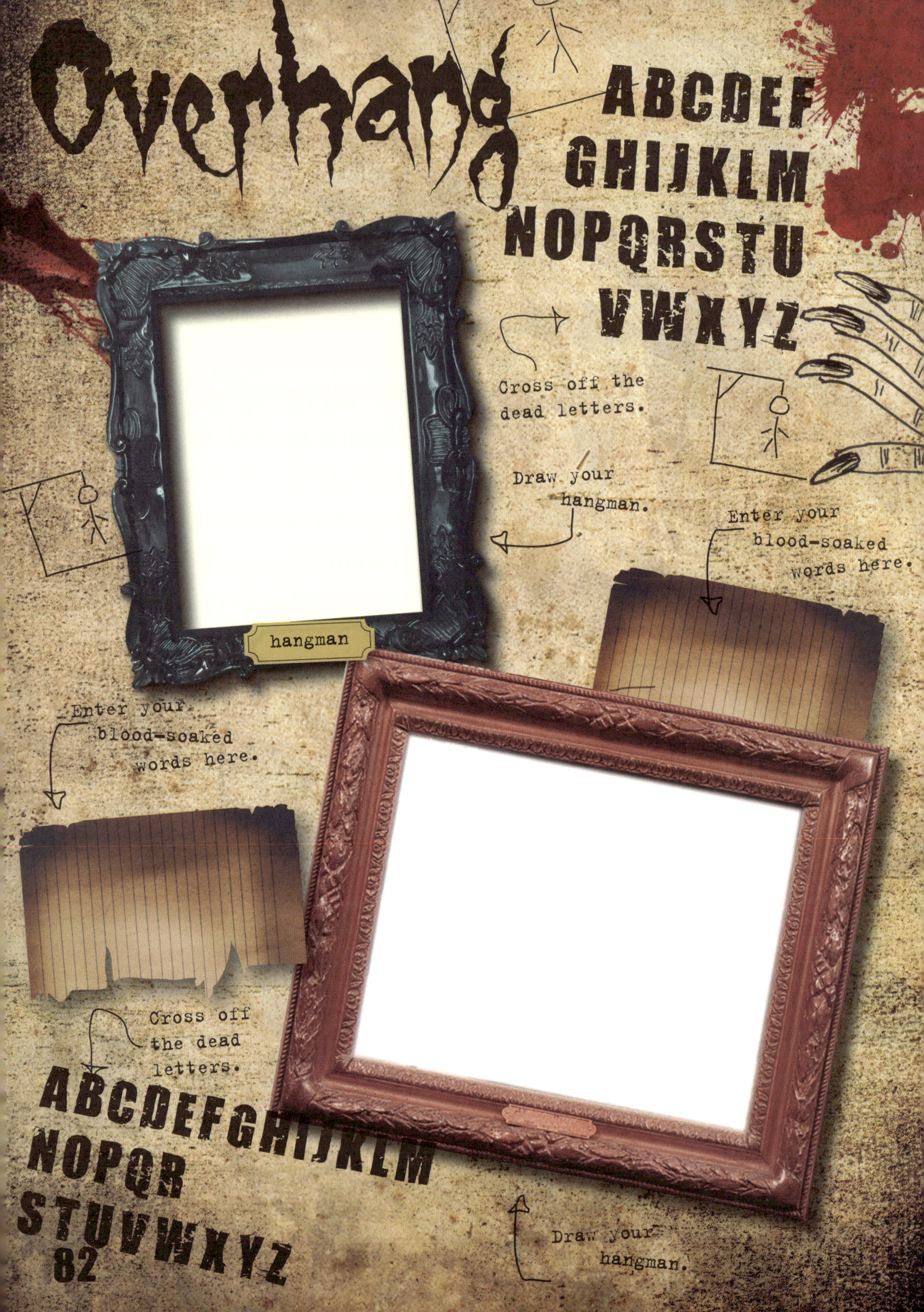
Overhang
ABCDEF
GHIJKLM
NOPQRSTU
VWXYZ
Cross off the
dead letters.
Draw your
hangman.
Enter your
blood-soaked
words here.
hangman
Enter your
blood-soaked
words here.
Cross off
the dead
letters.
ABCDEFGHIJKLM
NOPQR
STUVWXYZ
Draw your
hangman.

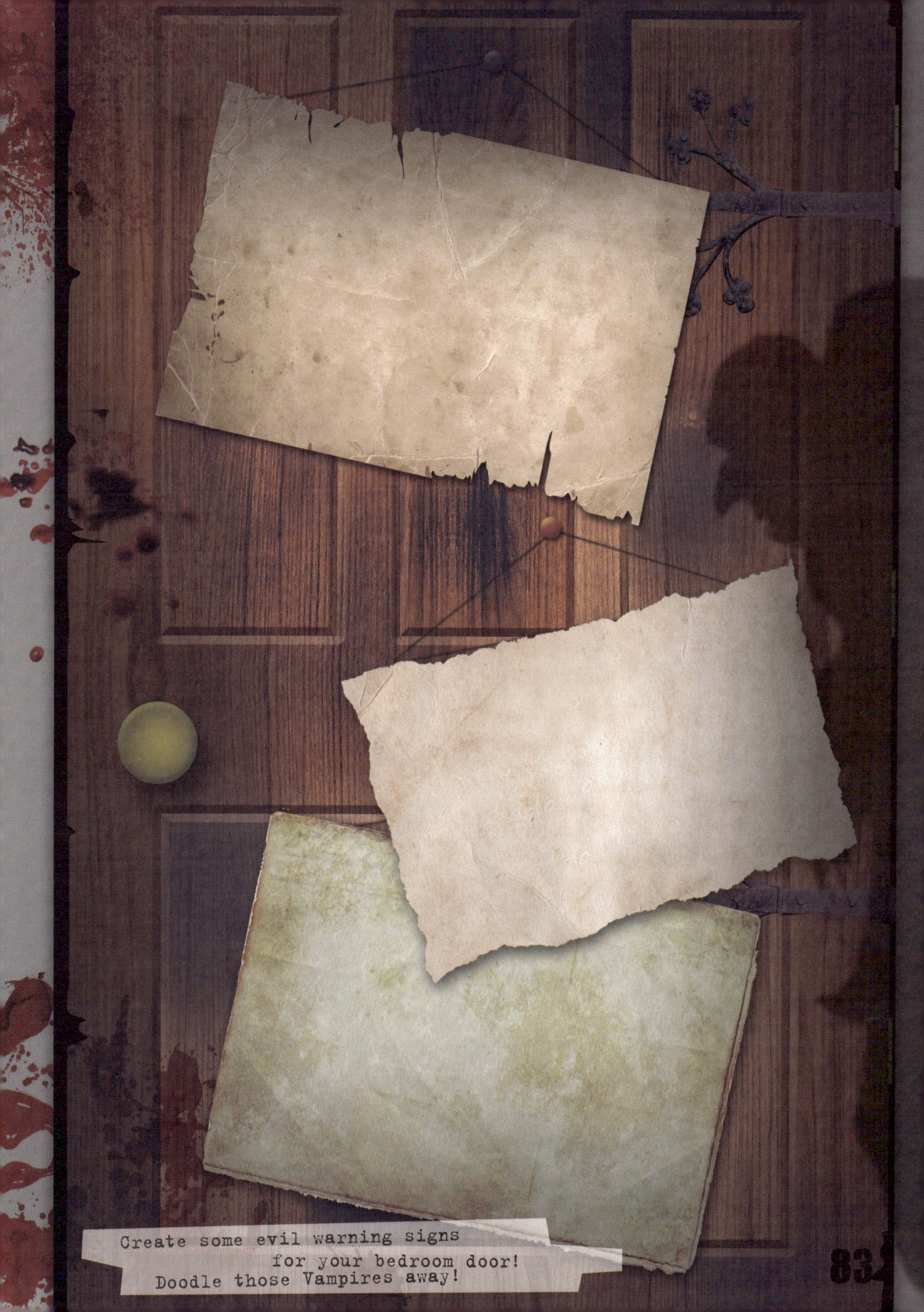

Create some evil warning signs
for your bedroom door!
Doodle those Vampires away!

Dot-to-Dot

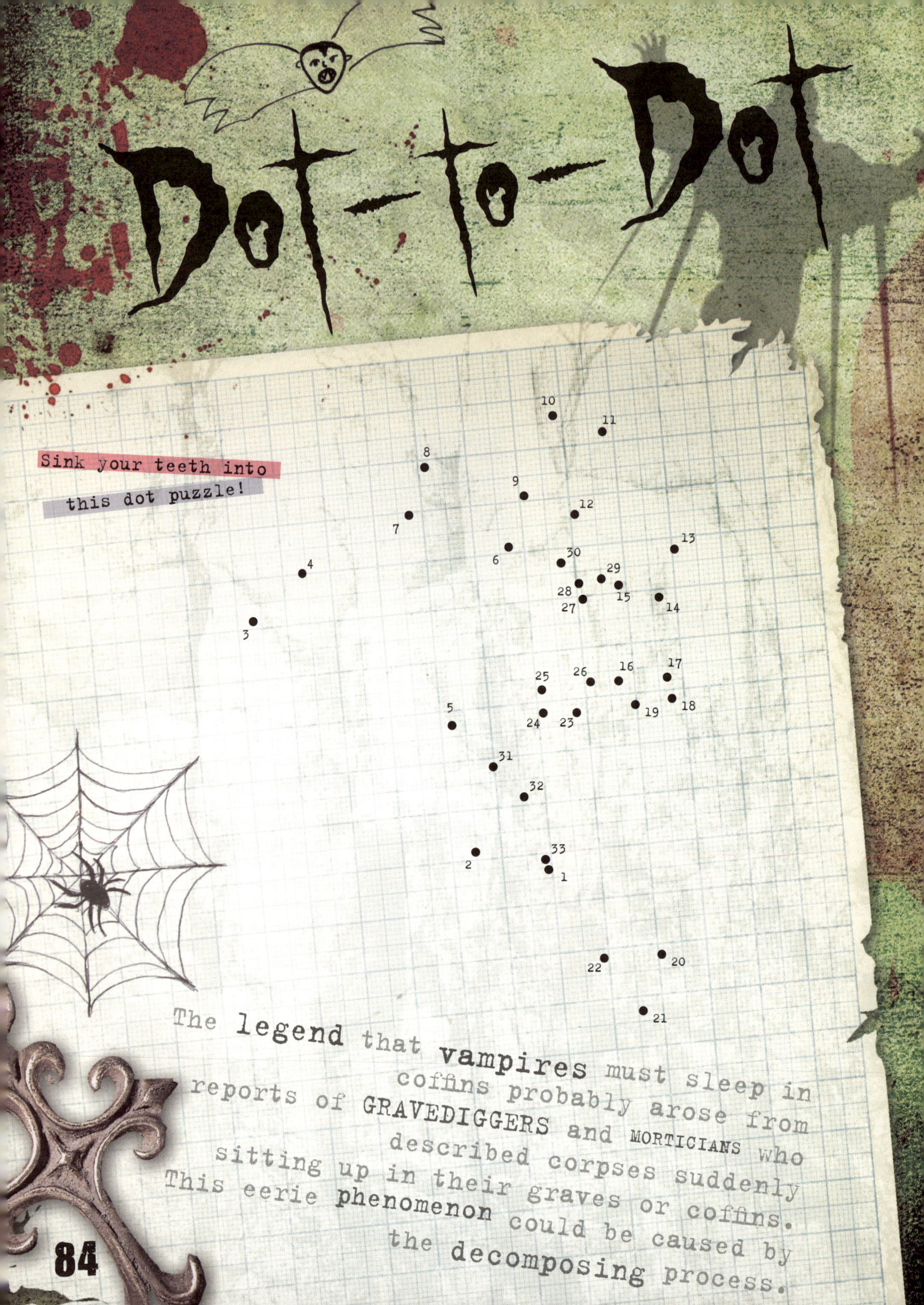

The legend that **vampires** must sleep in coffins probably arose from reports of GRAVEDIGGERS and MORTICIANS who described corpses suddenly sitting up in their graves or coffins. This eerie **phenomenon** could be caused by the **decomposing** process.

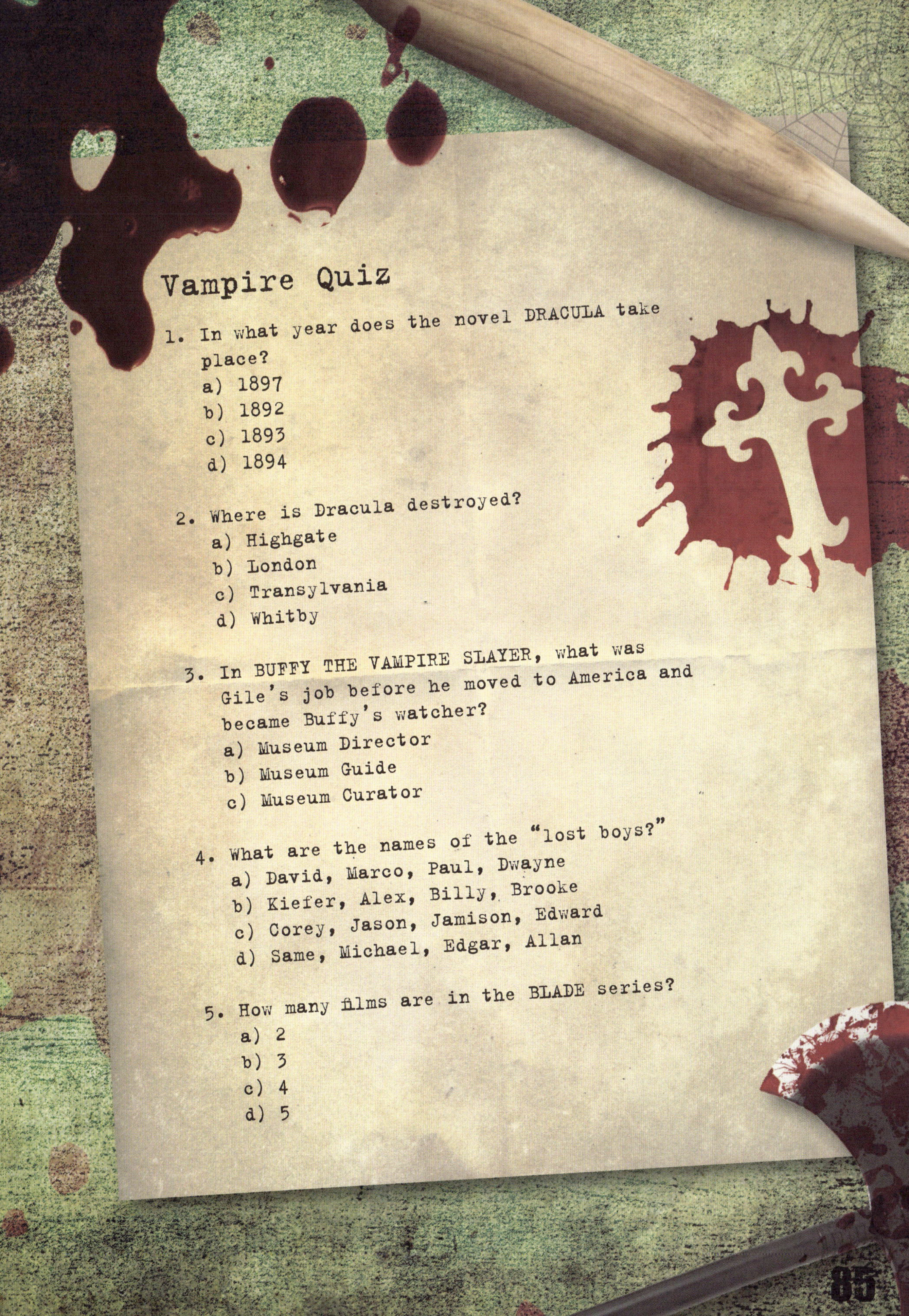

Vampire Quiz

1. In what year does the novel DRACULA take place?
   a) 1897
   b) 1892
   c) 1893
   d) 1894

2. Where is Dracula destroyed?
   a) Highgate
   b) London
   c) Transylvania
   d) Whitby

3. In BUFFY THE VAMPIRE SLAYER, what was Gile's job before he moved to America and became Buffy's watcher?
   a) Museum Director
   b) Museum Guide
   c) Museum Curator

4. What are the names of the "lost boys?"
   a) David, Marco, Paul, Dwayne
   b) Kiefer, Alex, Billy, Brooke
   c) Corey, Jason, Jamison, Edward
   d) Same, Michael, Edgar, Allan

5. How many films are in the BLADE series?
   a) 2
   b) 3
   c) 4
   d) 5

Vampire Quiz (continued)

6. 2008's LET THE RIGHT ONE IN is a film from which country?
   a) Sweden
   b) Russia
   c) Germany
   d) Italy

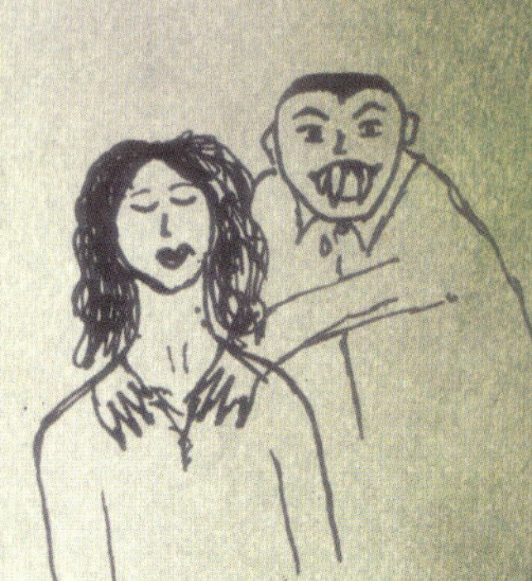

7. Who directed the 1922 masterpiece NOSFERATU?
   a) F.W. Murnau
   b) Fritz Lang
   c) Federico Fellini
   d) Marcel L'Herbier

8. Who directed FROM DUSK TILL DAWN?
   a) Quentin Tarantino
   b) Robert Rodriguez
   c) Tom Savani
   d) Bryan Singer

9. What is the real name of the Marvel charcter BLADE?
   a) Marv Wolfman
   b) Eric Brooks
   c) Gene Colan
   d) Wesley Snipes

10. Who starred as the vampire killer in FRIGHT NIGHT?
   a) Michael J. fox
   b) Roddy McDowell
   c) Richard Gere
   d) Harrison Ford

The Vampire Gig

Create a poster to promote the gothic vampire band Bloodsuckers.

Spot the Difference

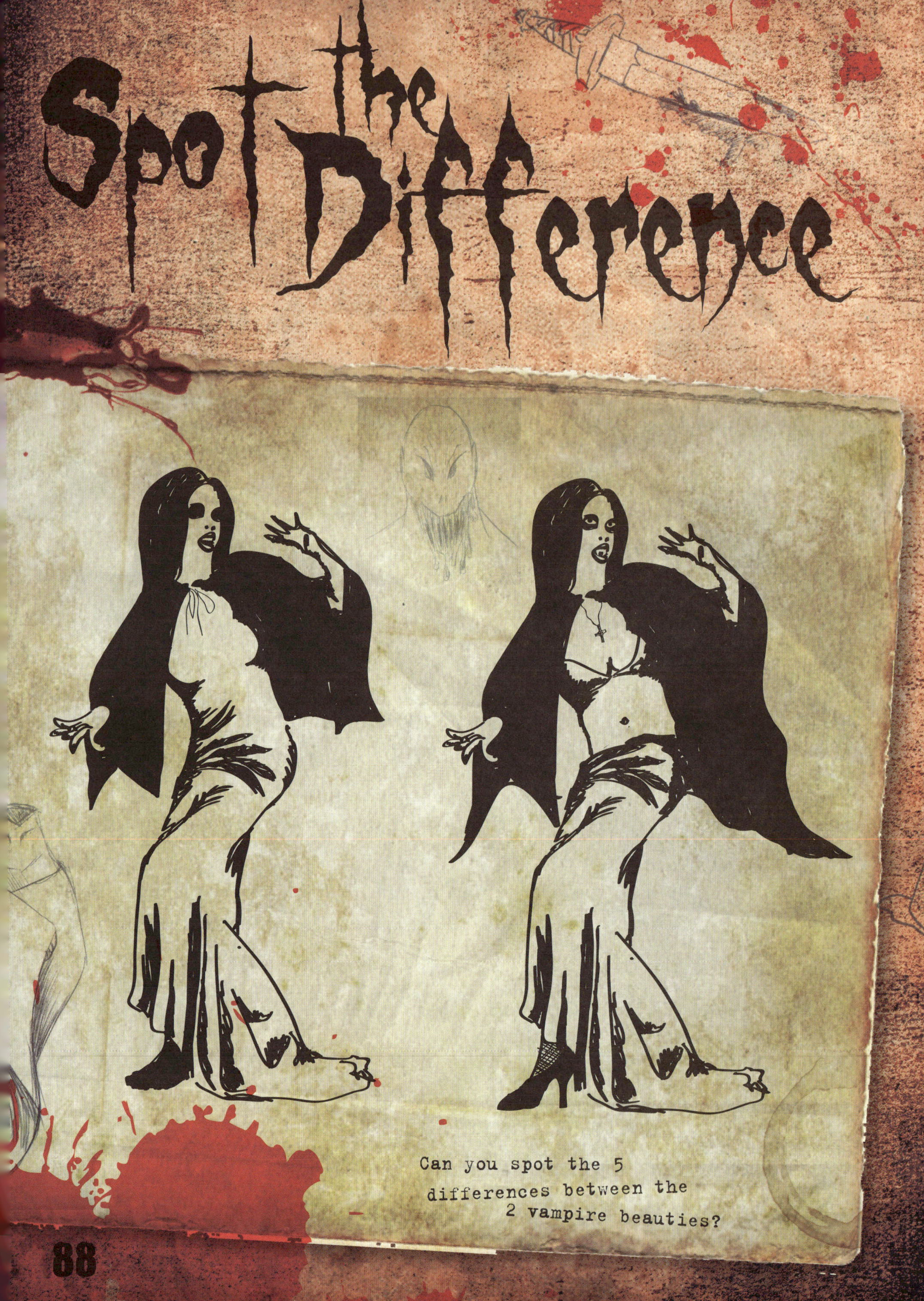

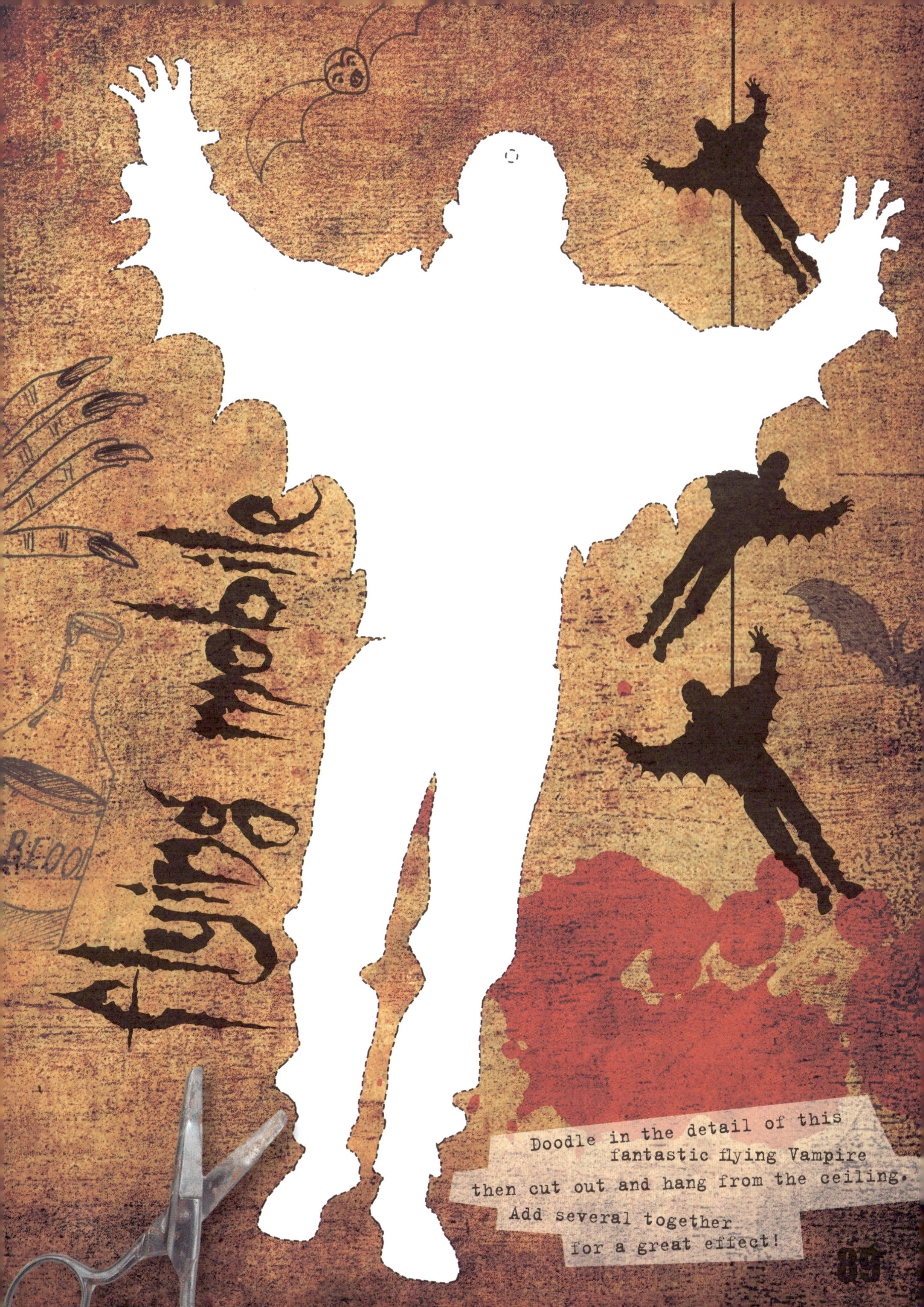
flying mobile
BLOOD
Doodle in the detail of this
fantastic flying Vampire
then cut out and hang from the ceiling.
Add several together
for a great effect!

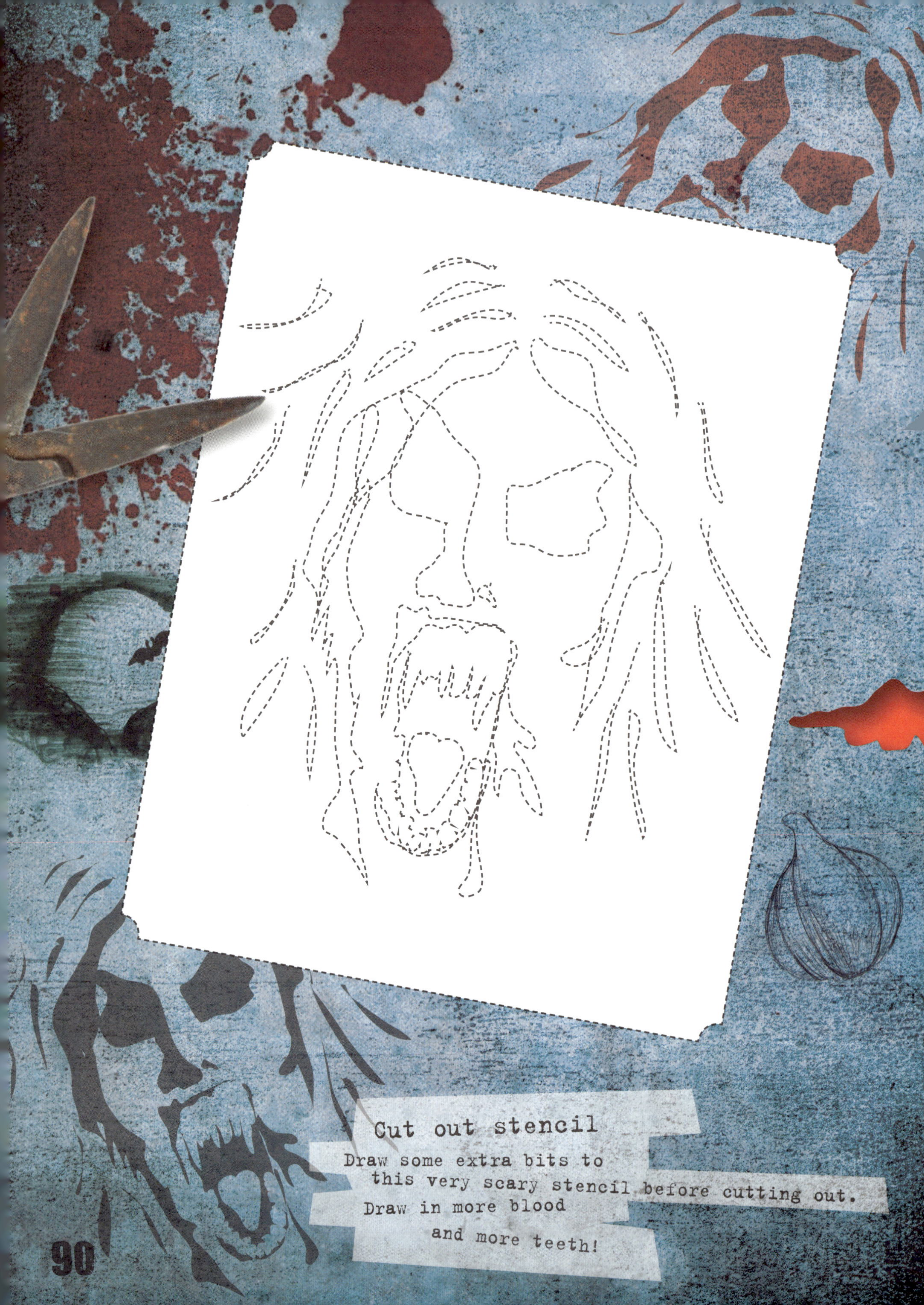

Cut out stencil

Draw some extra bits to this very scary stencil before cutting out. Draw in more blood and more teeth!

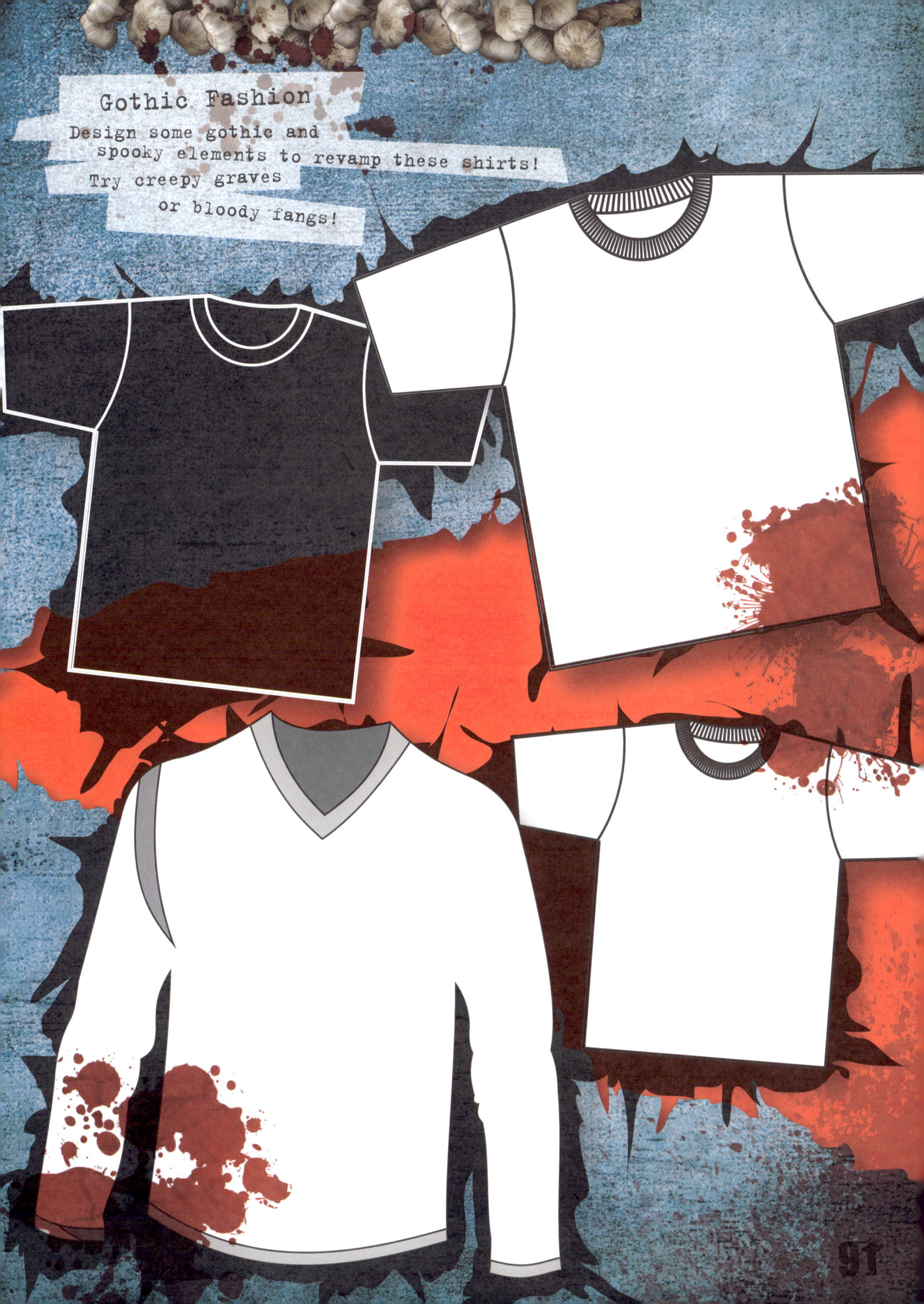
Gothic Fashion
Design some gothic and spooky elements to revamp these shirts! Try creepy graves or bloody fangs!
91

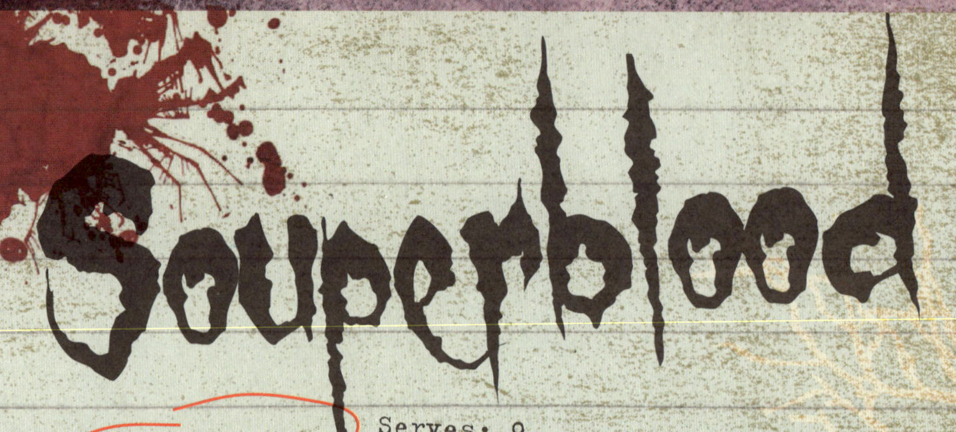

Souperblood

Serves: 9

Prep time: 15 mins

Cook time: 20 mins

Ingredients

1 tsp. olive oil, plus additional for pans
4 lb. red bell peppers, cored, halved lengthwise, and seeded
2 medium onions, thinly sliced
4 garlic cloves, finely chopped
2 1/2 cups hot chicken or vegetable broth
1 1/2 cups half-and-half
3 tbsp. balsamic vinegar
Bat toasts

Method

1. Preheat the broiler and arrange rack 5 to 6 inches from the heat. Lightly oil 2 shallow baking pans. Arrange the pepper halves, in a single layer, in the pans. Broil, turning occasionally, until the edges are charred, about 8 minutes. Transfer to a blender.

2. Heat the oil in a large nonstick skillet over moderate heat. Add the onions and garlic and cook, stirring occasionally, until softened, about 5 minutes. Transfer to a blender, add the broth and puree until smooth (use caution when blending hot liquids). Transfer the mixture to a large pan; whisk in 2 1/2 cups water and the half-and-half. Heat over moderate heat, whisking occasionally, until hot, about 5 minutes. Stir in the vinegar and salt and pepper to taste.

3. Ladle the soup into mugs and serve with bat toasts.

Warning
adult assistance
recommended for a safe result!

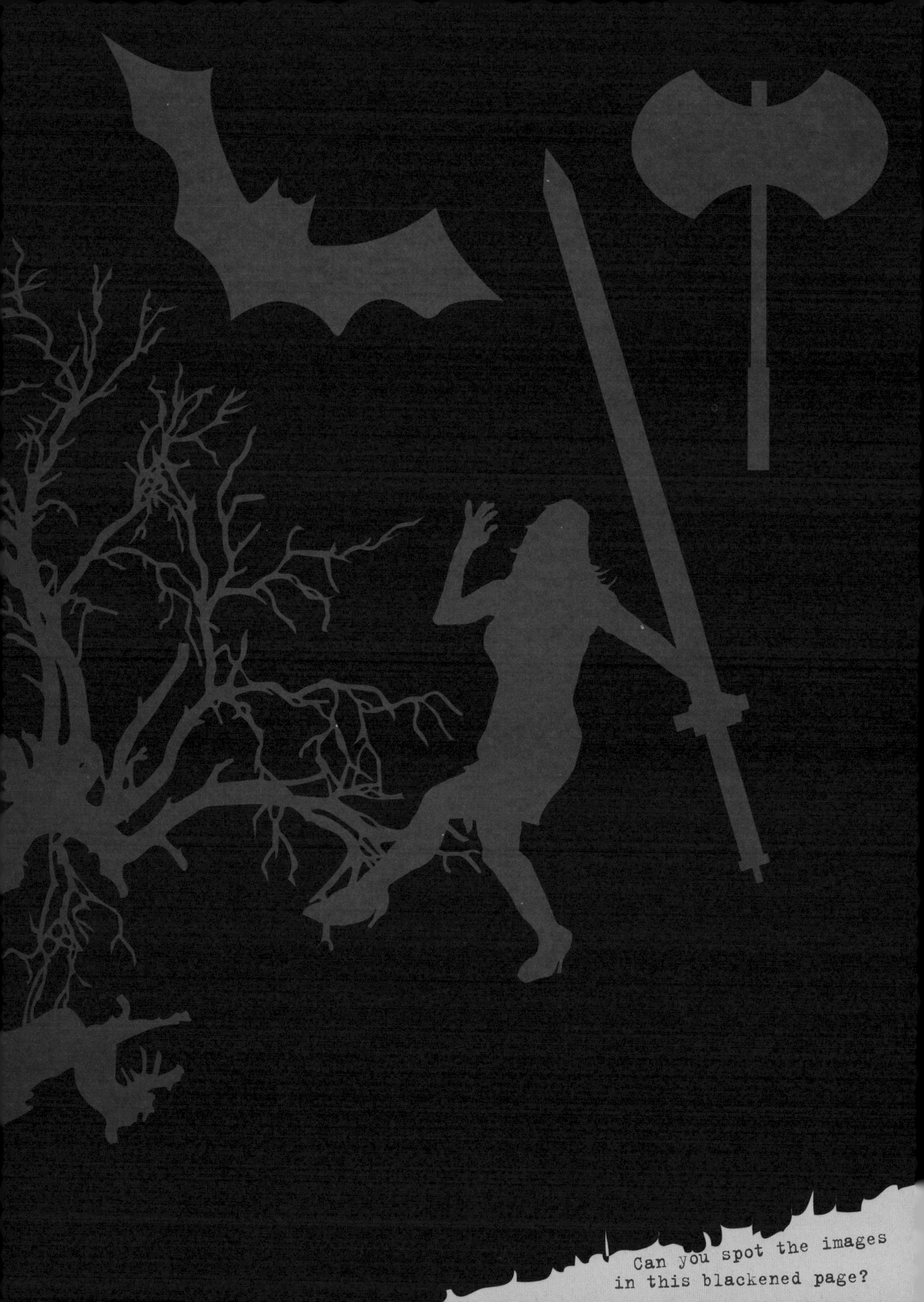
Can you spot the images
in this blackened page?

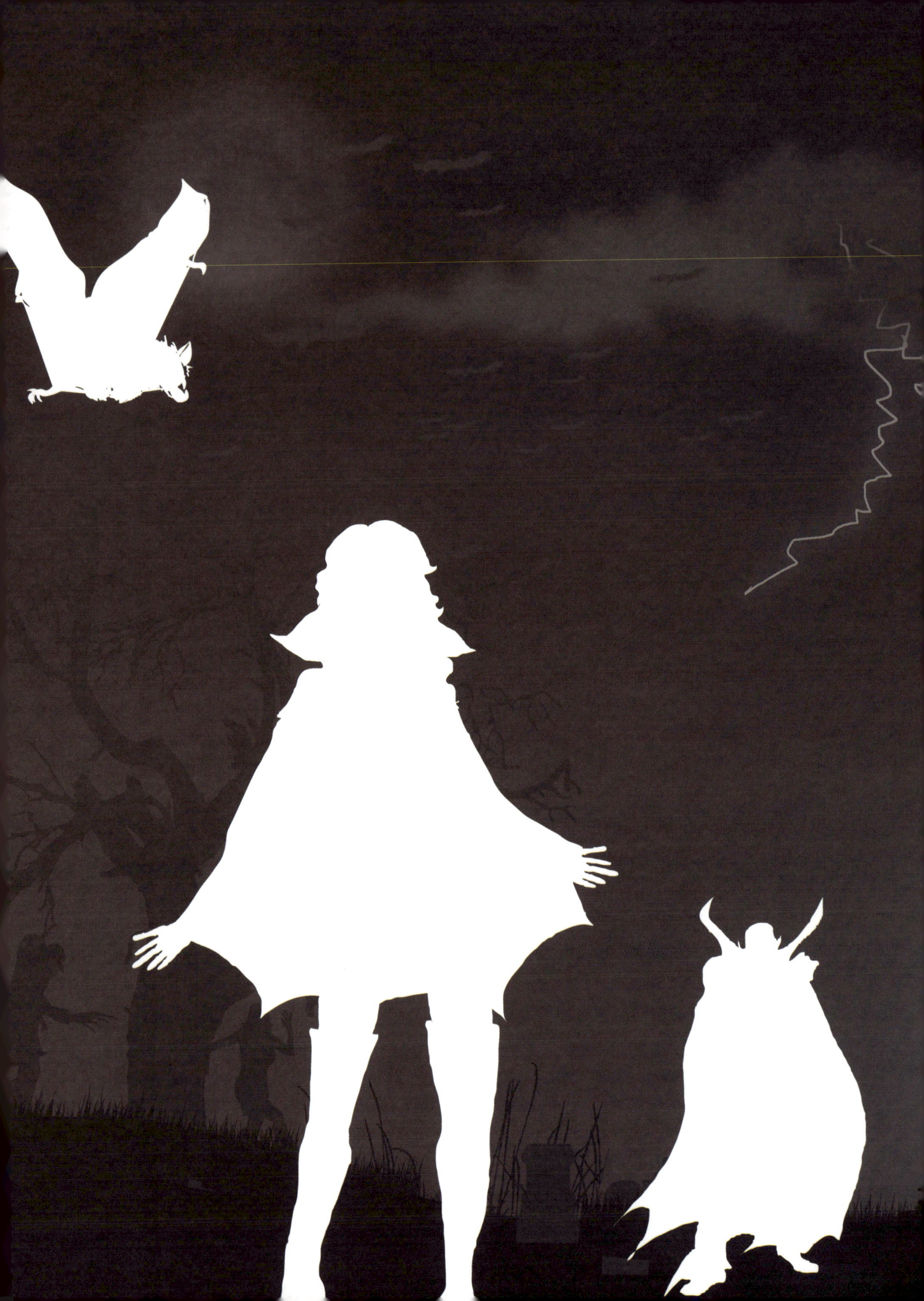

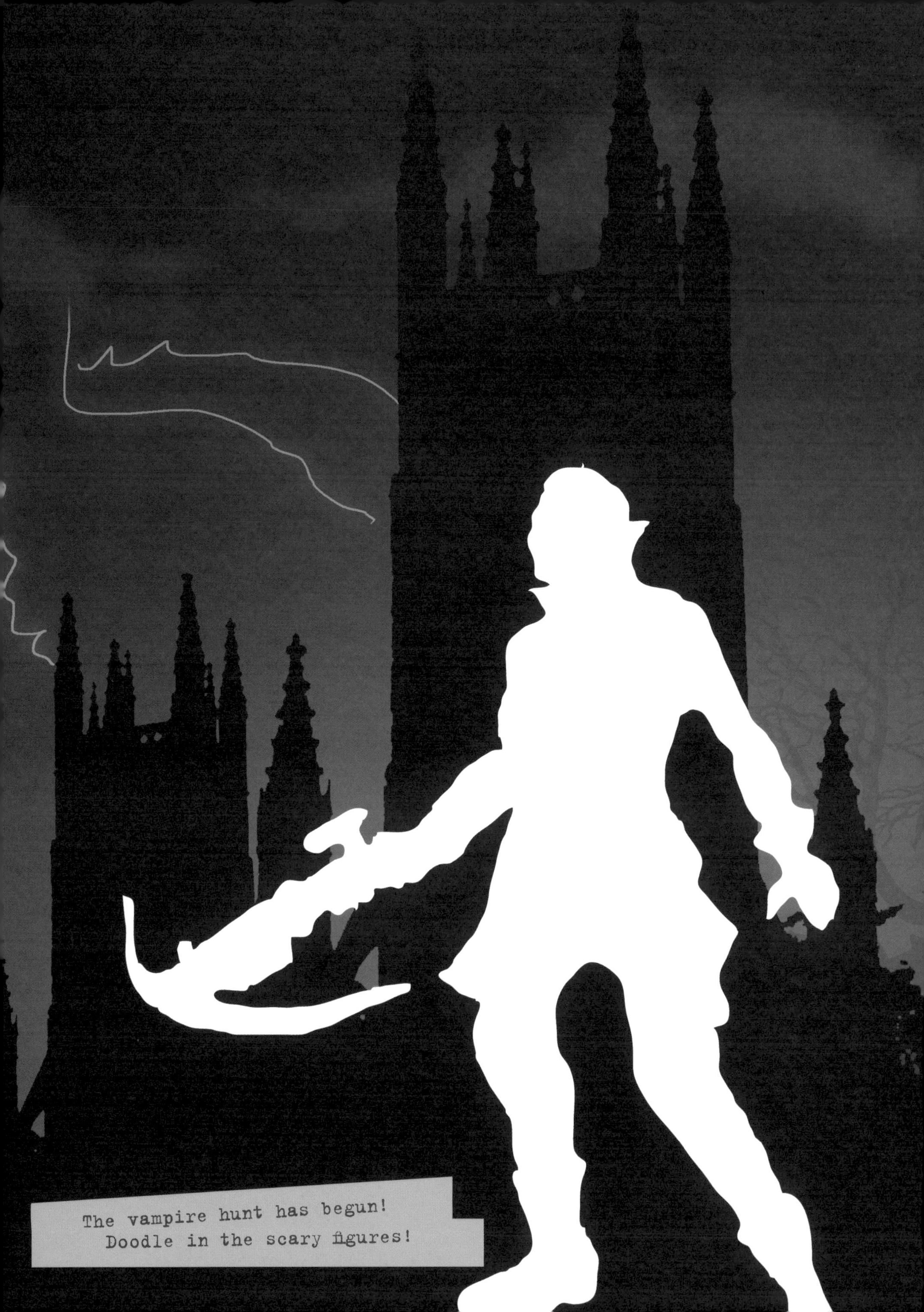
The vampire hunt has begun!
Doodle in the scary figures!

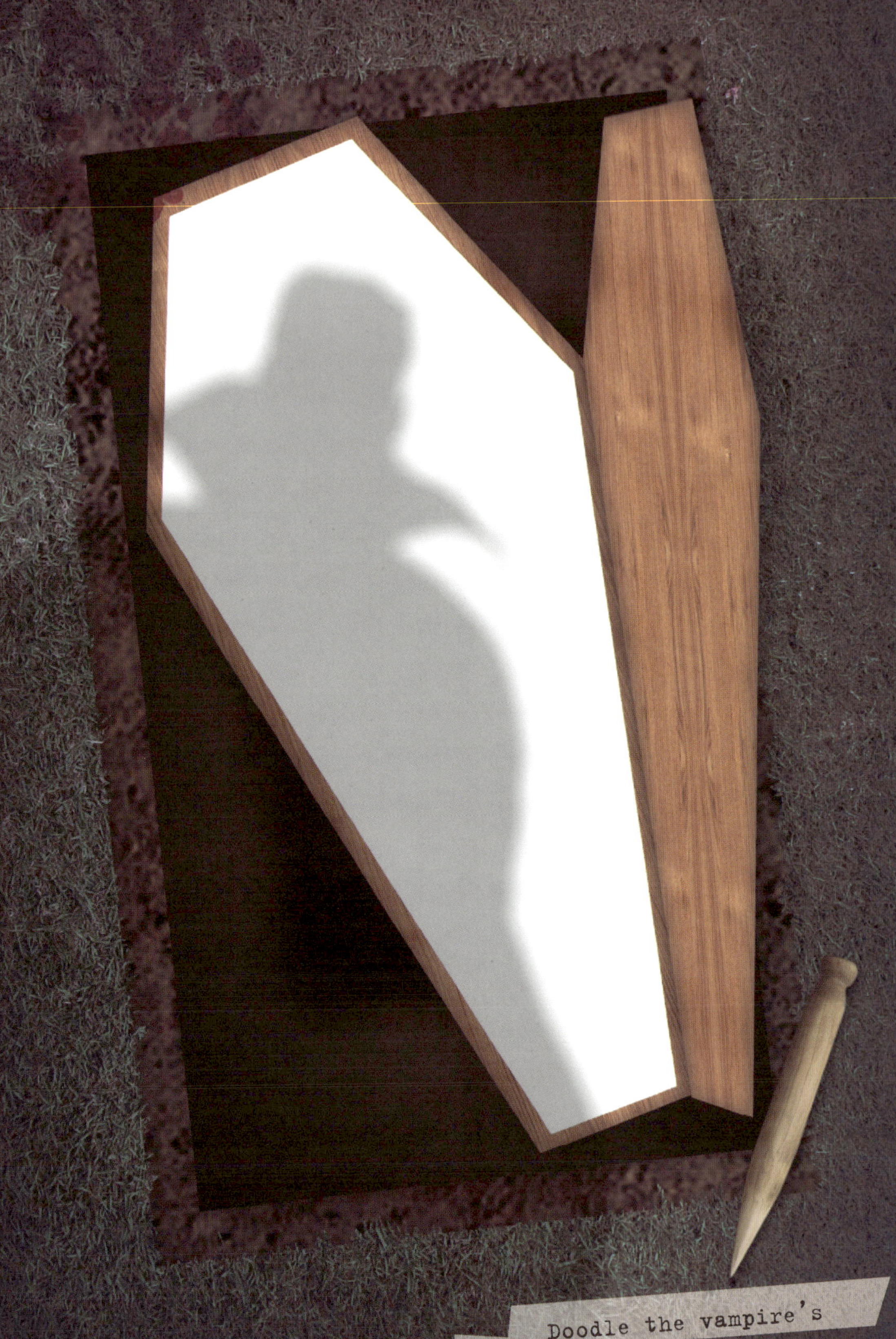

Doodle the vampire's

resting place...in the coffin!

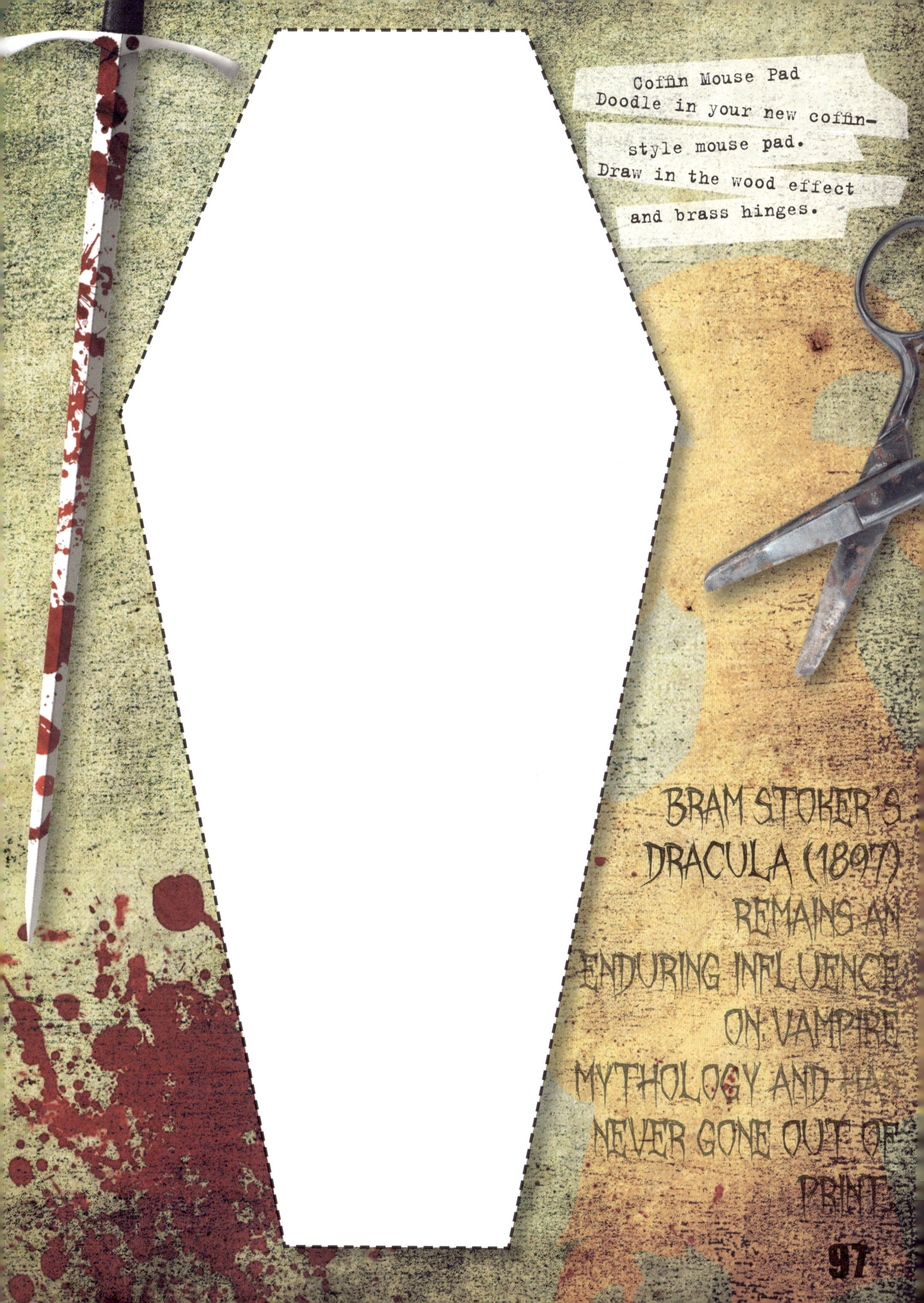
Coffin Mouse Pad
Doodle in your new coffin-style mouse pad.
Draw in the wood effect and brass hinges.
BRAM STOKER'S DRACULA (1897) REMAINS AN ENDURING INFLUENCE ON VAMPIRE MYTHOLOGY AND HAS NEVER GONE OUT OF PRINT.

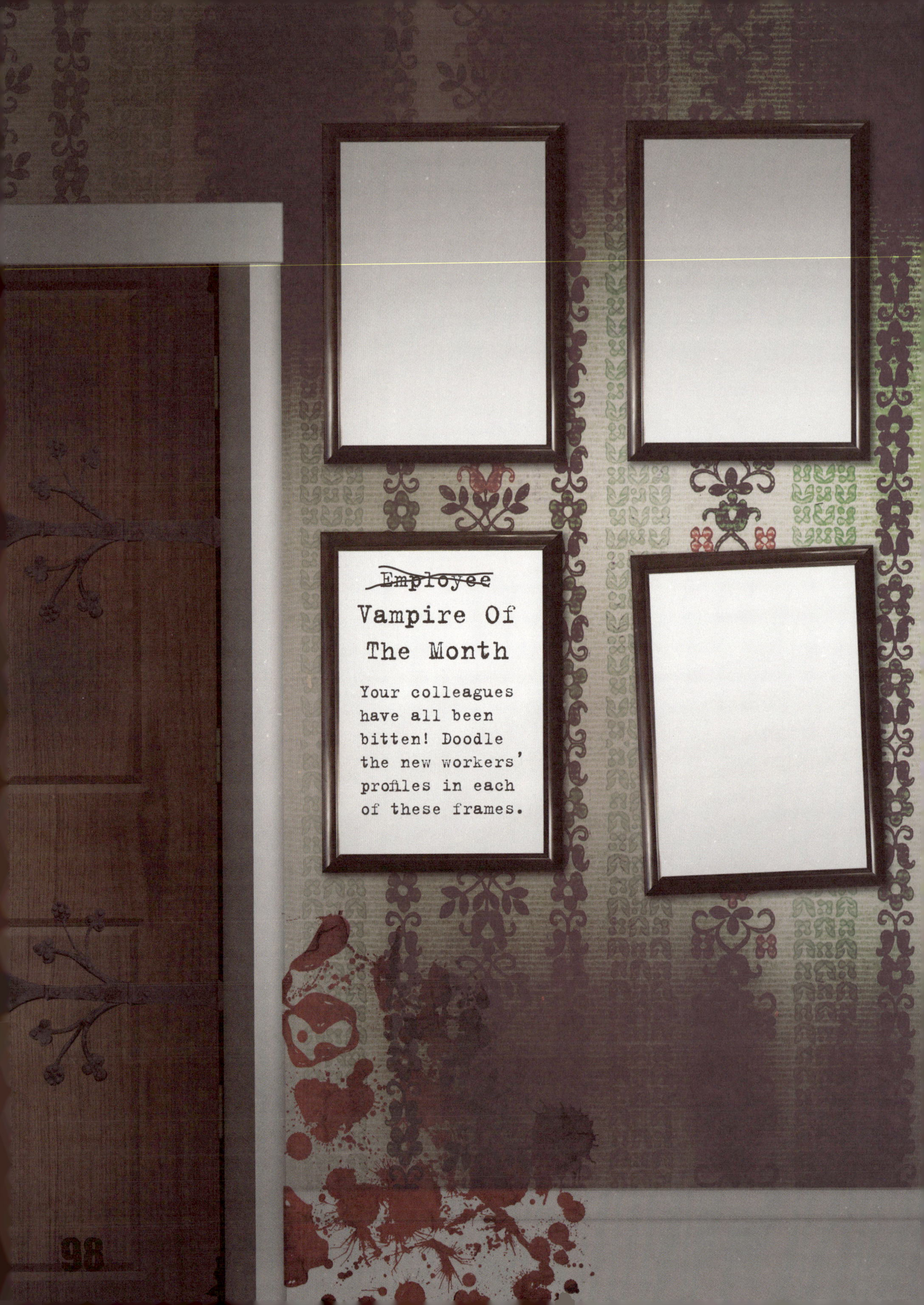
~~Employee~~
Vampire Of
The Month
Your colleagues have all been bitten! Doodle the new workers' profiles in each of these frames.

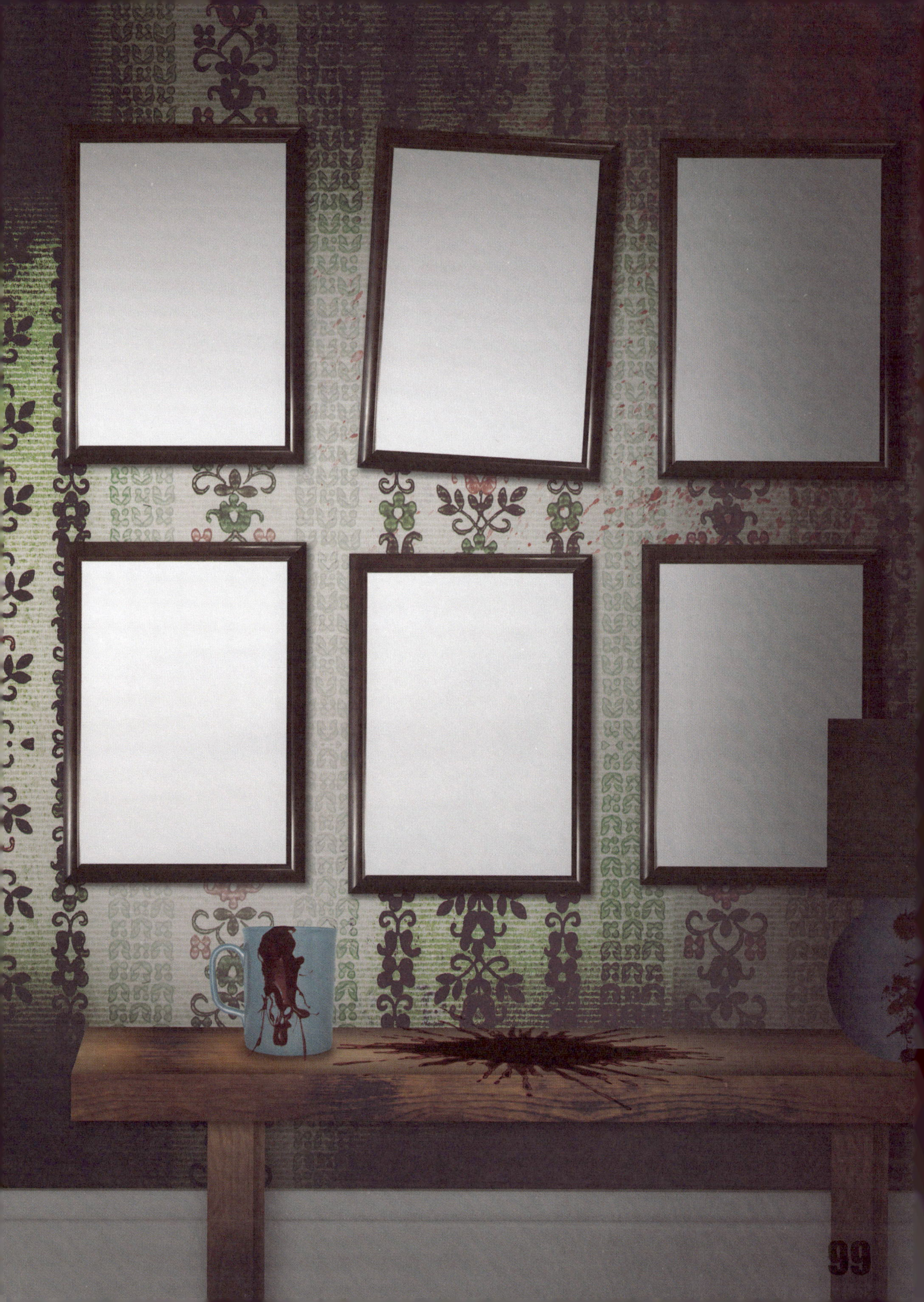

All your friends have turned
into vampires!
Doodle in their new vampire
portraits! Don't forget
to write their names too.

Word Search

creepy
crossbow
dusk
grave
holy water
moonlight
murder
neck
ultra violet

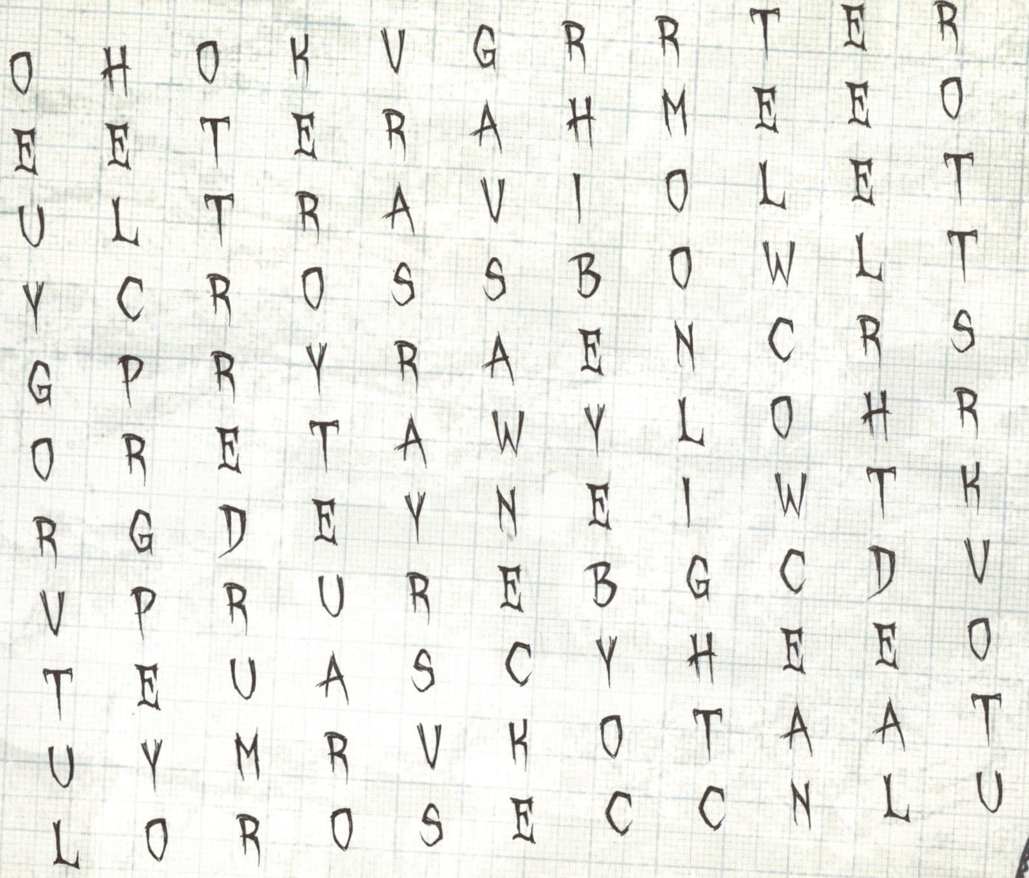

Draw some frightening monster bats on the old bits of paper below.

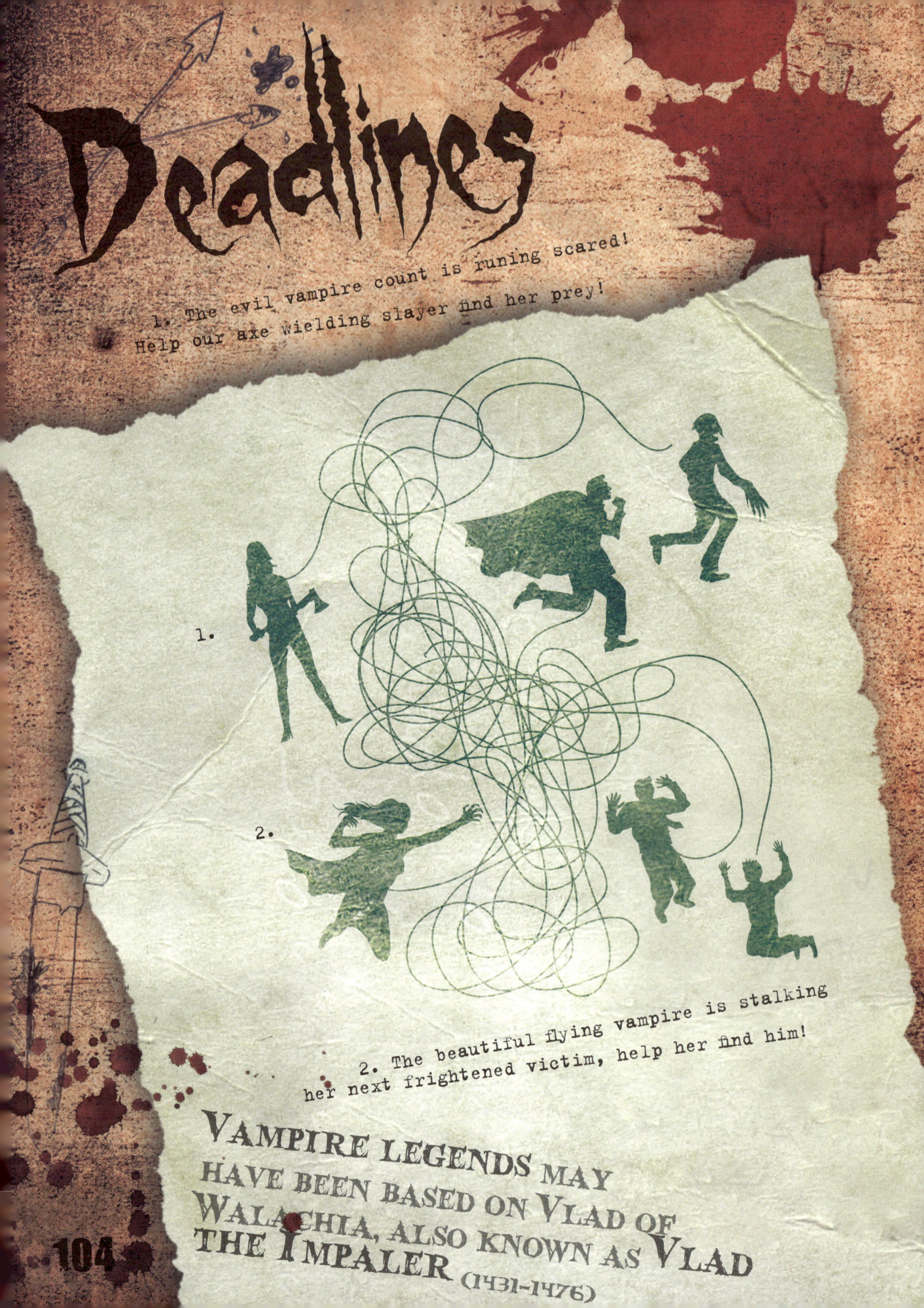

Deadlines
1. The evil vampire count is runing scared!
Help our axe wielding slayer find her prey!
1.
2.
2. The beautiful flying vampire is stalking
her next frightened victim, help her find him!
Vampire legends may
have been based on Vlad of
Walachia, also known as Vlad
the Impaler (1431-1476)

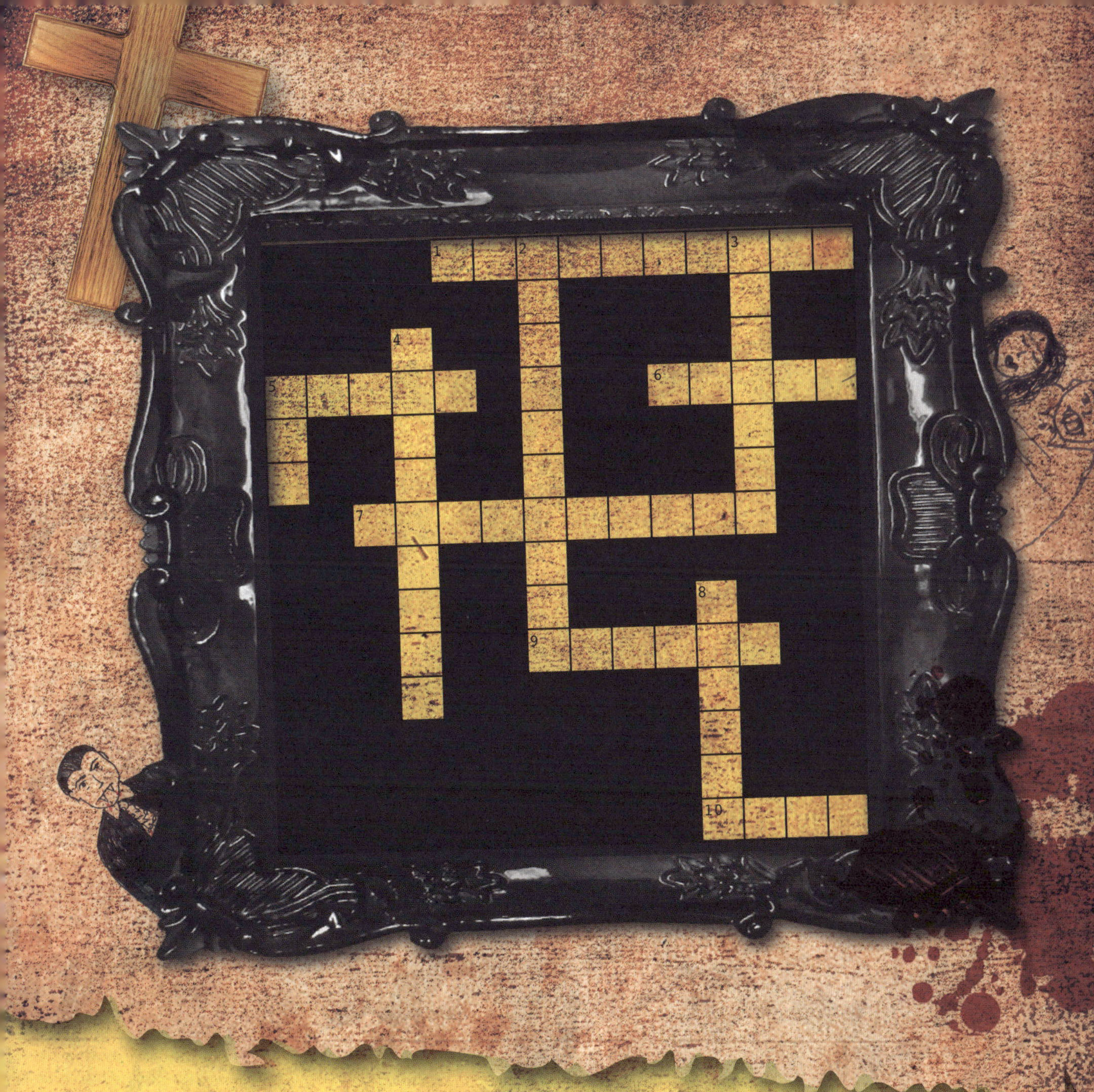

Across

1. Vampires cannot cross a threshold without an...
5. "I vant to suck your..."
6. Sharp wooden instrument used as protection against vampires
7. The author of the novel DRACULA
9. Herb used to fend off vampires
10. The most desirable part of a victim's body to a vampire

Down

2. Vampire slayer in the novel DRACULA
3. Vlad the...
4. The star of the film INTERVIEW WITH A VAMPIRE
5. Flying mammal often associated with vampires
8. The purest and most desired type of victim

Just Hanging

ABCDEFGHIJKLMNOPQRSTUVWXYZ

Cross off the dead letters.

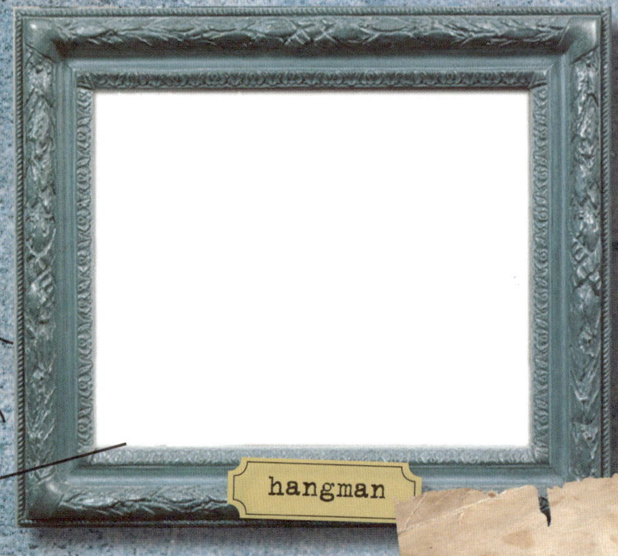

Draw your hangman.

Enter your blood-soaked words here.

ABCDEFG
HIJKLM
NOPQRST
UVWXYZ

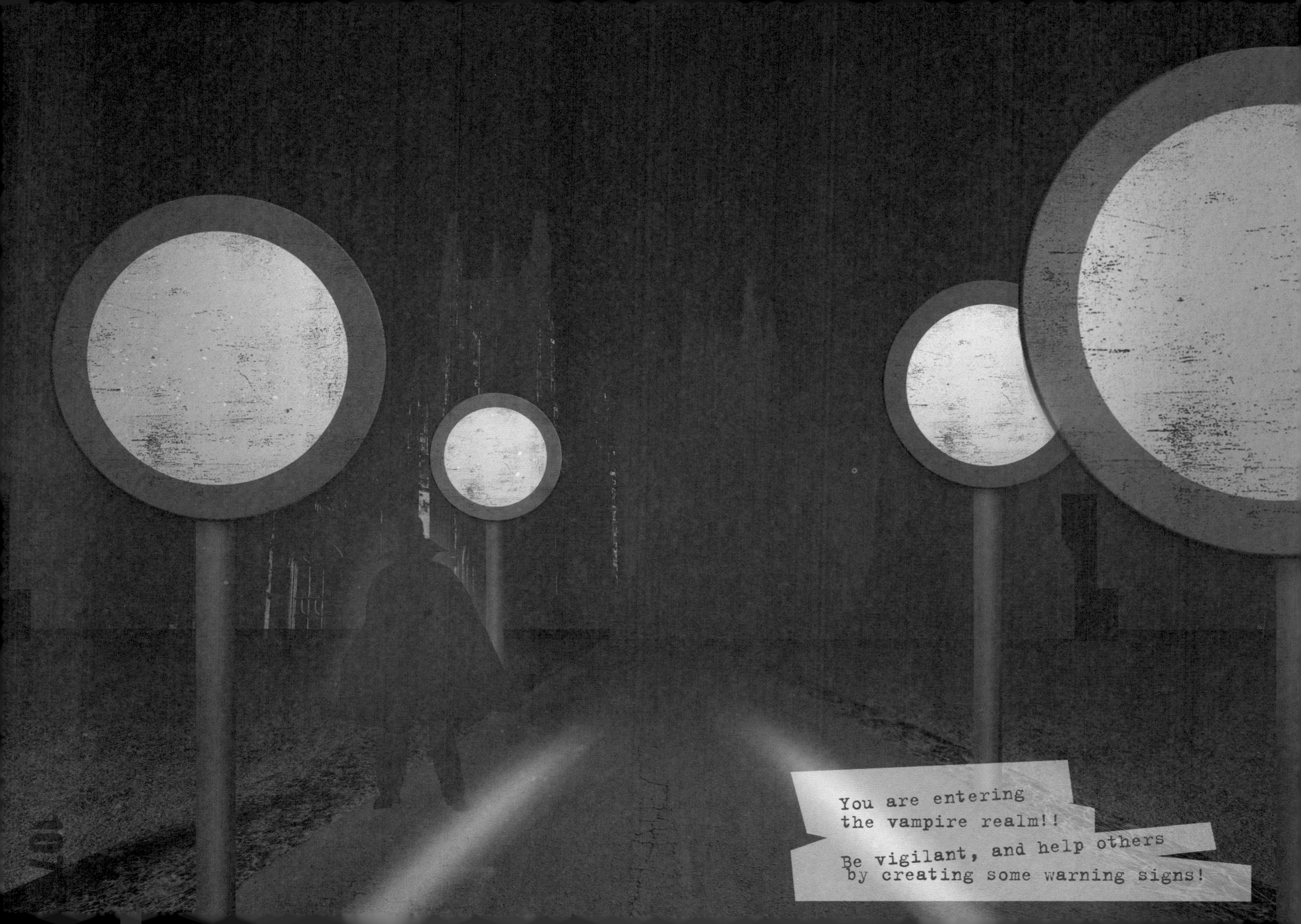

You are entering
the vampire realm!!

Be vigilant, and help others
by creating some warning signs!

Dot-to-Dot

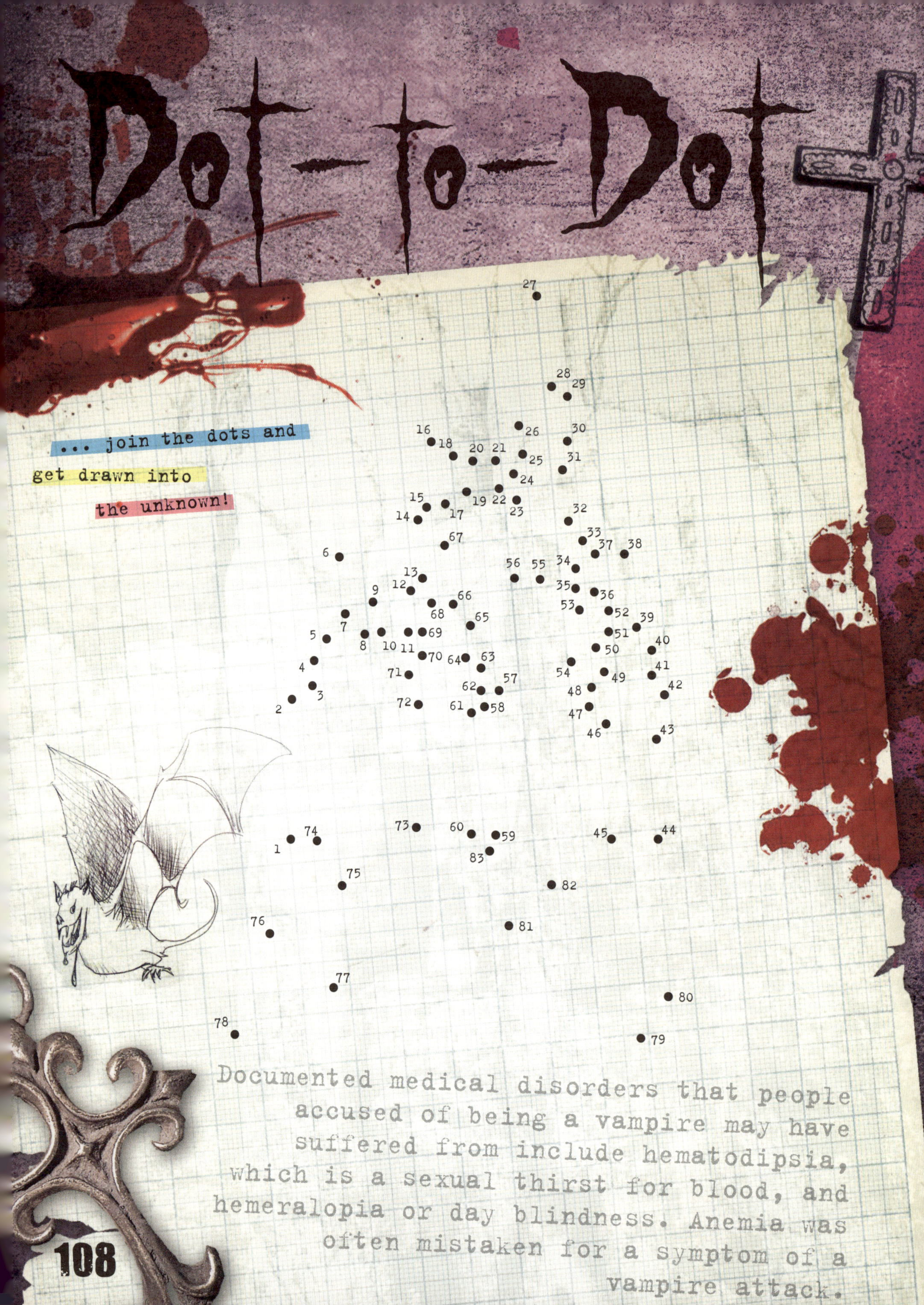

... join the dots and get drawn into the unknown!

Documented medical disorders that people accused of being a vampire may have suffered from include hematodipsia, which is a sexual thirst for blood, and hemeralopia or day blindness. Anemia was often mistaken for a symptom of a vampire attack.

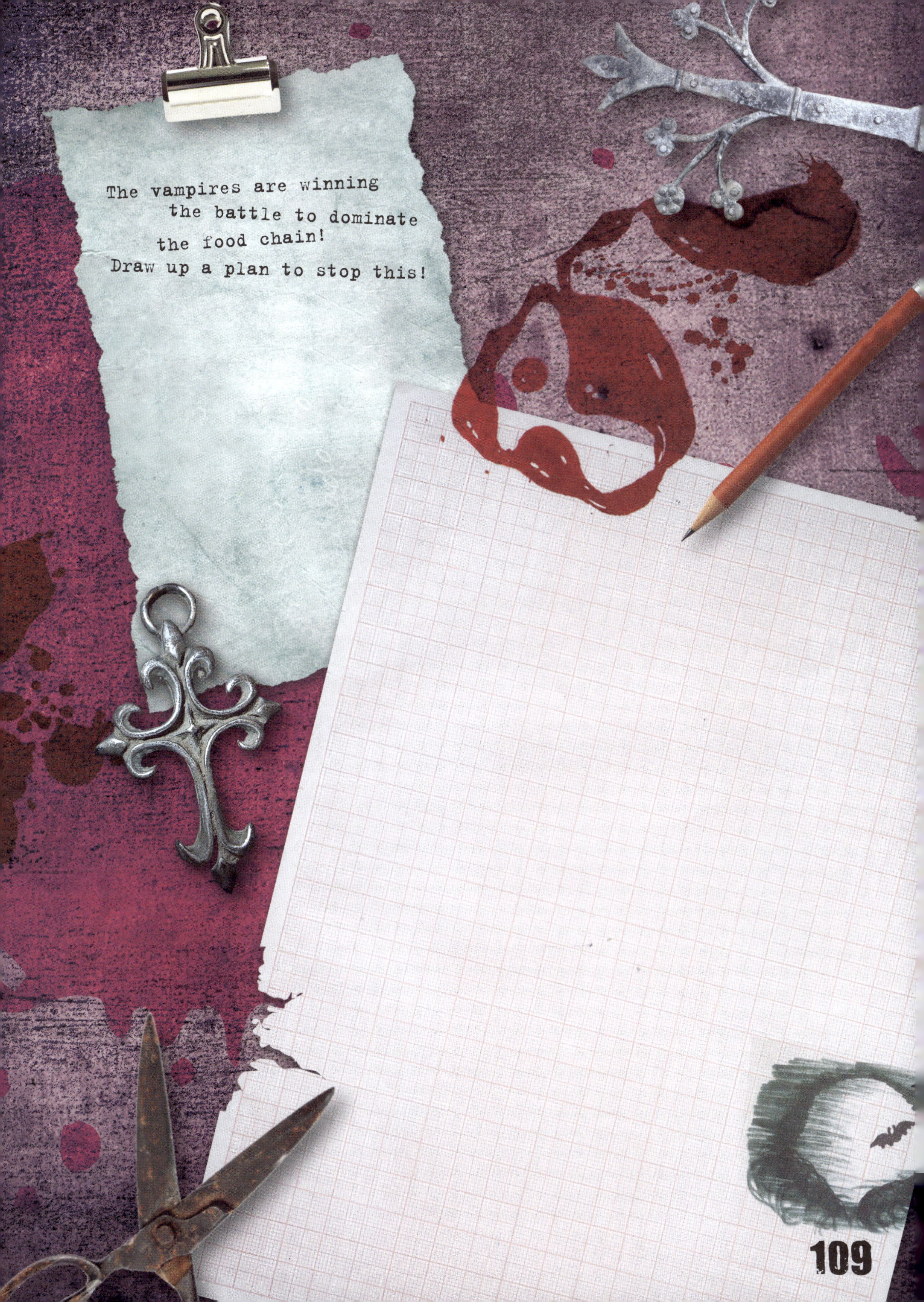

The vampires are winning the battle to dominate the food chain!
Draw up a plan to stop this!

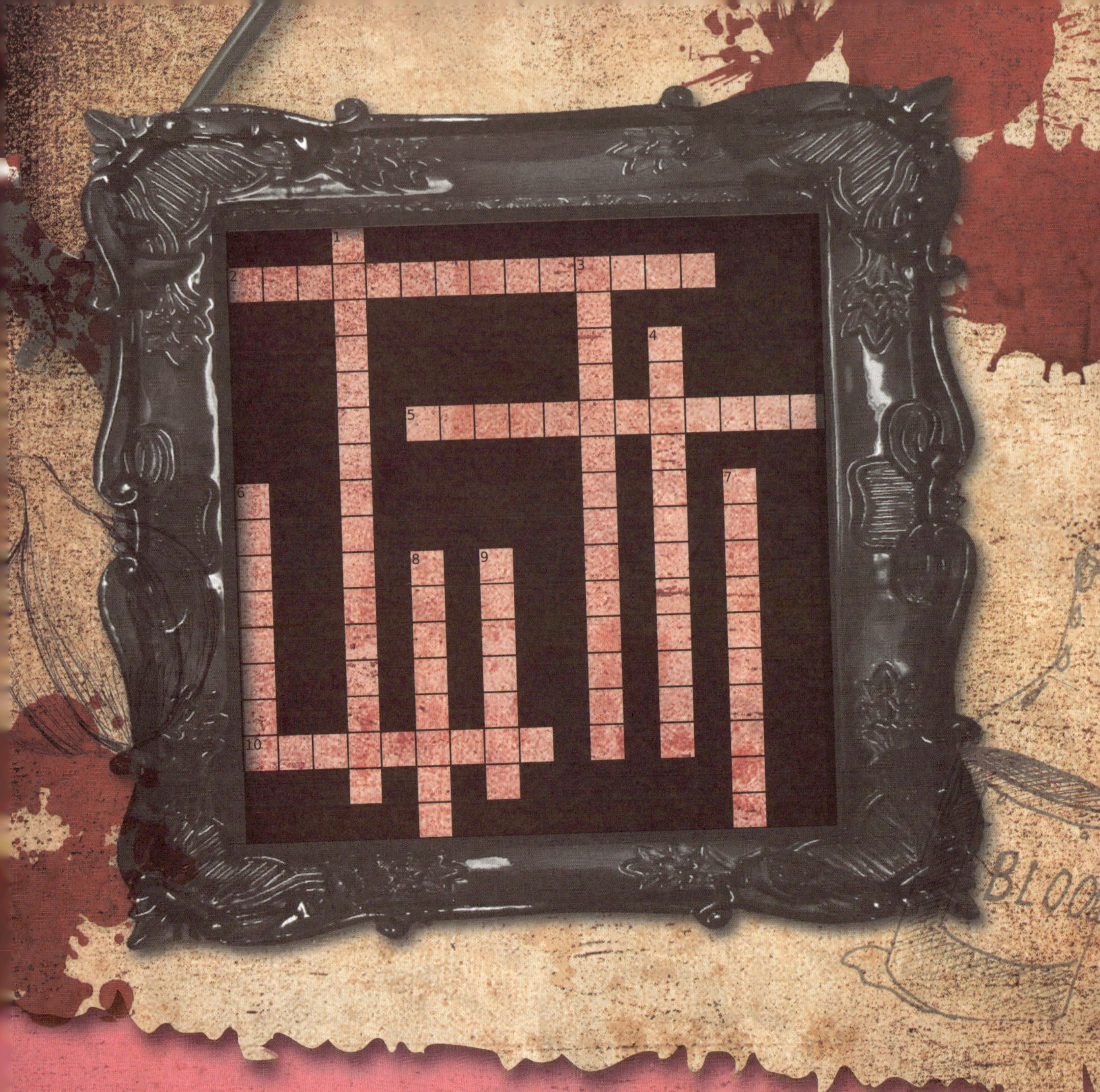

Across

2. Famous actor who played Dracula in the 1950s
5. Film spoof of the TWILIGHT saga
10. TV series starring Anna Paquin and Stephen Moyer

Down

1. Count Dracula's object of desire
3. Star of the film saga TWILIGHT
4. American actor who starred as Marvel hero BLADE
6. Vampires burn when in contact with
7. Creator of TV series BUFFY THE VAMPIRE SLAYER
8. Marvel character who is Blade's sidekick
9. Name of sequel to the film TWILIGHT

Design a vampire poster to scare the wits out of your friends!

WARNING POSTER

Vampire Mouse Pad

Get creative and doodle some gory vampire fun on the template above.

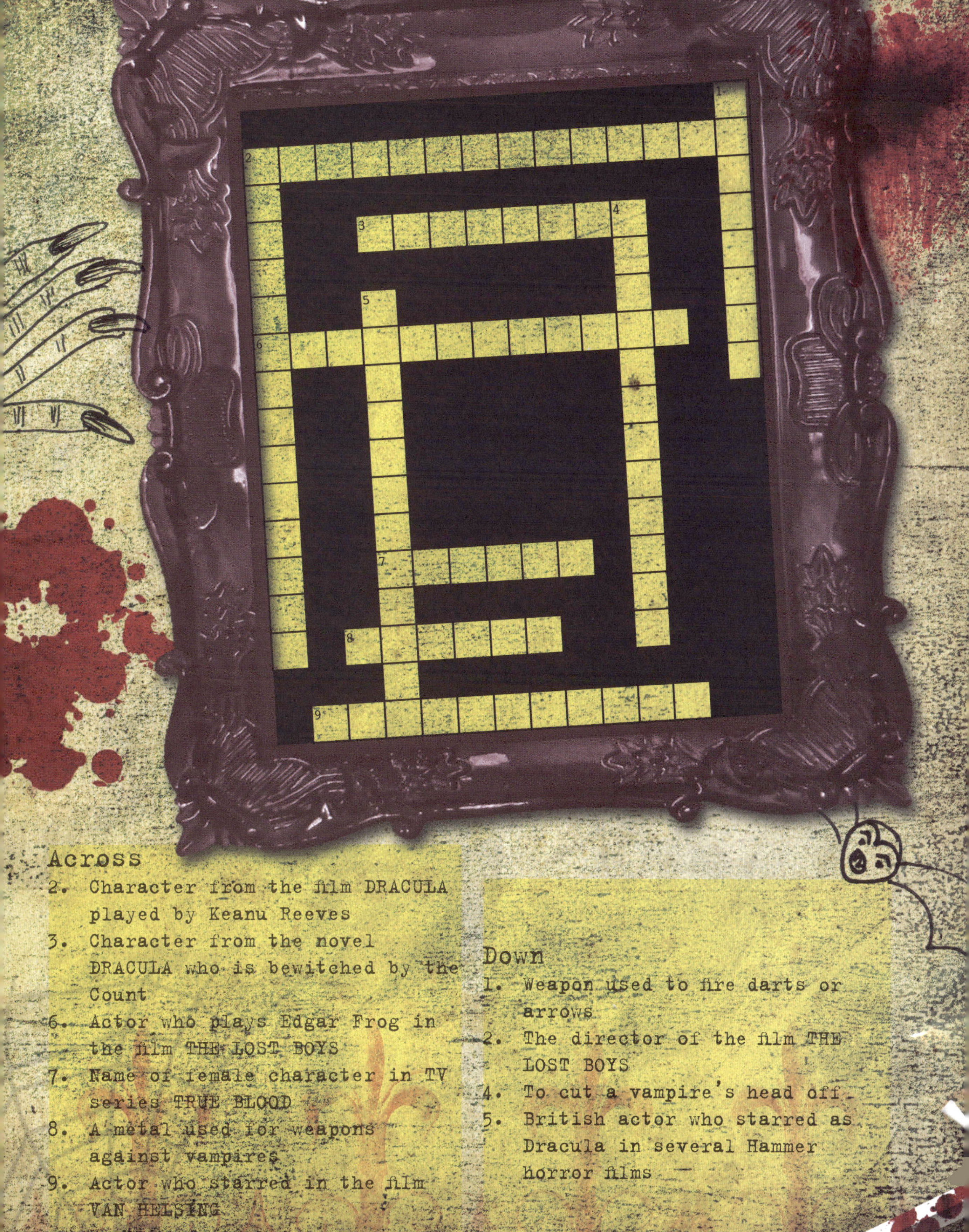

Across

2. Character from the film DRACULA played by Keanu Reeves
3. Character from the novel DRACULA who is bewitched by the Count
6. Actor who plays Edgar Frog in the film THE LOST BOYS
7. Name of female character in TV series TRUE BLOOD
8. A metal used for weapons against vampires
9. Actor who starred in the film VAN HELSING

Down

1. Weapon used to fire darts or arrows
2. The director of the film THE LOST BOYS
4. To cut a vampire's head off
5. British actor who starred as Dracula in several Hammer horror films

top ten lists

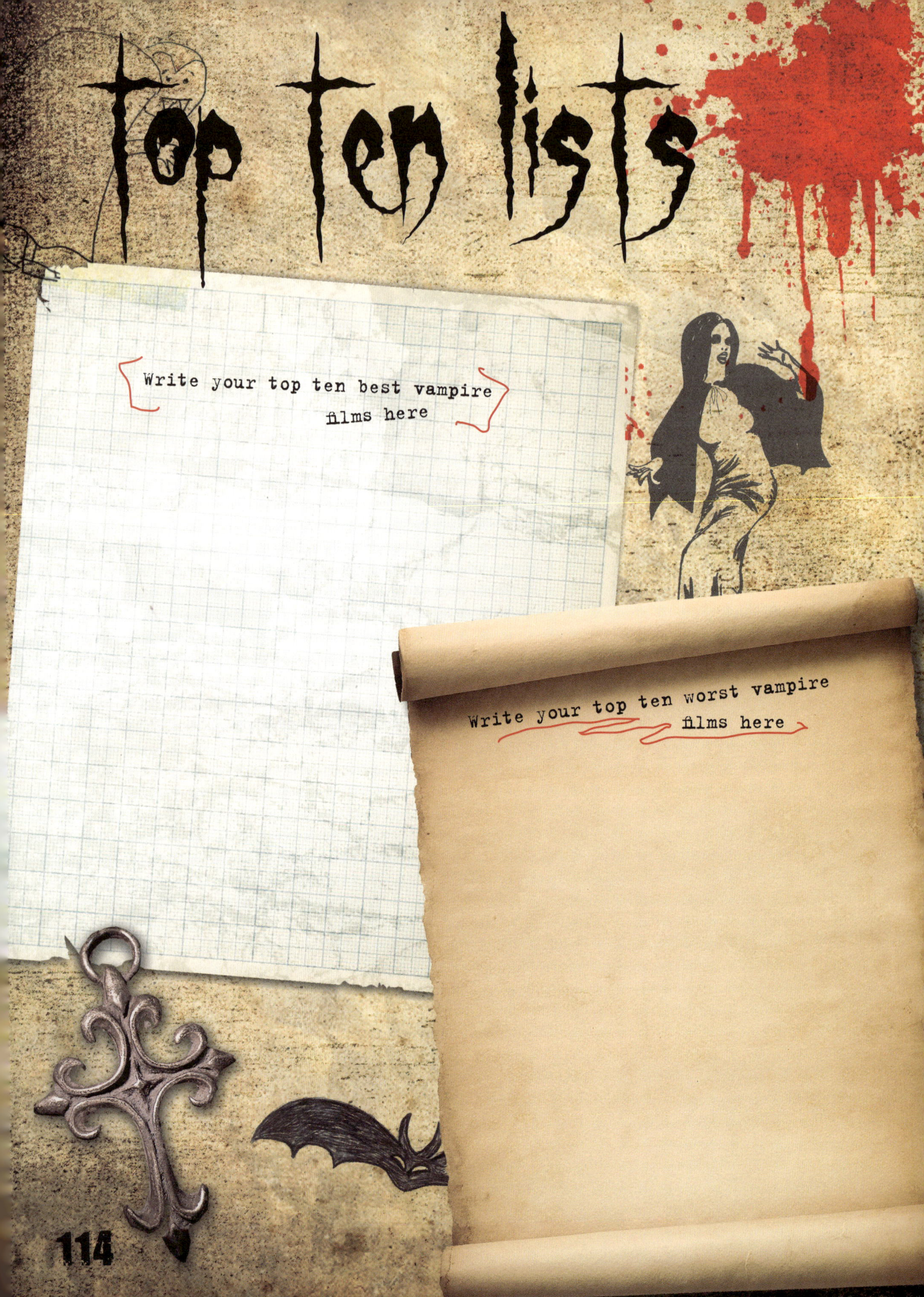

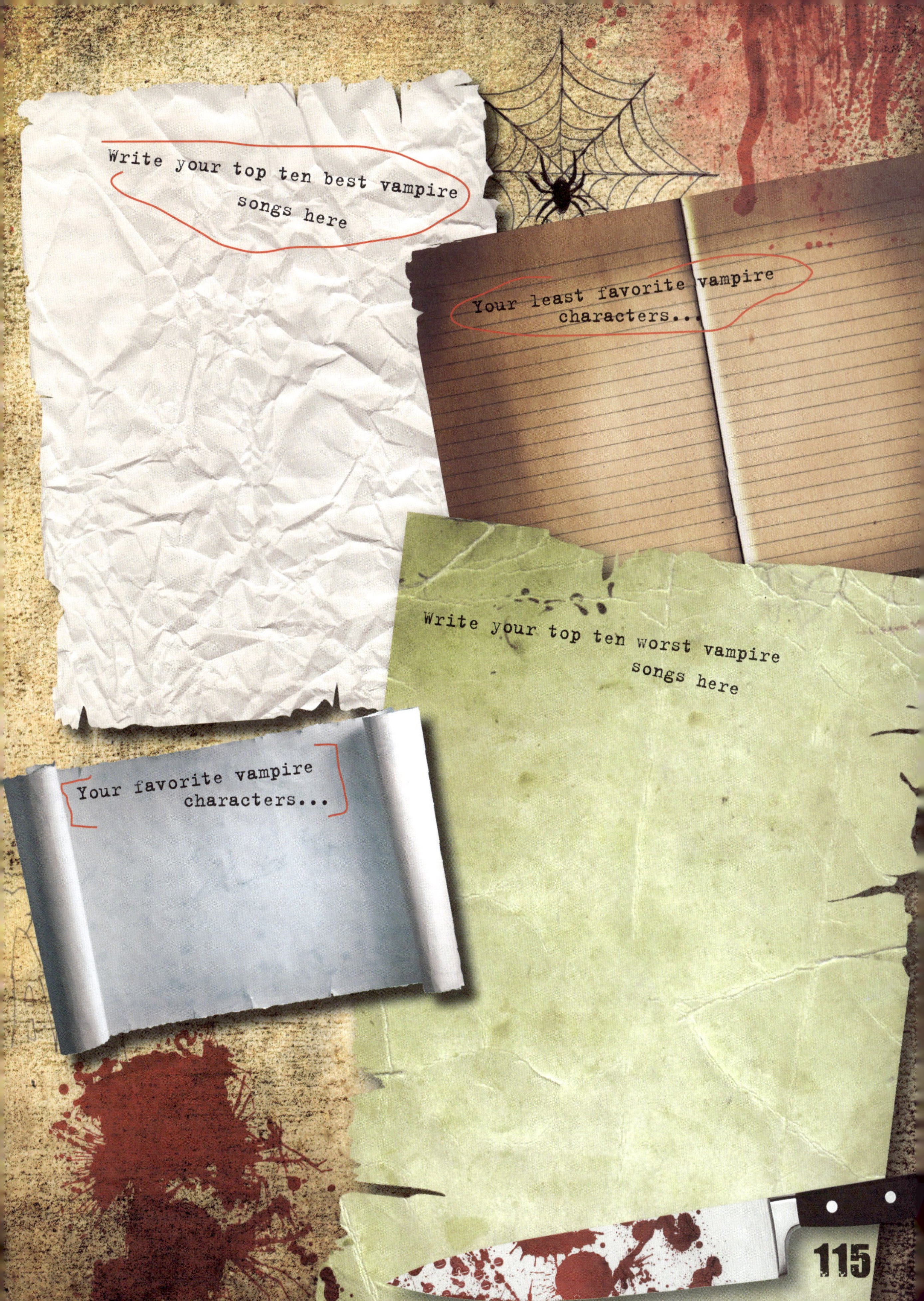
Write your top ten best vampire songs here
Your least favorite vampire characters...
Write your top ten worst vampire songs here
Your favorite vampire characters...

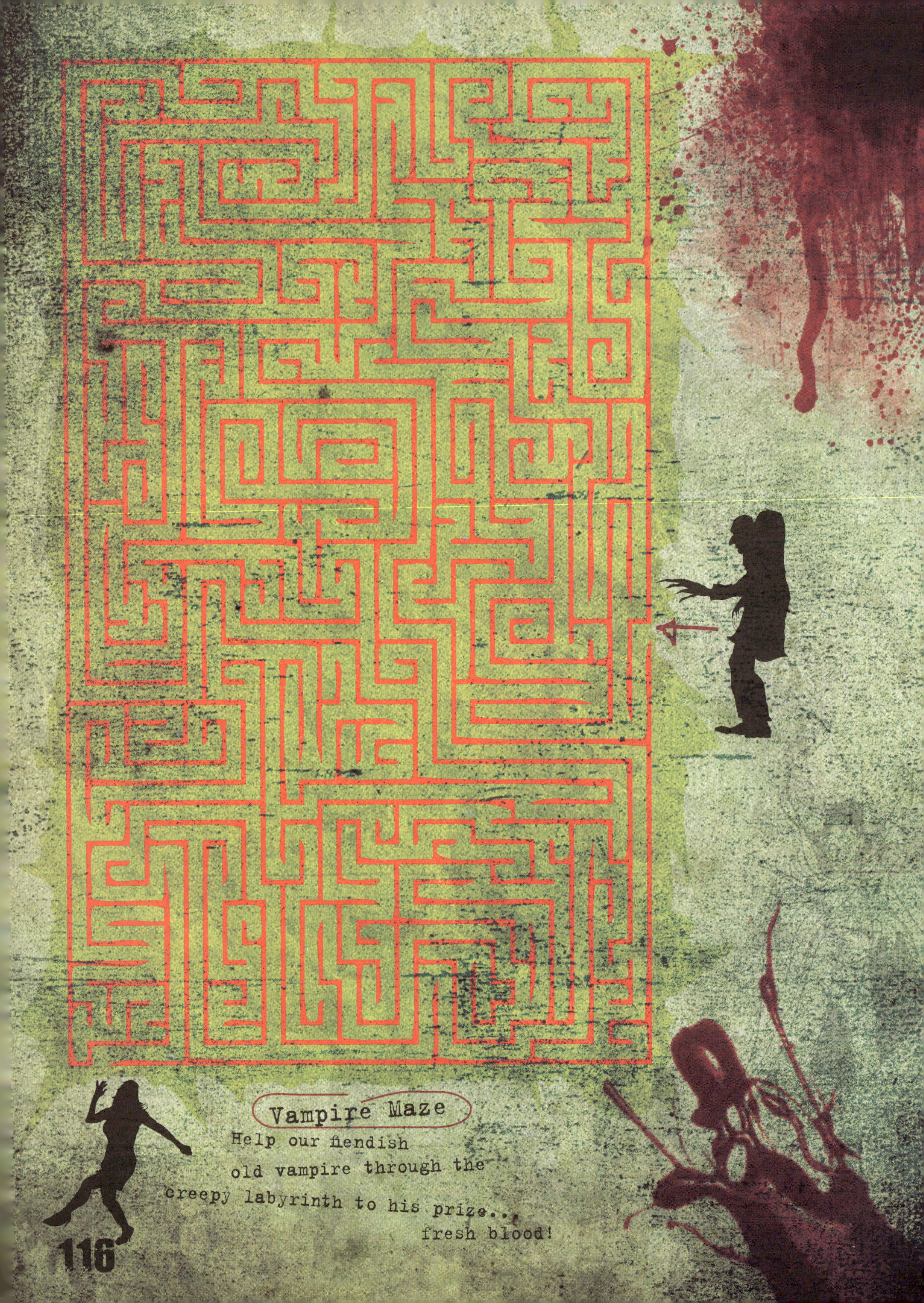

Vampire Maze

Help our fiendish old vampire through the creepy labyrinth to his prize... fresh blood!

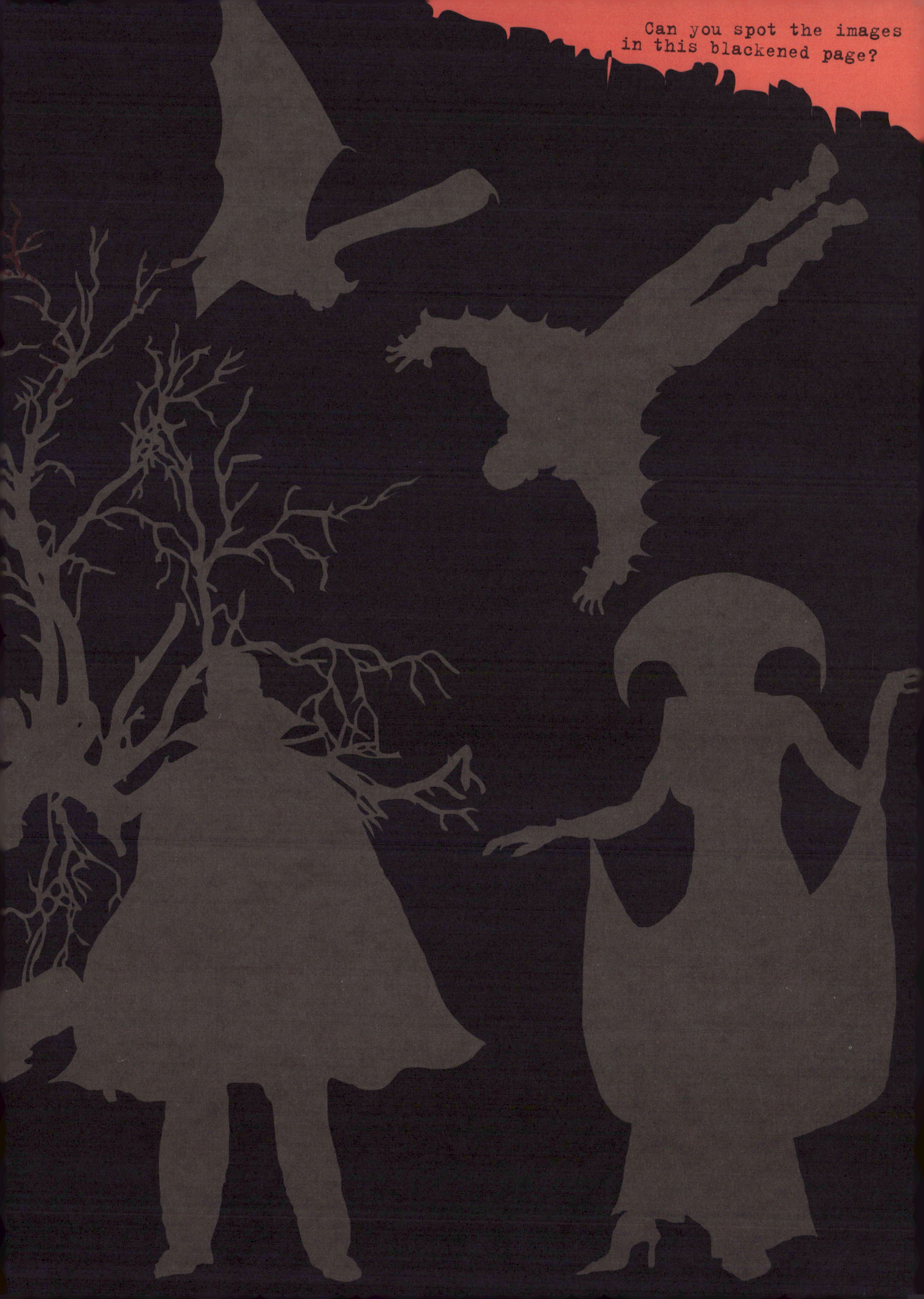
Can you spot the images
in this blackened page?

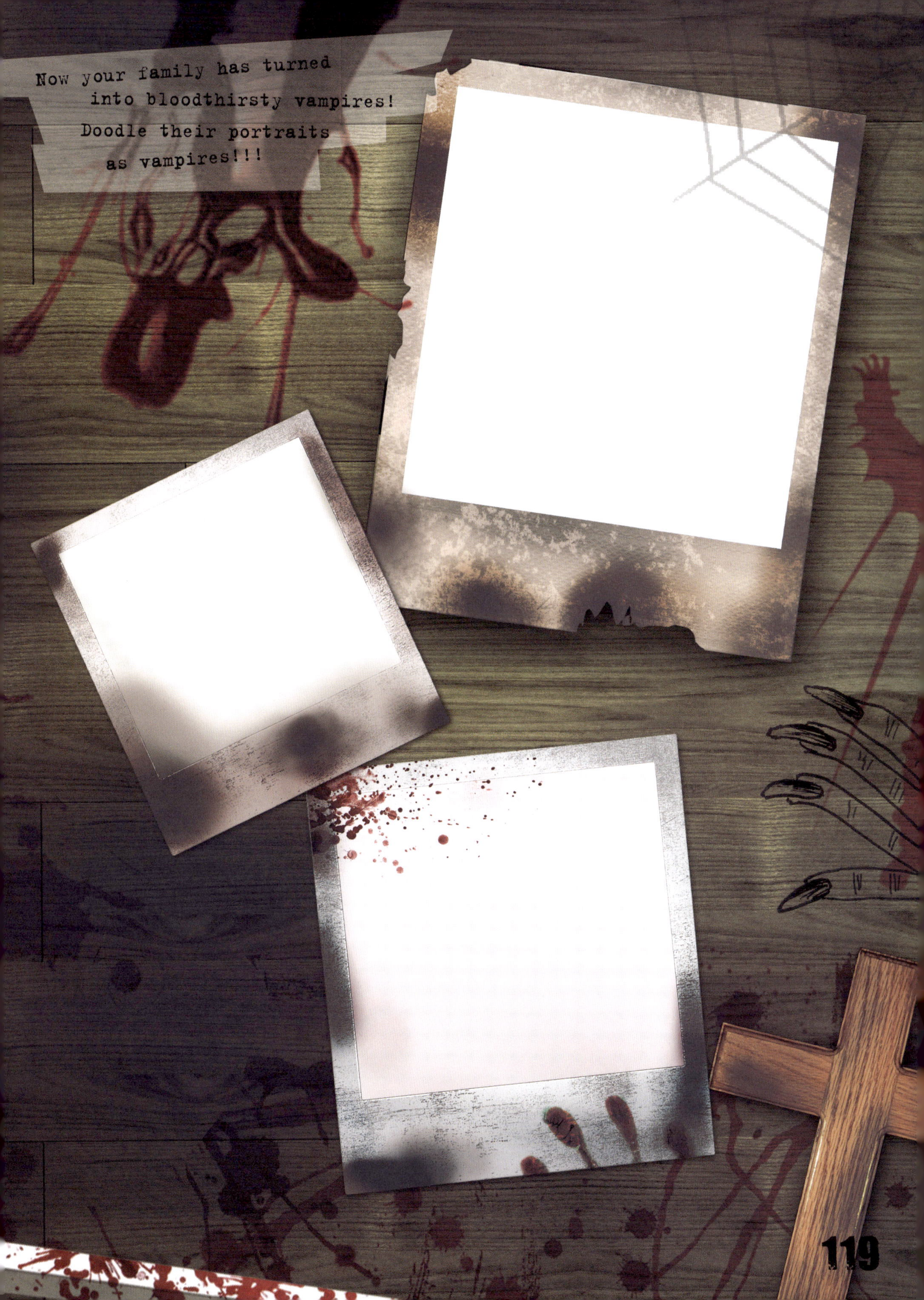
Now your family has turned
into bloodthirsty vampires!
Doodle their portraits
as vampires!!!

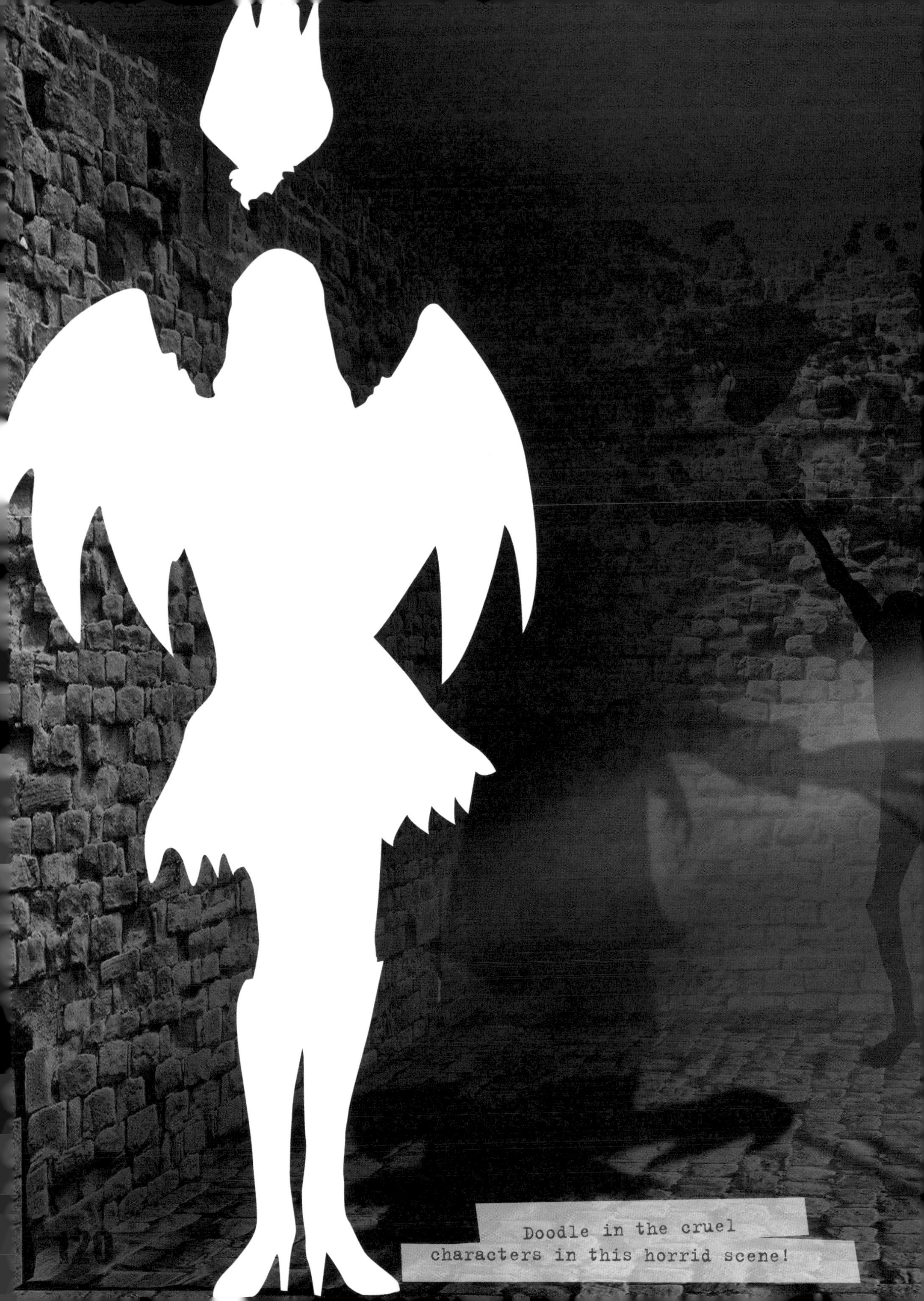
Doodle in the cruel
characters in this horrid scene!

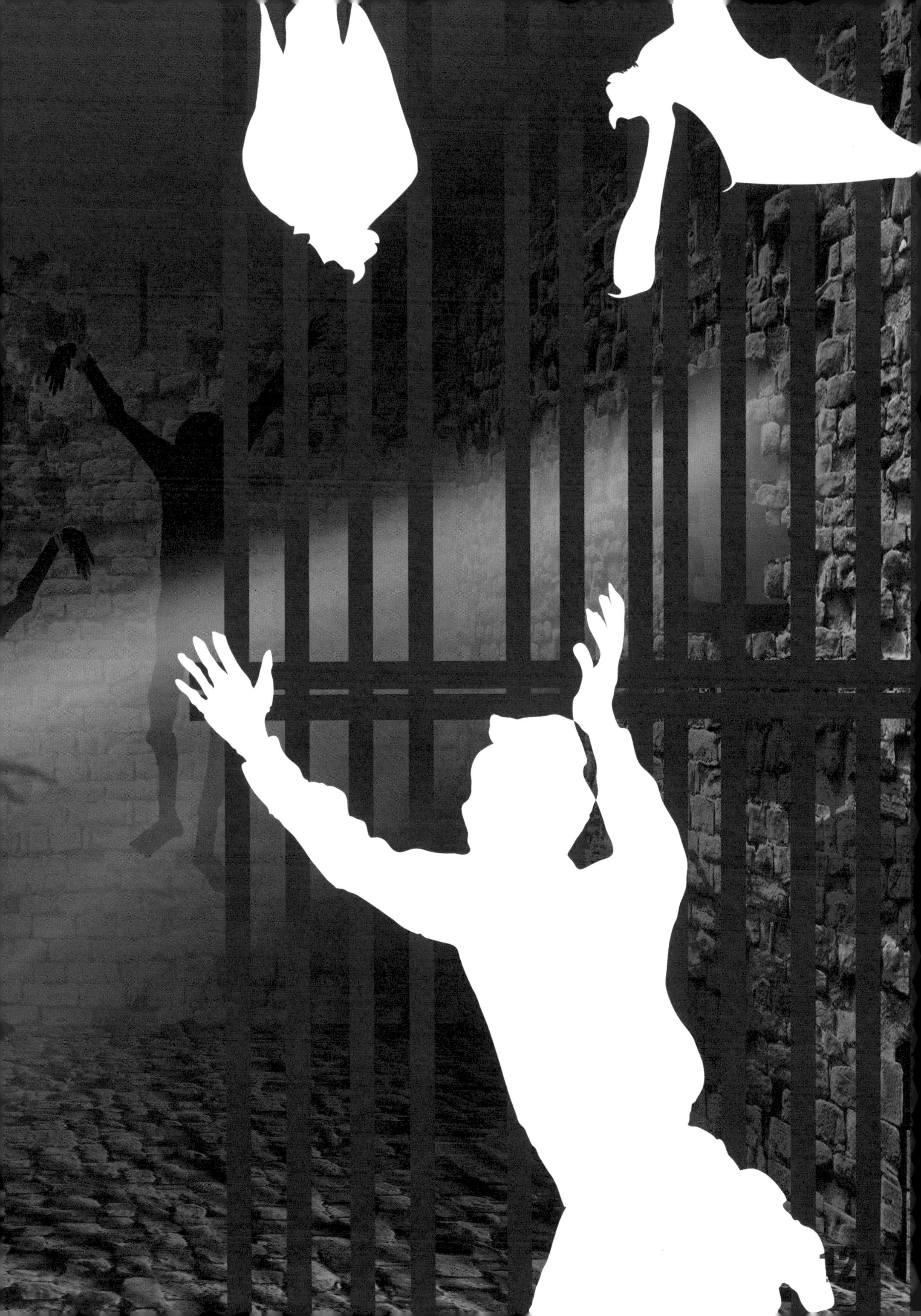

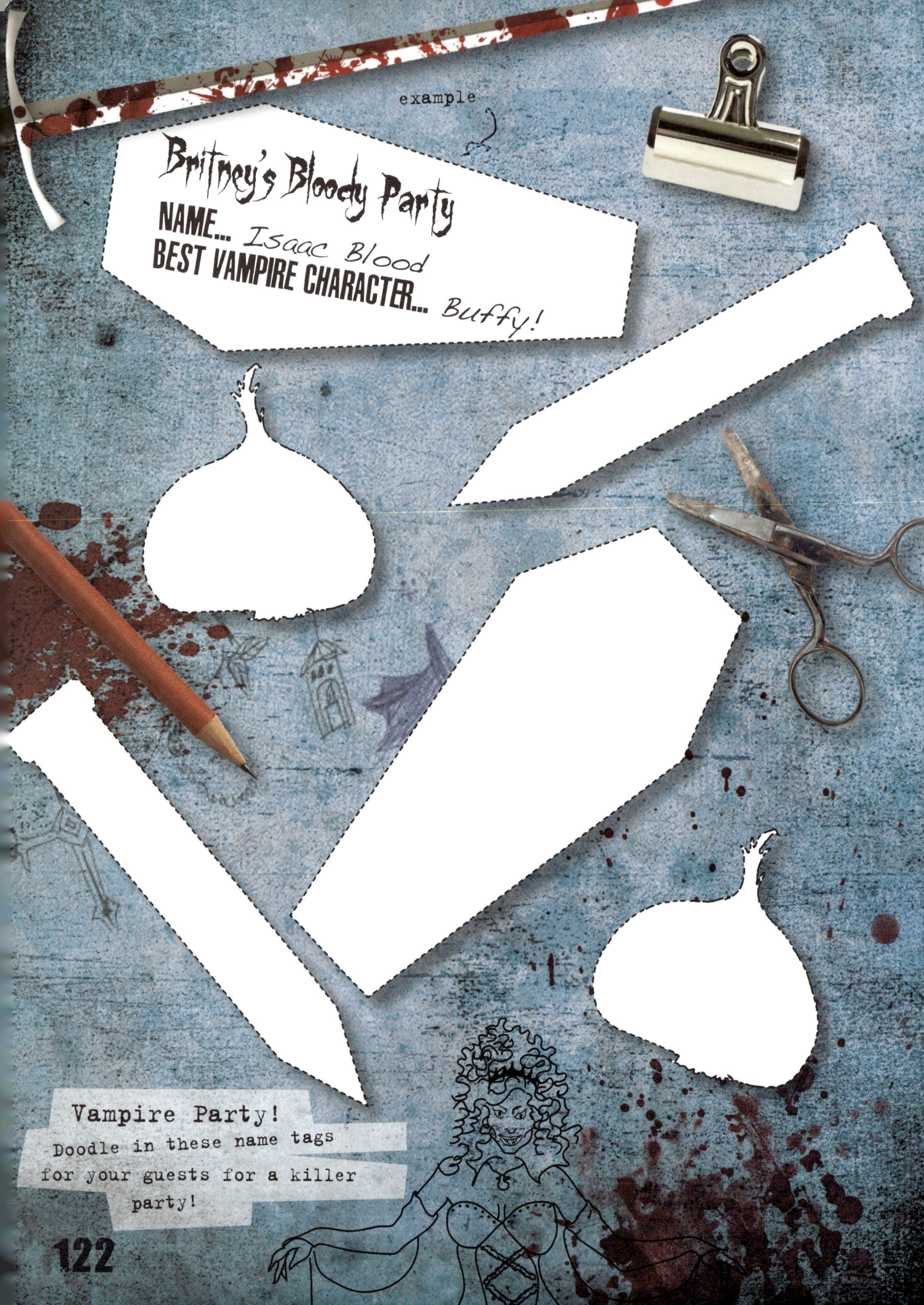

Vampire Party!

Doodle in these name tags for your guests for a killer party!

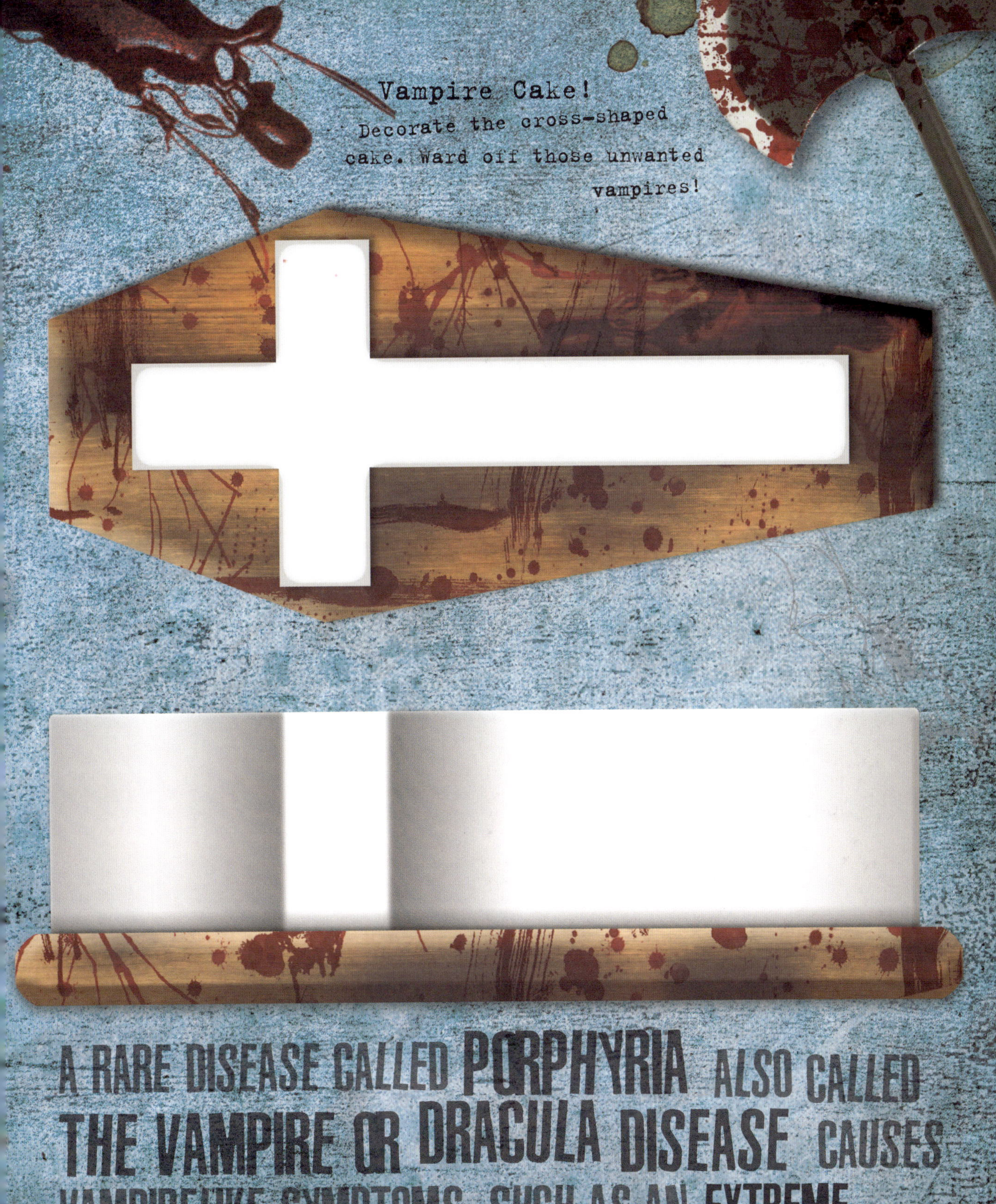

Vampire Cake!
Decorate the cross-shaped cake. Ward off those unwanted vampires!

A RARE DISEASE CALLED **PORPHYRIA** ALSO CALLED **THE VAMPIRE OR DRACULA DISEASE** CAUSES VAMPIRELIKE SYMPTOMS SUCH AS AN **EXTREME SENSITIVITY TO SUNLIGHT** AND SOMETIMES **HAIRINESS.**

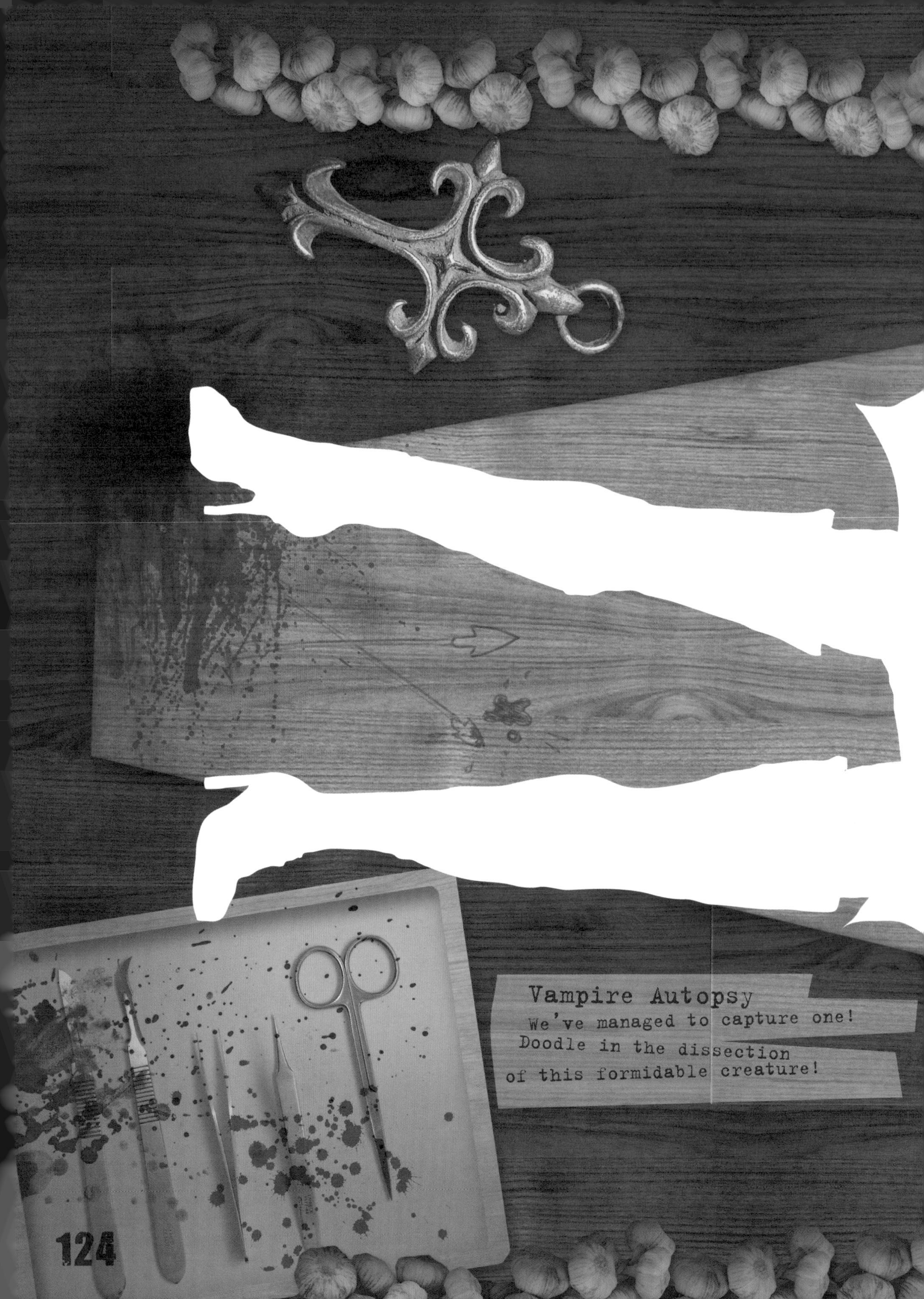

Vampire Autopsy

We've managed to capture one! Doodle in the dissection of this formidable creature!

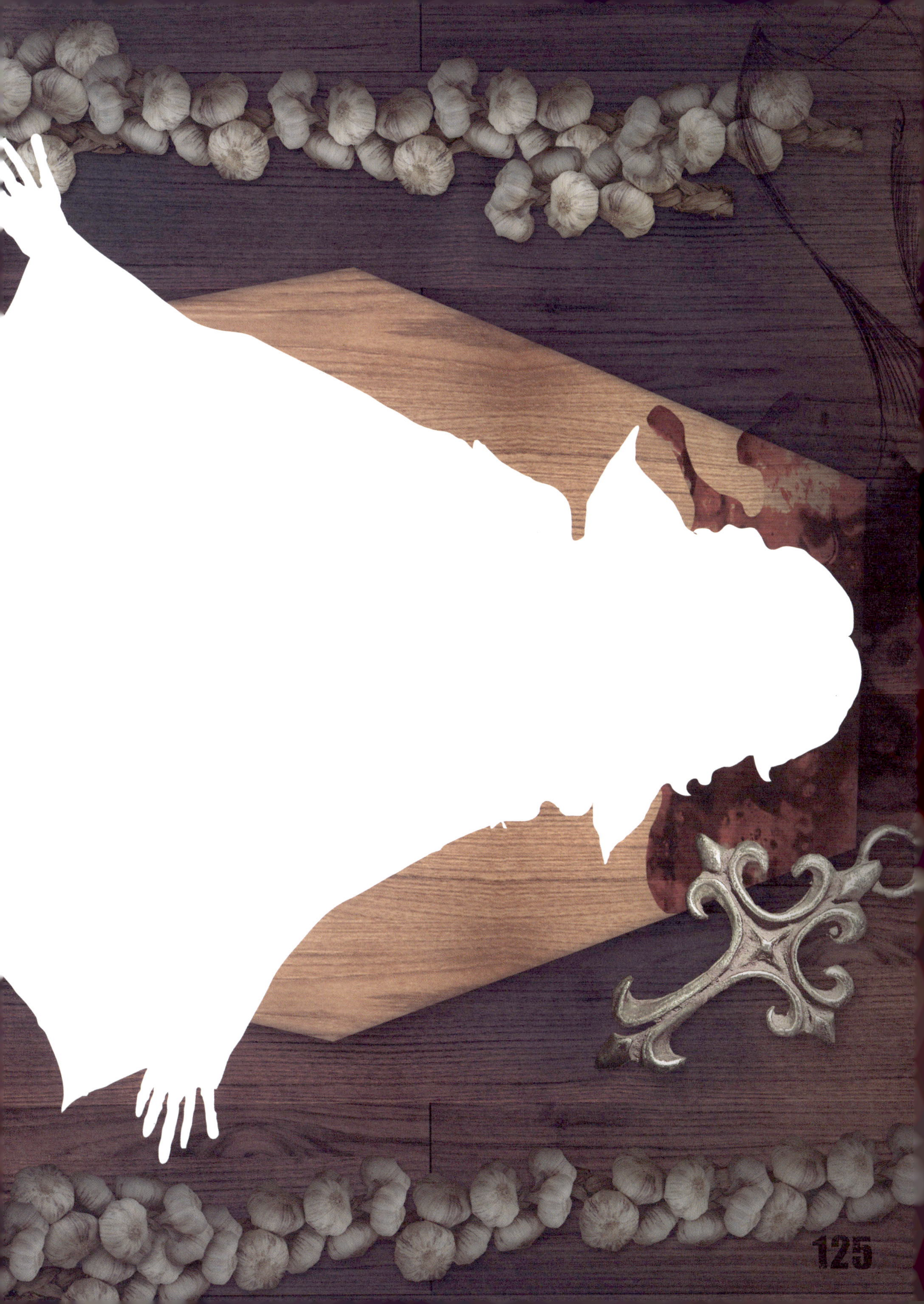

Answers

page 18

page 40

page 64

page 88

page 8

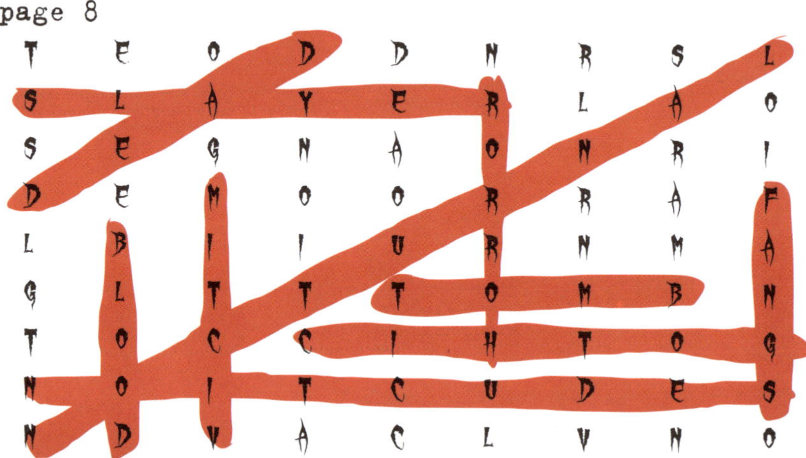

page 30

T H G E B T L W L E T O
B Y R D S L U A A A E E
S P O O K Y I W R Y I U
K N U O A P O Y G O I N
E O U I E N N A O D O N
L T W I L I G H T D I L
A I G O W K W T A F T D
N Z O H R D S E F T D P
R E K C U S D O O L B F
E U R R F N C I L R A G
T A E H U S H E E O T S
E A F S S T O N I N N N

page 54

r m i s r c s s l y
r i t l u o h o s r
m s e s x n r c r e
e s n r r o r r e t
t e r t e u n i i e
t l a h c a p e s m
i e r i p m a v e e
t f f r s r u e i c
r i m s a f s i s i
x l t t r v i s o r

page78

E R A T O T S K D L
T R D R A C U L A Y
N O I Y G E L F E R
K B E R A R K R D T
S I U S C R E A M S
C M L R R U M E T L
A S E L I S I R M S
R S I R E E A S L R
Y S E L S R D R I E
L S I E A E U U L A

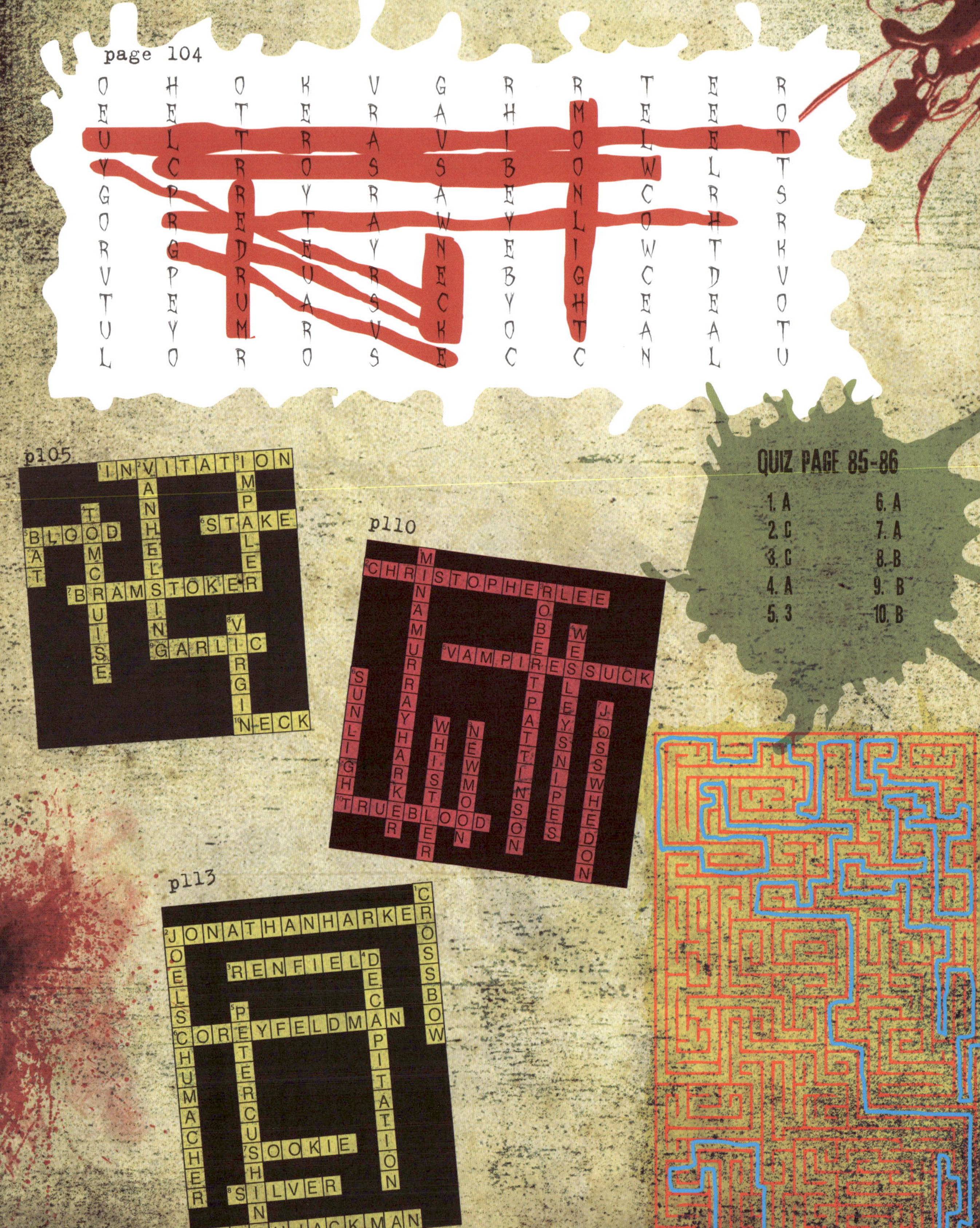

page 104
p105
INVITATION
IMPALE
STAKE
BLOOD
BAT
TOM CRUISE
BRAM STOKER
VAN HELSING
VIRGIN
GARLIC
NECK
p110
CHRISTOPHER LEE
MINA MURRAY HARKER
ROBERT PATTINSON
WESLEY SNIPES
VAMPIRES SUCK
SUNLIGHT
WHISTLER
NEW MOON
JOSS WHEDON
TRUE BLOOD
p113
JONATHAN HARKER
CROSSBOW
JOEL SCHUMACHER
RENFIELD
DECAPITATION
PETER CUSHING
COREY FELDMAN
SOOKIE
SILVER
HUGH JACKMAN
QUIZ PAGE 85-86
1. A
2. C
3. C
4. A
5. 3
6. A
7. A
8. B
9. B
10. B